Scribe Publications
THE VIEW FROM CONNOR'S HILL
South of Omeo.

Barry Heard was conscripted in Australia's first national service ballot, and served in Vietnam as an infantryman and radio operator. After completing his national service he returned home, where he found himself unable to settle down. He had ten different jobs in his first ten years back, worked as a teacher for a further ten years, and then held several mid-managerial posts before succumbing to a devastating breakdown due to severe post-traumatic stress disorder.

Since recovering, Barry Heard has decided to concentrate on his writing. His first book, *Well Done, Those Men*, dealt mainly with his Vietnam War-related experiences. He lives with his family in rural Victoria.

For Fraser and Ruby

The View from Connor's Hill

a memoir

BARRY HEARD

SCRIBE
Melbourne

Scribe Publications Pty Ltd
PO Box 523
Carlton North, Victoria, Australia 3054
Email: info@scribepub.com.au

First published by Scribe 2007

Typeset in 11.5/15.75pt Sabon by the publisher
Cover designed by Tamsyn Hutchinson
Printed and bound in Australia by Griffin Press

National Library of Australia
Cataloguing-in-Publication data

Heard, Barry.
 The view from Connor's Hill.

ISBN 9781921215483 (pbk.).

1. Heard, Barry. 2. Australia - Social life and customs
- 1945-1965 - Biography. I. Title.

994.05092

www.scribepublications.com.au

Contents

Introduction

IT WAS TEN YEARS AGO THAT THE BREAKTHROUGH HAPPENED. I had woken up not looking forward to my day, as usual. After lunch I found myself having a face-to-face discussion with my psychologist, which was never much fun. I was about to finish the session when she issued me with a straightforward, plain instruction: 'Write down how you feel, Baz.'

Sue, the psychologist, was having trouble getting me to talk. At that time I rarely wrote anything down, and certainly nothing private or personal. However, for some reason I took her advice. I returned to my room in the psychiatric ward and, for the first time, wrote about how I saw myself ... it was something we were continually being asked to do in group therapy.

'How do you see yourself? How do you feel?'

To my surprise, my timid initial jottings quickly became a habit. Mind you, I didn't share this little secret with anyone. A bloke writing—what a cop-out!

After several weeks, I found myself starting to write about painful scenes and incidents that I had witnessed as a young man, but I laboured to describe or explain the events: my shoulders would tense up, my forehead would jam with a rigid

1

frown, and I would hold the pen so tightly that it would almost snap. Then, one day, as I was writing my journal, something remarkable happened. Putting down the pen, I closed my eyes and pictured what I had been writing about. I saw a skinny young man in the jungle in Vietnam. He was very stressed, tired, concentrating, and looking quickly this way and that. Suddenly, a message squawked into his handset. He squeezed the receiver button and acknowledged the pilot.

'One, green smoke, Roger, out.'

The dust-off chopper came in.

His mate Kards was choppered out.

The young man now had the battalion radio in his hands ... and he was almost shaking with stress.

The scene was very clear in my head. Suddenly, like someone turning on a light, my own feeling of being stressed changed to something quite unfamiliar to me. I felt sadness. I wanted to enter that scene and comfort that young man, to offer him support and compassion. I wanted to explain to him that this bloody mess of a war was simply crazy. I wanted to tell him that he was okay, and that he was doing okay.

I was talking to myself ... some 30 years earlier.

Again, I picked up the pen. Now, though, my writing changed: I wrote with emotion. From anger to sadness and in between, I would sway and sometimes dash—always from my new vantage-point that enabled me to see this frightened young man, along with his mates, suffer through an appalling ordeal. Little did I realise at the time that I was purging my soul. Within a month I had written several hundred pages. Admittedly, I didn't show anyone my jottings for almost three years. It was too private for that.

However, it worked.

Today, that period of writing is gone, finished. In fact, I believe that after the first 12 months I had flushed out most of my demons. Sure, I was still fragile, and I showed all the outward signs of a tired, worn-out old man. But, inside, my spirit was starting to grow. Like a campfire that has struggled to start due to the pouring rain, I was on my way. In time, this fire could cook several dampers and boil a billy.

Today, for me, writing is like recalling a treasure, a unique incident, or a story. It leads me to explore my memory, my opinion, my feelings, and my life. My only regret is that I didn't hit upon this activity decades ago. Almost every day now, my pen hits the paper running. Come—let me share some of these precious recollections with you.

MANY PEOPLE contacted me after reading my first book, *Well Done, Those Men*. There were sections of the book that had appealed to them, such as its beginning, which described life in the country devoid of television and takeaways. Most people who corresponded wanted to read more about that era and the district out from Connor's Hill. As mentioned, over the last decade I had written at length about this period. Mainly, these were short pieces that I wrote for my own satisfaction. For me, and for many locals, returning to that period in written form has been a delight. I always felt proud to show them a story I had written. Sadly, that era has all but disappeared.

To produce this book, I put those pieces together. For authenticity, or to verify some of the yarns, I did many trips back to the high country, made numerous phone calls, and had a wonderful time. It was like turning back the clock—sitting around a table, having a cuppa, a scone, and simply talking. Many were surprised at my recall. That is a benefit of writing: delving into my mind for information invariably results in a totally forgotten memory coming to the surface.

I believe I grew up in a unique district, and that it had a profound effect on me. As a young person in the Omeo area, I always felt I was under a subtle form of scrutiny, a cultural check maybe, to ensure that I wasn't stepping out of line—not that I minded. Perhaps a good example was the time when I recall getting a tongue-lashing from my parents and being banned from driving their car for a month. I had been dobbed in by a local farmer. The night before, I had driven down Connor's Hill in my parent's car at a speed that now makes me shudder. I passed an old farmer in his Vauxhall Velox. With a lurch, I lost control of Mum's car. It went off the road, slewed on over a small hump, and then became airborne for some 20 feet before landing back on the bitumen. Fortunately, it corrected and we continued. There were five of us in the car. Death was but a stroke of luck away. The farmer reported me to my parents and, boy, did I cop it.

Living in the Omeo Shire was almost like having an extended family. Nowadays, most Australians grow up in cities; apart from immediate family, neighbours, work, or schoolmates, many have little idea of the diversity of the people who surround them. For me, during my youth, the high country was rich in characters and flushed with gossip, and the community was very close. From Glen Wills to Tambo Crossing, I knew every family in some way.

In normal day-to-day living, there were peculiarities such as people being typecast based on whether they lived above or below the Gap, as it was called. 'Above the Gap' referred to the higher, colder areas around Omeo and Benambra, where the inhabitants experienced snow and bitter, cold winds, and their stock did it tough in the winter. The area is famous for its fine wool and hardy Hereford cattle that have been reared on the open plains of the high country. People as far back as Banjo Paterson have been entranced by this beautiful, unique country. 'Below the Gap', where I grew up, was the Tambo Valley, consisting of Swifts Creek and Ensay, and many tiny locations such Tongio and Tambo Crossing. It was rare to have snow there, and our winters were milder, but our summers were much hotter. Yet it was only a five-mile drive from the lower to the higher open plains. The road that connected the two districts was called the Gap. It's where my parents' farm was located.

From early settlement, rivalry thrived between the two separate areas, particularly in sport. Other distinctive sub-cultures could be found throughout the entire shire. Farmers or graziers were the elite, while the majority of workers were employed in the many timber mills found in every town in the shire. Most farms also had labourers. Religion was a major influence, and subtle forces could be seen at play when it came to marriages and courting, religious instruction at school, and even funerals.

Mind you, I didn't realise that such things existed until I left to go into the army. But—and this is a big but—if this community was put under pressure, or if it had to cope with a disaster, it was as one. The peculiar quirks that superficially divided the areas disappeared, and the problem was met head-on—whether it was a death, a bushfire, a tragic accident, a house burnt down, or havoc caused by a freak flood. People were always there for each other.

Consequently, when I started writing for pleasure, particularly about those early times, I began to realise the benefit of having experienced that era, and I felt an inner satisfaction. I often smile as I relive a cherished period on paper. Countless times as a youngster, I remember enjoying a meal on the farm, or at home, when the table would come to life. There would be talking, laughter and, sometimes, a pack of cards. People had reputations as storytellers, and I always looked forward to their company. I never sat in a lounge room, as so many people do today, fixated on a box, staring at a beam of electrons in a vacuum.

There's no question that I spent my youth in a beautiful area that boasted many wonderful scenes and views. The film

The Man from Snowy River was made just over the hills from where I grew up. The young man who did all the spectacular riding in that film, Ken Connelly, comes from Benambra, just up the road. And Connor's Hill, mentioned so vividly in my first book, is not the most spectacular landmark when compared to the rest of the shire I lived in. However, for me it offered something special: it was the gateway to home. Many times, when returning from a trip away from the area, I always felt I was home once we reached the crest of Connor's Hill. People have told me of their similar feelings when they arrive at a railway station, or turn into a street, or spot a tower or a spire or the like that identifies their town. That, for me, was Connor's Hill. There were times when I just stopped and admired the awesome view. As a young lad, often while returning home after work, I would comment to my friends about the sunset or the low-hanging clouds. My friends at the time, Rover the dog or Swanee the horse, never answered me, but I'm sure they enjoyed the view as well. Much later in my life, this view returned to me in a fleeting moment that allowed me to return home. At the time, I was thousands of miles away and believed I was going to die. That, however, is another story altogether.

MY FIRST EFFORT at just writing for the joy of it was a short piece I wrote about Rover, a dog I had once owned and loved. I harboured countless fond memories of my times with him, but the idea of writing about my dog only arose after a chance meeting. Like many locals who knew me, the bloke I met realised I had been doing some writing, mainly for therapeutic reasons. He was very concerned about my health, and was pleased that I was finding writing such a benefit. It was a strange period of my life. People would say things to me like, 'You're looking younger, Baz' or, 'You're back, our Baz is back

... bless you, my boy' and, 'I haven't seen that cheeky grin for decades.' However, rarely would they talk about my illness—a mental breakdown—or the cause of the problem—Vietnam. Until this day, and this meeting.

To my surprise, the person almost challenged me to write about Rover ... for fun, for the very reasons stated above.

His name was Bill, or old Bill, as I called him. Let me explain.

I met old Bill, a dear old man from my past, in the mall near Safeway in Bairnsdale in the year 2000. As I approached the precinct, the first thing I spotted from some distance away was old Bill's familiar, thin, leathery face. The checked shirt, moleskin trousers, 1950s' Harris tweed sports coat, riding boots, and wide-brimmed Stetson hat he still wore also gave him away. It made me smile as I thought, *Still a gentleman—a neat, polite bushman who always doffs 'is lid to the ladies.* He sat alone on the bench seat in the mall, his head lowered, staring at the rollie between his nicotine-stained fingers.

He looked up as if sensing my approach and said, 'G'day, mate.'

'G'day, Bill, ya old blighter. How's things?'

'Good, mate. Yourself? Ya spelling improved yet?'

'Yeah, good. You know, Bill, I wouldn't have believed it, but the older you get, the uglier you get. You sure you weren't from Omeo, mate?'

'Steady on, Baz. Anyhow, I can do up me shoe laces. You learnt that yet, mate?'

This was a typical greeting. We discussed the weather, stock prices, and the possible closing of the old Benambra store. I had first met Bill about 40 years before, while working in a shearing shed. I was the rouseabout and Bill was a shearer—and a good one at that. He is retired now, and lives in the small country city of Bairnsdale. I see him whenever I go down the street, which is not too often. On this day he gave me some lip about my footy skills, or lack of them, when I'd played for Ensay; Bill always enjoyed reminding me how bloody useless I'd been. Then, as usual, I'd turn to the subject of Bill's shearing. There is no doubt he was one of the best shearers I'd ever picked up for when I used to rouseabout. But he was a bloody mollydooker—a left-hander—and it was difficult to pick up his fleece when he finished shearing his sheep.

Even though we usually had the same discussion every time we met, our conversation was enjoyable, created a few laughs, and reinforced the strong bond of friendship we shared. It's funny how insults affirm camaraderie in the bush. Yet, for all our yakking, I sensed a deeper resolve. Bill lived alone now. Doris, his wife of around 50 years, had died some ten years back. I also noticed that his old dog, Tattle, wasn't sitting beside his boots.

So, with some concern, I awkwardly asked, 'How's things, Bill? Looking after yourself?'

He hesitated, looked down, and said, 'Can't bring Tattle downs the town any more, Baz. He just used to get excited when he saw other dogs, but then this lady complained and reckoned she would get him banned, ya know? So now I don't bring him. Bit rough, I reckon. Poor old fella, he knows when I gets dressed up and I is going downs the street. He whines and then sits at the front gate and looks real sad, like. He's still there when I go back. Pity, the kids downs here love him.'

I was taken aback. This didn't seem fair. Tattle was Bill's best mate, a kelpie-cross sheepdog that was reputed to have been a brilliant yard dog in his day. It didn't seem right that they deny Bill the company of his mate. Reaching over to old Bill, I put my hand on his shoulder. 'Geez, mate, that's a bit rough.'

'Yeah, I know. Poor old Tattle. I only ever seen one better dog than him, and that was the dog you had, Baz. Remember him, mate?'

I looked away. How could I forget? The powerful memories of my own special dog flooded back. Bill continued talking about Rover, that unique dog I once owned. He not only recalled many of his characteristics; he also remembered in detail the peculiar markings of that strange-looking dog.

Bill, like many of the old people up home, was aware I had been real crook for the last couple of years. After a period of silence, in a low voice, he mentioned my writing. I guessed that, like most, he had heard that it had helped with my recovery, and he knew I had been doing a lot of it. He muttered something I didn't quite get. He seemed embarrassed until, with a cough, he asked, 'Ever put the story of Rover on paper, mate?'

'No,' I replied. 'I haven't.'

'You should, mate.'

I changed the subject. We continued to speak of other characters, and recalled those wonderful days in the 1950s and 1960s in the bush. I still feel lucky to harbour such delightful memories.

I returned home that same day, half determined to write about the dog and to acknowledge the wonderful companionship I had experienced by having owned such an animal. Later the same day, I was in my shed working on a piece of old furniture. It was a simple task—sanding back the top—but I was continually distracted. Old Bill's enquiries earlier that day about Rover really nagged at me. At one stage I stopped, walked outside, and sat in the shade of the old rivergum that grows in our backyard. Pondering those good times years ago, and that exceptional dog, I asked myself, 'Surely just the memory alone is worth the effort?'

So, as a dedication to Bill and to a wonderful dog I once owned, I decided to write the account he had requested. I wanted to re-live on paper that special time in my life.

That night, I put pen to paper. Several hours later, I had finished the rough draft and cherished re-living that era, and that unique dog and his part in my life—or should that be the other way around? It was only ten pages long, and the exercise made me realise how special it is to write about a treasured memory. I was keen to show old Bill; I thought I might pop around for a cuppa and give Tattle a pat. As it turned out, old Bill loved the story—he reckons he read it to Tattle. I hope you enjoy it, too.

chapter one
Rover

I MET ROVER ON A SHEEP-AND-CATTLE FARM. MY INITIAL impression was that if I was ever going to have a dog, it would be a lot smarter than this mutt and, hopefully, not as ugly.

It was during my first week at a farm called Kanangra that I spotted the dog. He was sitting up in the front seat of a blue Desoto ute. His master, old Jack Moy, was doing his block and calling the dog names that I wouldn't put on paper.

I'd just started work on the farm as a labourer, in my first paid job. I would be 'kept', which meant that I'd live and work on the farm from Monday to Friday. It was late 1961, and I was sixteen years old.

Now, Jack Moy, Rover's owner, was a rotund old man of 70-odd years. He owned the farm next door to where I worked, and he had the misfortune of owning this ugly, brindled part-kelpie dog called Rover. In fact, I thought old Jack was pretty tolerant with the dog. Perhaps it was his pet as well. Like me, old Jack Moy lived at Kanangra from Monday to Friday. We shared two bungalows out the back of the main homestead, and we both ate all our meals with the owners of the farm.

I'll never forget the first meal I had on that Monday night. Although it wasn't a special night, it was like a banquet—perhaps put on for my benefit, I first imagined. Initially I was quite chuffed. In time, I discovered that most meals consisted of at least three courses, completely different from home where we had large, simple meals with little variety. There was a another big difference: at home, Mum had insisted that we bathe once a week, and we only got dressed up for dances, barbeques, and balls. Now, in this new job, I was showering every night. Everyone also got dressed up for tea, which started with an appetiser and a sherry.

The meal that first night on the new farm was a bit daunting, really. At the table, bamboozled by the array of knives and forks in front of me, I sat not moving a muscle. Then there was a bit of cloth wrapped up in a metal ring. I watched every move that the others made.

We were up to the main course when old Jack, Rover's owner, arrived. Although he was quite late, he joined us for tea. He had been down to the post office to collect the mail, which he did most nights. Naturally, old Jack couldn't go past the pub on the way back, so he walked in with a slight lean to one side and a lop-sided grin to the other. He lunged towards the table, sat on the sideways-turned chair, and then plopped the napkin on his lap. Grunting, he turned his chair and pushed it back, which enabled him to slide his sizable belly under the edge of the table and lean forward on his elbows. He then began eating.

I was fascinated, especially by old Jack's table manners. I had never seen a display like it before; it was amazing. His substantial stomach increased the distance from the plate to his mouth, so he sat well back from the table. Then, leaning forward, he would pivot his food towards this mouth while his elbows rested on the table. Naturally, his arms were a fraction too short, so the last half-inch could be best described as a lunge, a fling, or a flick in the general direction. Actually, to be fair, over time, I noticed he was quite accurate. Most went in. This night, with his skill levels lowered by the intake of a few ales, the food went, let's just say, *towards* his mouth.

The first time I saw him swivel his food and gulp, I blushed with embarrassment as I struggled to stop a giggle coming out. It reminded me of my three-year-old young brother feeding himself. Mind you, it didn't bother old Jack; he hoed into the lamb cutlets and salad with gusto. In fact, I was amazed that the boss, a gentleman, didn't point out to the old fellow that he had a piece of lettuce hanging off his bushy eyebrow. Then again, before I started at the farm, Mum had told me old Jack was a shire councillor, and an ex-shire president as well.

'Call him Mister,' said Mum.

So my guess was that you didn't mention things like stray food to such an esteemed gentleman. Still, when a piece of beetroot landed on the left shoulder of his clean, newly starched shirt, I thought something should be said. But I believe the boss either didn't possess the courage or had too much respect for him to do so.

I went to bed that night with a head full of old Jack's eating prowess, doubts about the order in which one should use the assortment of knives, forks, and spoons and, to top it off, instructions from the boss to rise at about 6.00 a.m., milk the cows, separate the cream, and come in for breakfast at 7.00 a.m. Fortunately, I could do all those things. As for the dining etiquette, that was a different matter. My first day on the farm was a steep learning-curve.

The next morning I got up half an hour early. Old Jack in the next bungalow also stirred. He opened the door, and Rover emerged; he'd also slept in the room. I'd never known a dog allowed in a house before, let alone a bedroom. Old Jack appeared on the top step in his dressing gown. He stooped and then, with a grunt, patted Rover. They seemed good mates. He stretched, reached inside his pocket, and started another ritual that was far more intriguing than his eating habits. He began a weird charade of rolling a fag. I'd known a smoker before, but I'd never seen a smoke rolled while the roller had a convulsion, and I'd certainly never seen anyone finish a whole cigarette in one deep drag. Meanwhile, Rover disappeared briefly, piddling on every post within 25 yards of our bungalows. The dog shook himself vigorously and then returned hurriedly. Did he enjoy the fag-rolling as well?

In the meantime, old Jack unscrewed the round, orange lid on his tin of Log Cabin, plucked out a small wad of tobacco, and rubbed it around in his palms. The smell—a pleasant, rich odour—wafted in my direction.

Temporarily, his lips held a cigarette paper. Gradually, a small, blurting cough—a sort of a choking sound like a two-stroke engine refusing to start—emerged from his mouth. With this rhythm established, the volume increased to a squawk and then a splutter, spraying saliva in a circle of roughly six feet all over the concrete and Rover.

Old Jack then pulled the cigarette paper from his mouth and coughed some more. By this time, it was a deep, loud, rumbling, gut-wrenching growl like a possum in the mating season. His body started to bend forward and wobble, the cough got deeper and louder, and the process of rolling the cigarette continued. By now, my mouth was agape. This was incredible.

Finally, with his belly flopping up and down, his face red, his eyes bulging, and his hands reaching for the matches, old Jack spat out an oyster-like, solid piece of phlegm the size of a large grape. *Thwack!* It hit the saliva-sprayed concrete, and Rover barked. I was stunned. The dog sniffed at the vile globule warily.

I'd never seen anything like it. I felt like applauding this exhausting feat of human endurance. But the show wasn't over yet—this was only act one.

To finish his oyster-ejection spit and rasping convulsion, old Jack, with his head lolling over his belly and his belly jammed between his knees, shoved the rolled cigarette into his mouth, struck a match, and lit 'er up. By the time he was vertical, he'd sucked the fag down to his lips and thrown it away. A large *ahhh* then came out of his mouth, he thumped his chest, and started rolling another.

I guessed that, for old Jack, this was the perfect start to the day. As for me, well, I reckoned I should've clapped. But being a young farm labourer who wasn't exactly known for bursting into spontaneous applause, I remained quiet. Rover also just sat, mouth agape, head twisted to one side in a look of admiration, I thought. Thankfully, he didn't touch the repulsive blob of spit.

So in the one day I had met an esteemed gentleman with fascinating eating habits who smoked non-stop all day, and had a foul tongue and a worthless, ugly dog.

Despite all this, old Jack seemed content on his farm doing small jobs, tinkering in the woolshed, and driving around with Rover perched up in the front seat of the blue ute. He would often talk away to Rover and pat the dog's head. I admit the dog didn't answer, but there was eye contact between them.

Over time, I could see that old Jack struggled when it came to doing the stock work on his farm. No wonder, as he and Rover were both useless—old Jack being too crotchety, and Rover having no idea. Whenever I watched old Jack trying to muster, very quickly there would be swearing. His voice would grow louder as he spat out numerous confusing commands like a passionate, browned-off footy supporter. Meanwhile, the dog tried to round up the sheep while turning to look desperately at his owner. There was only one command that Rover appeared to obey and that was, 'Git in tha ute, ya hopeless ugly bugger of a bloody thing.'

Now, I didn't own a dog—just a slow, old horse. But after only a couple of weeks, I soon found myself helping old Jack in the paddock. This usually happened after I finished work. He would sidle up to me and quietly ask, 'Can you give us a hand mustering some sheep, mate?'

I obliged if I wasn't busy. Then it was always the same routine—the three of us, Rover, old Jack, and me, in the front of the ute, heading up into a paddock somewhere. After several opening and shutting of gates, we would be within sight of a mob of sheep. To be fair, old Jack would always try Rover first. He'd call the dog out of the ute and then shout, 'Come here, go way out, go back, come round, speak up, sit, sit, you brindle bastard, sit!' He would bellow as the sheep split up and ran everywhere. Rover seemed to run in decreasing, confused circles, barking occasionally. He had no idea.

'Go back, come 'ere, come 'ere! Ah, shit. Go back! Sit! Sit! Useless bloody brindle bastard. Git in tha ute.'

Rover would then leap through the open window and sit on the seat. Old Jack would turn to me. 'Baz, can you head off those bloody ewes, mate?'

Would you believe, I then did my sheepdog-impersonation act. It must have looked hilarious. Running and flapping my arms and making tugboat noises while copping abuse was exhausting, but it was a lot of fun and I became very fit.

As the sheep started to move along, old Jack would sit in his blue ute with hopeless bloody Rover beside him, his tongue hanging out, while I did all the dog's work, except for the sitting. Old Jack tried it once and I think he meant it, but I drew the line at 'Sit!'

Over the months, old Jack and I became really good mates. He let me drive his blue ute, and talked a lot about his days growing up as a youngster on the farm. He had done it tough. I enjoyed his yarns about horses and carts, the stagecoach, and when 'gold fever' hit the district. Listening to old Jack was like reading a good book.

It was usually as we were driving in the ute somewhere that he would begin a yarn. The funny thing was, I reckon Rover enjoyed them as well. His tongue would loll about, and there was always a gleam in his eyes.

But there came a time when I realised that old Jack had been away for about three weeks. Mind you, I didn't give this much thought until the boss told me that old Jack was really crook: he had inoperable cancer and didn't have long to live. That was a shock. Old Jack was a loveable character.

The other thing that was a bit of a surprise was that, before he went away, old Jack left a message with the boss. When he died, I was to have Rover. This was a strange request, and I found it a bit embarrassing. What good would a mutt like that be?

Several weeks later, poor old Jack died, and I became Rover's new owner. To be honest, I was at a bit of a loss. The unwritten law about ineffective dogs on a farm was to give them 'lead poisoning'—that's right, take them up the back paddock and shoot them. But I recalled the weird friendship that old Jack had established with Rover, and I decided I would find another owner for the dog; someone who wanted a house pet, maybe.

The problem of Rover bothered me all the next week. I kept the dog chained up most of the time, only letting him off just before I fed him each night. That way, I knew he'd come when called—and he did, straight away. Then, one night, I asked the boss to tell me a bit about old Jack's dog.

'He was trained by one of the best trainers around, a bloke from Bairnsdale,' the boss said. 'In fact, old Jack paid a top quid for him as one of the best. But that's the way it goes sometimes. No matter how well trained, the dog turns out a dud; a one-man dog that won't work for anyone else. No damn good, in other words. That's what old Jack got—a worthless mongrel.'

Come Friday, it was time to head home. During the week, I'd decided I would take the dog home. Maybe something would turn up. We had an old, black dog at home called Darky. He was a house pet and, well, maybe he would welcome a mate.

So, with Rover seated on the potato bag I had wrapped around the bar of my pushbike for his comfort, I warily pushed off for the four-mile ride home. As a precaution, I also had a long rope; just in case he wouldn't stay on the bike, I'd let him run beside me. Then, with his front paws resting on the handlebars, and his back legs on the bar below, I peddled for home.

What I thought would be a frustrating ride, with Rover trying to get off, didn't happen. He sat quietly. Many thoughts about the dog filled my head as I peddled along on the bike. I vaguely recall stopping for a break and showing him the view from the top of Connor's Hill. It was magnificent. To be honest, I hoped that an answer to the dog dilemma would eventuate at home; Mum was fond of animals, and maybe she'd look after him for a time.

It was a pleasant, 30-minute ride to our house on the Tambo River. My brother Peter, aged three, was there to greet me as usual. He immediately fell in love with Rover, and in no time was hugging him and leading him around with a length of hayband (a light rope). Mum liked the dog, too. Good—that might mean he'd have a home. Phew! I was pleased, as I didn't want to take him back to the farm.

Peter played with Rover all weekend, and Mum said that he was a quiet dog with a nice personality. She decided to keep him for the meantime.

On Monday, I rode to work believing that old Jack would be happy that his brindle mutt had a home, even if it was only a temporary one.

Several weeks passed, and I barely gave the dog a thought. Come the Friday, I rode the Malvern Star home and was pleasantly surprised to find Rover in an old pram, wrapped in a blanket, and wearing a bonnet. He was Peter's baby, and Peter was babbling to him. Rover, his tongue hanging out, was lapping up the attention. I thought, *Good. The dog's fitted in.*

Then my brother John, who also lived at home, came outside and commented, 'Check out what Rover can do, Baz.'

John pursed his lips and then whistled Rover out of the pram, flicked his fingers, and pointed towards the kids' new toy. Curiosity found me watching Rover rocking in a toy rocker. He sat in the seat, paws on the handles, just like on my bike, and rocked. Amazing. Then, another whistle from John, and Rover sat at his feet. John, who was enjoying this, told Peter to go and hide. Giggling, Peter scampered off and hid behind a fruit tree. Rover lay on the ground with his paws over his eyes.

'Find Peter,' he said.

It was obvious that Rover knew exactly where Peter was hiding, but he pretended otherwise. He wandered off aimlessly, looking and sniffing roughly in my youngest brother's direction. A fit of giggles from Peter forced Rover to show his hand (or should that be paw?).

After much hugging and a belly scratch as the dog lay down on his back, John announced it was Rover's turn to hide. He gave the instruction, and Rover went to another fruit tree and stood behind the trunk with his back to Peter. Peter hid his eyes, counted roughly to ten, and then declared in baby talk, 'Coming, ready or not!'

Rover stood very still, his head slightly turned so he could watch the proceedings. After 30 seconds, Peter had no idea where the dog was. Rover shook his collar and gave his position away, much to Peter's delight. He thought he had found him. Mum, looking through the kitchen window, laughed.

I was puzzled. Maybe this dog had some potential. John said it had only taken him a couple of weeks to train Rover to do these tricks. Consequently, after a bit of pondering, I cautiously decided to try Rover on the farm.

He seemed pleased to sit up on my pushbike when I headed off on that Monday. Again, he was the perfect passenger. And again, I stopped at the top of Connor's Hill. It was an exhausting ride up that long, steep incline with a dog on board. We both admired the early-morning mist that covered the Tambo Valley. The low clouds must have been 15 miles across, with just mountain peaks protruding here and there.

We were drenching sheep on the farm. The boss had normally done all the required mustering and I did the yard work. He was away this particular day, and there was one last mob to bring into the woolshed. I decided, *Well, here goes—I'll try to muster the mob of young ewes with Rover.* There was no one about, and I had nothing to lose. Cautiously, I walked with him into the lucerne paddock, left the gate open, and stood beside the strainer post. Hesitantly, I said, 'Go way out.'

Rover ran along the fence, behind the sheep.

'Speak up.'

A good dog will bark, and force the sheep to run into a mob. Rover barked twice, and the sheep herded together.

'Come over here.'

He started to come towards me when some of the sheep broke away.

'Go back!' I shouted, fearing this would be one test he wouldn't pass.

He not only went back; he headed them. Then, knowing where I planned to take the sheep, he started to quietly push them towards the gate. Within an hour, to my amazement, I realised this dog was good—very good. I realsied that Rover was a good paddock dog, which made me very happy. I gave him a cautious pat.

Getting sheep to the woolshed and yards efficiently was

an enormous time-saver on a farm. Then, with the mustering finished, you'd go and get the yard dog. A yard dog has to be forceful, aggressive, and tough. It runs across the sheep's backs, and turns them towards the desired direction. It has to have almost perfect balance. Many times, in a small yard packed with sheep, a dog will fall, disappearing underneath. At times, the dog is trampled quite severely. Most farms have two or three dogs—a cattle dog, one for the paddock, and another for the yards. Rover was better in the yard than the paddock. He was an all-round stock dog. In fact, he was a champion. It made sense that old Jack had paid a top quid for him.

I returned home to Mum and Dad at the end of the week with Rover proudly perched up with his paws on the handlebars. No sooner had I walked in the back door than I burst out with tales of the remarkable abilities and skills that this rather ugly-looking, part-Kelpie dog had shown. Admittedly, both of my parents had never owned or worked a sheepdog. They simply had to take my word for it that Rover was an exceptional dog.

It wasn't long before he was able to prove me correct. It was later that same year, I recall, after my parents had purchased a farm at Tongio. Here was my opportunity—when we put our first sheep on our new property. Mum had bought the sheep, a mob of fine-woolled merino wethers, at a sale. A truck had dropped all five hundred of them at our yards during the week, and Mum had gone up and let them out into the ridge paddock. This paddock had a bit of bush and a very steep, large ridge. Dad and I didn't get to see the sheep, as we were busy for the next two weeks.

It was the third weekend before I first saw the wethers. Dad, Mum, and I went up to the farm. I was going to muster them with Rover, check them for flystrike and any dags, and decide if they needed crutching. On the drive to the farm, Rover sat on the floor in the front of the Land Rover at my feet. That is what he'd been trained to do. Apparently, old Jack had taken ages to entice Rover onto the seat of his blue ute.

On arrival, we all got out and walked down by the small creek from where we could see the sheep. Sure enough, they were way up high on a very steep ridge. Both my parents looked in my direction, half expecting me to say, 'Wait there. Rover and I will go up the ridge and return with the sheep.'

I had a different plan; I was simply busting to show them what this remarkable dog could do. I knew I could send him into any paddock. He, in turn, would carefully check the entire area and return with all the sheep. So, raising my right arm, I pointed and said to Rover, 'Go. Way away out.'

Now, this paddock was huge. To walk around the boundary would take at least 45 minutes. Rover cast out very wide, and vanished through the small clump of bush. He emerged halfway up the grassy ridge and finally disappeared over the crest of the hill. Meanwhile the sheep, which were near the top, ran together. We could just make them out; they were peering at Rover over the other side somewhere. I waited proudly. I knew Rover would find this task a piece of cake. The sheep on top of the ridge remained fixated on what I guessed must have been Rover way down the other side, bringing up the stragglers.

Then something strange happened. The sheep we could see—I might add that they were some 500 yards away, on top of a long spur—stopped looking. They returned to their task of walking slowly while nibbling away at the grass. We waited and waited until Dad said, 'What's going on?'

I had no idea, and remarked as much. It was a bit awkward for me, after all the bragging and boasting I had done about my Rover. Finally, after quite a wait, I decided to walk over the ridge and see what was going on. It was a long, hard climb. I couldn't work out what the dog had done. Had he become frightened in this unfamiliar area and cleared off home? That was hard to believe; home was fourteen miles away. Then again, a farmer I knew at Ensay had a dog that was a good worker, but very timid. If this bloke yelled at his dog, it would put its tail between its legs and trot home gracefully. Maybe Rover had found a rabbit or a wombat, and had decided to give chase. There were many rabbits on the farm.

Finally, puffing profusely, I reached the top of the high ridge and started over the other side, and there was Rover. He was sitting about 20 yards away from a very badly flyblown sheep. I couldn't believe it. The sheep had become so weak that it couldn't walk. I guessed it must have run off on its own when it spotted the dog. Rover had given chase, and the sheep had run until it was exhausted. In Rover's mind, because of his training, a dog must never leave a sheep behind. I was so proud—I called him to me and tried to indicate that it was the smartest thing I'd ever seen a dog do. I'm not sure if he was impressed, but I was. He hesitated when I called him away from the flyblown sheep.

We then mustered the remainder, finally got them into the yards, and I went about my job.

Several hours later, I returned with some shears and a bottle of blowfly oil, and attended the sick sheep. It was quite an effort climbing back up that steep ridge because I was carrying all the gear as well as some water. On my arrival, the sheep looked very weak and hollow. Just on dark, it got to its feet and quietly walked back to the mob. Thanks to Rover, the sheep survived.

As I mentioned, buying the sheep property at Tongio was exciting. My parents, particularly Mum, told all and sundry that Rover was the best dog on earth.

Certainly, the mustering, yard work, and sheep management on our new farm was easy. Every other weekend I did stock work with Rover, and he made it all a delight. However, the first major problem we faced at the Tongio farm was rabbits. They were in plague proportions all over the farm. Dad told people, 'There are so many rabbits that when you clap your hands the farm jumps backwards three feet!'

At first, we tried ripping burrows with the bulldozer, but this made no difference. Someone suggested 'myxo', so I caught a number of rabbits and had them tagged to make sure I could return them to the correct burrow. All up, I had 20 rabbits when I visited the lands department in Swifts Creek. They inoculated the rabbits with myxomatosis.

Returning to the farm, I let the rabbits go near their burrows and we waited. We hoped for rain, because mosquitoes spread the myxomatosis virus; the moisture aids their breeding. Typical of most trials using that virus, initially there was a good kill. Then, over an eighteen-month period, the number of rabbits went back to where we'd started from. Finally, later that same year, with the introduction of 1080 bait, the rabbit problem vanished. In a matter of months, after we'd used several free feeds of carrots and then the poisoned batch, the rabbits disappeared almost overnight. It made a big difference to the farm. It carried a lot more sheep, and Bob, a good builder, planned to build a woolshed with yards.

By the time Rover turned four-and-a-half, I'd had him for more than eighteen months. He was a brilliant stock dog with sheep or cattle, and a dear friend. He would work tirelessly and never let me down. Well, that's not quite true; there was one day …

It was a very hot summer's day, and Rover and I had been working in the yards drenching sheep on the farm at Ensay. With a pen just completed, we headed back out to the paddock to collect the next mob. He rounded up a lively mob of two-tooth ewes, and we were about to move them through the laneway paddock. As I un-snibbed the gate, I nodded to Rover; the heat was oppressive, and he just looked at me and kept panting away. But there was a reason I nodded at the dog. Both of us had to have our wits about us. With other sheep in the same paddock, there was always a risk. As we moved the mob through the gateway, I would send Rover around the other sheep. He, in turn, would force them across the dry creek bed and into a corner of the laneway. That meant we were free to quickly progress down the paddock, making sure we held our mob tight as they moved along the opposite fence. You had to have a good dog; otherwise, if the mob I was mustering mixed, or 'boxed', with the others, it would cause many problems. Even determining which sheep came from which mob could take ages.

Rover was doing his usual job—effortlessly controlling the mob—when something happened. Never before had he done this. Suddenly he left the mob, ducked beneath the wire fence, and tore up another paddock with blistering speed. I whistled frantically, but he simply ignored me. Hell's bells! There was the dog going in the wrong direction, and the mob heading towards the other sheep in the paddock—what was I to do? Stunned, I did nothing. Then, all of a sudden, it dawned on me. Rover was heading for a cattle trough. He dived in and rushed along the length of the metal trough with his mouth wide-open, gulping water until he reached the other end. Leaping out, he turned and headed back towards the mob of sheep, and rounded them up just before a disaster happened. The blighter—he worked them back into a tight mob and then for the first time gave me eye contact. It was a very sheepish look. That poor, bloody dog—he'd been dying of thirst. He couldn't turn on a tap like the one I did at the woolshed and have a long drink. Cunning beggar—I reckoned he worked out exactly when to leave the sheep and tear up the paddock for that precious drink. I didn't pat him. Instead, I got off Swanee, my horse, and called Rover and gave him a hug.

There was no question that I loved this dog. His loyalty was total. Nevertheless, he had a couple of infuriating habits. One was farting, which I'll come to later. The other habit was indulged in so often that there were times when I nearly fell off Swanee while craning my head trying to find him. Yes, Rover continually walked with his damn head between the horse's hind legs, so close that I couldn't see him. Knowing Swanee, I bet he was a party to this. There I'd be on the horse heading up the paddock, turning, stretching, looking, just making sure Rover was with me. If it was midday with the sun overhead, I had no hope. Earlier or later, I would see his shadow bobbing along. Yet once we were in the proximity of the sheep, I would whistle, point in a direction and, suddenly, like magic, he would appear. The following year, when we went droving and spent day in and day out wandering behind the calves, I wouldn't see him for hours. A lot of working dogs have this habit.

Like most animals, including humans, Rover enjoyed praise and pats. But, most of all, he enjoyed travelling. Many dogs do. He sat on the bonnet of the tractor, or with me on the saddle of the horse, particularly if he was weary. He loved the Land Rover, a four-wheel-drive vehicle I drove when fencing or doing practical jobs. Rover would stand with his head out of the sliding window, his ears flapping, and his drool running down the door.

Most of all, he loved my new motorbike. Yes, I had updated from the pushbike. We had so much fun. I had no helmet or protective gear, and I rode it with typical teenage bravado and stupidity: flat out and then a sliding stop were the only speeds I used on the 175cc Super Bantam. About 40 miles per hour was 'flat out'. Rover sat on the fuel tank, between my arms. We had quite a few prangs in the paddocks, but we were never hurt—just bruised. He loved the Bantam, and whenever I said, 'The bike, mate,' he would grin, rush over, and sit beside it.

However, when things got a bit hairy on the Bantam, I was on my own. Rover had a knack of abandoning the bike just before I skidded across wet grass backwards, the motorbike beside me bumping along with its engine screaming. But it wasn't always good fun. One day, as he was about to hop onto the bike, he put both his paws on the red-hot exhaust pipe. I got a very dirty look. Would I ever get him on the bike again? Typically, Rover decided the best way to do it was to sprint at the motorbike and leap into the air from about three yards away. My part was to catch him. It worked, the smart blighter!

A good farm sheepdog has many skills. However, the thing I admired the most in Rover was the way he worked at lambing time. I loved lambing down on a farm. Every morning, very early, you'd go around to the ewes and their new lambs. If everything was going well, you'd move the ewes that had lambed that night into an adjoining paddock. It was hard; the dog had to separate the new mothers by wandering quietly through the mob. You hoped that the dog could bring the lambs along as well, but this rarely happened. Nevertheless, some dogs invented ways to catch the lambs. Bonny, the boss's dog, would hold them in her mouth until he came over and picked up the lamb. Typically, Rover was different. He would knock them over and gently put a paw on the lamb until I came over and carried the lamb quietly behind its mother.

Like any good sheepdog that's well known in a district, Rover enabled me to get work away from the farm, like rouseabouting — working as a handyman in a woolshed picking up fleeces, sweeping, penning up, and doing many other jobs. The word soon got around that not only could I rouseabout but, more importantly, I came with a very handy dog, and so could help before and after a day's shearing as well. This meant that we got a lot of woolshed work around the district. Thanks to Rover, I was getting work that paid better. Fortunately, the boss didn't mind.

Every year I had more woolshed work, and shearing time couldn't come quickly enough for me. Most runs lasted two or three weeks. Then the bales of wool were loaded onto a semitrailer and taken to the sales in Melbourne or Geelong. On the last day, there would be a break-up. The owners would put on beer and food while the workers created the atmosphere, and it was great fun. Then I would move on to another shed.

Over the years, I met most of the district's shearers, wool classers, and wool pressers. I enjoyed the atmosphere of the woolshed. I would live on the owner's farm during shearing, as most had shearers' quarters. At daybreak, Rover and I would help the farmer muster and pen up. Then, after shearing, I'd brand the shorn sheep and return them to their paddocks that night. By most evenings, Rover was exhausted, and I always asked the shearers' cook for any scraps. Rover enjoyed many a hearty meal. Then at bedtime, just like old Jack, I let him sleep in my room in the shearers' quarters. He would disgrace himself with ripe, heavy farts—always with a smirk on his dial, the blighter, but I tolerated the foul air. It only became a problem sometime later ...

The dog's status spread, and I vividly recall the day when local legend Alan Taylor asked me to work as a drover. He was the head drover responsible for all the cattle and sheep taken long distances from the remote areas of the high country to the railhead at Bairnsdale, and he asked *me* to do some cattle droving. What a privilege. Here was a chance to drove hundreds of calves from the isolation of Benambra to Bairnsdale, and I'd be paid for it. I couldn't wait. The first time I did the trip, my job was at the tail end—I was the last person at the back of the mob, with a packhorse as my companion. At times, I would lead cars through the mob and do some droving. I was very young, and the boss drover was checking me out. It was almost like a test.

I enjoyed unloading the bulky, canvas-covered load on the draught horse each night. I would put out the swags, the camp oven, and the cooking gear and frame that held the oven over the fire. It was my job to collect firewood, light a fire, and help prepare the food. However, first things first—I would put the billy on and make a brew. Our water was in waterbags, and at times I rode down to the river to fill them up. Other times, a local homestead provided the water. With the drovers all enjoying a cuppa, I would feed the dogs, and would finally join the men around an open fire and hoe into a glorious meal. It was a treat.

The following year I became a drover with my own small mob. The first calf sales were always at Benambra. This year, the three of us—Rover, Swanee, and I—had arrived quite early at the yards. I brushed Swanee, and I gave Rover the large bone I'd hidden in the saddlebag. As the last pen went to auction, I mounted up, my freshly oiled stockwhip hanging over my right arm as we waited. Rover had dashed away for three nervous pees. Once the sale ended, the calves would be let out of the yards in no time, and then it was the drovers' time. We couldn't wait. Local talk had it that this year the Benambra area and the high plains had enjoyed a good spring and summer, particularly in the bush. It had been a good sale: the calves had sold for record prices, and they were in prime, sappy condition. It also meant they would be brisk, energetic, and harder to control.

Picture these young calves—most of them not long separated from their mothers—calling out frantically, panting almost to the point of exhaustion in the eerie, noisy environment of the sale yards. The auctioneer and his minders would walk along the top rail of the yards after each pen was knocked down to the highest bidder. The auctioneer almost sang as if performing the lead role in a comic opera. Bids would be thrown in rapidly while the chorus or the auctioneer's scouts called 'yes!' or 'hep!' in a loud voice. With a clap of the hands, the final bid was announced and everyone would move to the next pen. It was quite a performance. The first time I saw a sale, I thought they were all drunk. Imagine how the calves felt, with a strange voice bellowing weird noises overhead as dozens of people peered at them through rails or while perched on top.

The Benambra sale finished early. With the last pen sold, these frightened young calves were drafted, organised, and counted. Some would only be travelling small distances to local farms; these would stay in the yards overnight. The remainder, the bulk of them, would be herded together in a large yard, and rushed through open gates without warning onto an open road, only to face strange horses and smart, sharp, loud dogs, cracking whips, and men giving orders. There would be several hundred calves, all about to start the long journey to Bairnsdale. You could sense the fear building in these young animals. They needed a strong hand, guidance, and compassion. Always, the drover's first job was to settle them, circle them, talk to them, calm them, and avoid haste. If possible, this happened quickly, and the boss's instructions were always to keep them in a tight pack. This not only required cool heads from the drovers; attentive dogs and watchful horses also played a part. It was like an event with an audience.

The first fifteen minutes had the potential at any moment to erupt. Then it would be a true test. Word had it that this year these calves were bigger and livelier than usual. Even in the yards, the calves were anxious and wide-eyed, their flanks jerking up and down as they sucked in short breaths. As the wooden gates were about to be swung open to let the calves run onto the road, bystanders watched intently. Many locals were perched up on the yards waiting in anticipation, their legs hooked over the top rail, hats pushed back, chins on clenched fists, elbows on knees. It was a common scene at any sale, with the audience almost hoping for something to go wrong—anything that would test the drovers' mettle and create an exciting, chaotic scene. Maybe there'd be a mini-stampede or a rogue calf—a frenzied young Hereford steer—tearing down the road, bellowing in fear, which could crash through any fence and cause many problems for the drovers. Old-timers told stories of such scenes. It would only take a car horn, a slamming door, or a loud shout to ignite the pent-up jitters of these calves. No one would dare …

Rover, as I expected, was alert. Like a champion footballer, he anticipated movement. Working in yards at the sales was familiar to him. Many months before, I had used him in several sales, and he had done well. However, this was our first time droving a large mob; the packhorse had another young fellow leading him. Yes, now I would be a drover with my own section to look after.

The gates creaked open and the calves ran out—but they didn't rush. Alan Taylor had to count them as they ran out onto the road. As mentioned, always, at the start, some calves would attempt to run off, play the leader and, invariably, others would follow. It happened this time, too, and a drover quickly headed them in the right direction. A stray calf ran off, and Rover immediately earned his colours. It was exciting. A few whips were cracked, but only when necessary.

After some order was established, we headed the mob across the plains past Hinnomunjie and down to Omeo. It was a striking sight. The calves sold in these sales were always in prime condition, of good breeding and, apart from the odd one, always Herefords. At Omeo, there would be more calves from that sale. Within a day, Rover was a veteran. I kept looking, learning, and receiving instructions. Again, we were camping out and cooking our meals around an open fire. Several drovers mentioned Rover that first night. The boss liked what he saw.

From Omeo, it was down the Gap to Swifts Creek and then on to Ensay, all the way picking up more calves from annual sales. By now, the mob had swelled into the hundreds.

After Swifts Creek, Rover, Swanee, and I felt at home in the middle of the mob. I was enjoying looking after my own small herd. Already I had detected some calves that had certain traits and characteristics. There was a leader, a wanderer, a dopey one that walked into posts, and a couple that hung back, seemingly enjoying being near my two mates and myself.

However, as we went further, Rover's paws became a problem. At first, I thought it was a thorn, or maybe a small pebble, that had lodged in them. But, on inspection, it was worse. His front paws were very tender, the pads so worn that one had started to bleed. As I probed and tried to look for something foreign, he pulled away, ran off, and sat under Swanee. Concerned, I spoke to the boss. Poor Rover—I had to hold him very tight as several of the blokes had a look. They all came to the same conclusion: because there were now more sealed roads, his poor old feet were bleeding from twisting and turning on the bitumen. He was a tireless worker those first few days.

It was time to rest my dog. I picked him up and sat him up on Swanee. Initially, Rover had his ears back, sitting warily. He had been up on Swanee's back before, but always in my arms; this time, he was on his lonesome. Swanee made no protest; maybe he sensed there was a problem with Rover. In fact, the horse walked somewhat more slowly than normal. This must have been hard for Swanee, as he more often than not churned out a walk that took a good jog for me to keep up with. The dog soon settled. However, Rover's feet were a concern. There was still quite a way to go. From Ensay, there was a long and winding road through the bush to Tambo Crossing and on to Bruthen. Bairnsdale was the final leg, but that was another five days away.

The new calves settled quickly after the Ensay sale. It was the last sale; the new calves picked up there were well and truly outnumbered, and in no time swayed along to the pleasant pace we'd established. For the first time, we were leaving the open farming country and entering the bush. The bellowing had stopped, the rhythmic plodding was almost trance-like, and the whole scene had the characteristics of an army march. This meant the drovers could take it a little easier. It also meant I could walk along leading Swanee, my horse, simply flicking the stockwhip occasionally. Rover, still with sore feet, confidently sat in the saddle having a well-earned rest. If needed, he could work for half an hour, particularly if we lost a calf over a steep bank. However, he spent most of his time up on Swanee. This somehow appealed to people driving along the roads. They would stop their vehicles, get out, and want to take photographs of this likeable dog. It was odd, but they always asked his name. I would tell them it was 'Rover' (such a rare name for a dog) and then add that he was such a good dog he had been promoted—to a stockman—and he could ride a horse. I'm sure Rover smiled at that remark.

Just before Tambo Crossing, the day after Ensay, one of the drovers hailed down a local in his ute, and they discussed the problem of Rover's paws. Several remedies were offered. The bloke in the ute drove off, indicating he would return later. That night, after counting the calves into a paddock just past Tambo Crossing at Sandy's Flat, we attended to the horses and fed the dogs. By this time, it was dusk. I rolled out my World War I canvas sleeping bag and put the saddle at the head. This was my pillow. Within minutes, Rover was asleep on the bag—my own electric blanket. After a generous stew, followed by the perfect cuppa (one of many through the night), Jim sat beside me. His mate in the ute had turned up.

'Call ya dog, mate,' he said.

Rover trotted over. The next half-hour saw a curious Rover lifting one front leg, then the other. By midnight, between the three of us we had made four canvas boots—or booties. All it had taken was a few crude measurements, a canvas pattern, scissors, a waxed thread, and some darning needles. Not only did they fit, but they were held in place with a bright orange leather thong. It was quite a fashion statement.

That night I curled up, very pleased, my head on the upside-down saddle, and Rover on my feet. If it got too cold, he came in the bag with me. Mind you, it had to be pretty damn cold for me to let him in—I reckoned he saved his best farts for that bag. (Two nights before, I'd let him into the bag, and he didn't hesitate as it was very cold. He dropped a clanger. This foul fart almost choked me. It ended up in a standoff, as Rover was very reluctant to leave the warm sleeping bag. I weakened, but warned him he only had one more chance!)

The next morning, with my packing done and the calves let out, I knelt down and put Rover's booties on him. In disgust, he'd chewed them off, and I got a dirty look. I reckon even Swanee shook his head; well, we did try!

ROVER AND I did several trips to Bairnsdale over the years, but his paws always gave him trouble. I would work him in short stretches, particularly at the beginning. Having both Rover and Swanee made a formidable combination when it came to droving. They were both outstanding with stock. I knew I would have work for as long as I owned both of them.

The love I felt for this wonderful dog only came to the surface when tragedy stepped in. I was a rouseabout in a three-stand woolshed. As the only shed hand, I was flat out. Typically, Rover was asleep on a wool pack having a well-earned break. However, whenever I needed him, after a short whistle from me he would run to the swinging doors, ready to fill the catching pen.

On this morning, just before smoko, I was about to pick up a fleece when I noticed Rover moving towards me. He was staggering, losing his sense of direction, but determined to get to me. Farm dogs normally never cross the woolshed floor. I quickly dropped the fleece. He reached my feet and tried to sit as he usually did, but this time he fell over. I reached down to pat him. He shook, his eyes fixed on mine, and then he went limp and died.

The shearers turned off their machines. Someone turned off the petrol engine. The woolshed went quiet.

I picked up my sweet dog, hoping he would lick my face and be Rover again. He was warm, soft, and beautiful. I looked up for something: a miracle, some hope. One of the shearers, Bill, had tears running down his cheeks. He used to sneak Rover biscuits at morning tea, while I pretended not to notice. Tom, another shearer, walked outside shaking his lowered head as he reached for his handkerchief.

Time stopped.

I put Rover on his favourite wool pack. Both Bill and I patted him with tender, loving strokes.

'What happened, Baz?'

'I don't know. He's only a young dog,' I replied in my strongest tearful voice.

'I reckon the vet should see him, just in case it's dangerous,' the farm owner said.

I carefully put Rover in the boot of the farmer's car, and he drove off. It would be a long drive to Bairnsdale. Bill and I had put several blankets under my Rover to make it more comfortable for him. I watched the boot as the car disappeared in a cloud of dust down the long dirt driveway.

The vet said it was 'hard pads' disease, caused by the constant paw trouble Rover had had from droving and mustering. Somehow, his infected paws had poisoned his blood, or something like that.

Rover returned to me the next day. I brushed him, wrapped him in a warm blanket, and took him down to the creek where I had dug a hole the day before. I buried him with affection and dignity, and then raked the mound neatly. I cut a branch from a Weeping Willow tree, drove it in the ground, and hung a sign that simply said: 'My good friend Rover.'

TWENTY YEARS LATER, with a wife and three kids, I was driving up the same winding road I had driven cattle on with Rover. I was telling them about my precious companion, when I found myself saying, 'Let's visit the old fella.'

I hadn't been up that remote road since Rover had died. We parked just above the small stream. Staring at the creek with tears in my eyes, I was suddenly overcome with emotion. My family surrounded me. They thought the grieving was for Rover. But it was something else that had triggered my reaction: a magnificent Weeping Willow tree had grown from the small branch I had stuck in the ground all those years ago. It is still there today.

Rover deserved that.

chapter two
A kid in Melbourne

WRITING ABOUT MY PRECIOUS DOG HAS, INEVITABLY, TAKEN me way ahead of myself. It's time for me to take you back to the start, a long time before Rover, to the haziest of all my beginnings.

I was born in Melbourne in 1945. My father died when I was barely eighteen months old. Sadly, I don't remember him, the funeral, or the grief that surrounds such an event. Our family lived at the corner of 23 Smith Street and Little Victoria Street, Collingwood.

Before his death, my immediate family consisted of Mum, Dad, my older brother Ian, and me, a bub. Under the same roof lived Nana Heard, my father's mother, and her five adult children. It was the Heard family house, rented by Grandma Heard. Grandpa Heard had absconded, cleared out, shot through—whatever term you want to use. However he thought of it, he offered no further help to his family. Perhaps, after the experience of the Depression, he did what many dads did. During that tough time, within a family—a poor family, that is—many a husband not only left home to hunt for work, but also promised to send money home. Secretly, many a husband stayed away during those times, pretending to have absconded, because deserted mothers had preference when it came to what little support there was available to poor households from churches and other aid organisations. Sadly, after the severity of the Depression subsided, some husbands chose to stay away—particularly those who had offered little help to their family. I believe my pop fitted into that category somewhere.

The dwelling at Smith Street wasn't actually a house. The entrance was by a side street, and the front of the dwelling was a pawn shop, or op-shop. Typical of so many families who had suffered through the Depression, my father's family had been evicted four times; their stay in Smith Street became the longest they had ever stayed at the one address.

World War II saw the young men in the Heard family join the services—my father into the army, and his brother Cliff, the navy. On return from one leave, he married Mum. They moved into the tiny room at the Smith Street house; Nana Heard now slept under the staircase. The other five Heards had to fit into the remaining two bedrooms, but that arrangement didn't last. Baby Ian arrived, and my parents moved to the big bedroom downstairs.

Dad was then posted to Townsville, and he was there when it was bombed. Darwin, Broome, and Townsville were all targets of Japanese bombing during that stage of the war. Yet, as so often happens, our politicians kept knowledge of most of this from the Australian public.

It was during his time in Townsville that my father became very ill with a blood disorder. At the time, this was diagnosed as having stemmed from his multiple broken noses. He had managed to break it several times while competing as an amateur boxer representing the army in inter-service bouts. He was ill for many months. The army, unable to offer any further medical assistance, discharged him from the hospital and the service. He returned to 23 Smith Street. It was 1944; the end of the war was in sight.

Not long after he arrived home, Mum became pregnant with me. Dad immediately returned to civilian employment, but his health never really improved or changed for almost two years. Consequently, he struggled to keep working as an upholsterer. Between them, the entire Heard family eked out a living that paid the rent and put food on the table, but nothing more.

By early 1945, I was born, and Ian had a young brother. Now it was my parents and we two boys in the *big* room. In January 1946, Mum fell pregnant again. Within months, my father's lingering blood disorder attacked a major organ—his heart. He stopped work, and his health deteriorated rapidly. His brother Cliff, who still lived at Smith Street at the time, vividly remembers carrying my dad through the house and along the street to catch a tram to the hospital. He told me that, at the most, my father would have weighed roughly six stone. He died within days. Although Dad was given the simplest funeral, I know from enquiries and from talking to family members that, when my father died, the entire Heard clan was almost penniless and destitute.

Three months after my father's death, my brother Robbie was born. He was a blue baby—for him to live after birth required a full blood transfusion. Life for my mother must have been hell.

The Heards all rallied together—one of the plans had been to adopt us three boys into the other Heard families, since by now three of them had married or planned to marry. Then help came in the way of Legacy. My father, being in the army, had been away during a lot of the war. He didn't go outside Australia, but somehow his circumstances fitted Legacy's requirements. Mum got a pension, and we remained in Smith Street.

Oblivious to all of this, I thought my life as a youngster had been good. I can still remember Nana Heard, the house, and the upstairs area—the tiny room, and the alcove under the staircase. They are all fond memories, yet most of the time we lived life as paupers.

The following year, Mum, my brothers Ian and Robbie, and I moved to Ringwood. We would be living in a house near Mum's parents, who had arranged rental accommodation for us. The address was on the corner of Great Ryrie Street and Bedford Road. Known as 'Corbett's Orchid', it was our first real house. It was a half-acre block with a huge yard.

They were an odd couple, my mum's parents, Nana Roy and Uncle Jock. Uncle Jock, Nan's second husband, was a tall, bonny Scot with a broad accent and a beaming smile. He enjoyed life and loved us kids. Nana Roy, Mum's mum, by comparison was tiny, grey-haired, and always busy. Their house was always spotless. She continually nagged Uncle Jock, yet his smile remained firmly planted.

After a brief stay in the Great Ryrie Street house, we moved to Wilana Street in Ringwood, right next to Nana Roy's. My first memory of this new address was vivid. It happened several days after moving into our new old-weatherboard house. I would have been about three or four. I recall lying on my back on the front lawn, staring up at a huge, tall, dead tree. There were clouds rushing across the sky. It was quite windy. Suddenly, the tree started to fall. I got up, rushed inside, and screamed the news to my mother. We ran outside. The tree was big enough to hit the house if it fell in that direction. Yet, when Mum rushed outside, the tree hadn't moved. I'm sure I muttered something like, 'It must have gone back up, Mum.'

It was many years later that I realised the tree hadn't gone back up. Like another train in the station that makes you believe you're moving when in fact you're stationary, I'd imagined the clouds had stopped and the tree was falling. Such a fright for any youngster is bound to be one of their first memories.

There were four of us living in this seemingly large weatherboard house (many years later, I discovered it was tiny) with a radio. Yes, it was just Mum and her three boys; I was the middle one.

It's funny, but in years to come the sound of the radio would always be my first recollection of that house. It was always switched on. Mum used to listen to the radio serials: D24, which was a Hector Crawford production, Hop Harrigan, and others.

Ringwood was an outer suburb of Melbourne—the last major suburb east of the city, and a 30-minute train trip from Flinders Street Station. I loved this new environment. Nana Heard would also visit regularly, and we often returned to Smith Street. The train trip was always exciting. Ringwood was different from Collingwood in many ways. For instance, instead of us having to go to a shop to buy bread, milk, and ice at Ringwood, a horse and cart delivered those items.

Then there was the lavatory. Smith Street had had one with a chain that you pulled when you finished your business. It not only flushed; it made a low, hollow, bopping noise for ages. However, at Ringwood there was a whole industry involved around the humble lavatory, which was in a small room out the back. Once a week, at dawn, a man wearing a beret and a strange-looking leather cover on his shoulder would appear. He would run into our backyard carrying a can, open a rear flap to our lavatory, and remove the can inside it. Then he would unlatch the lid on the empty can he carried, attach the lid on the full one, and put the empty one under the lavatory seat. Closing the rear door, he'd heave the full one onto his leather-covered shoulder. The full can seemed to be very heavy. The man would sprint to the truck—commonly called the 'night cart'—shove our can onto the tray, and then the truck would move to the next house. There would be two men operating either side of the street; I watched them every time they came to our house for the first few weeks.

Suddenly, our life changed yet again: our mother re-married. His name was Bob and he was a plumber—a dark-haired bloke from two streets away, near where we had first moved when we came to Ringwood. It was weird; I had never noticed him before. Mum continually prompted us to call this new man 'Dad'. This seemed strange to me, because life seemed complete and without any need for this drastic alteration.

I gather, from our relations and others, that we three boys were very close at the time. Robbie, my younger brother, was born in 1946, a year after me. Ian, my older brother, was more than four years older than I was, and yet we stuck together like glue. I know that, for me, it was a confusing time having a new father.

After the move to Wilana Street, I started at the local kindergarten. This was located at the back of the Church of England, about three streets away, just near the railway underpass.

Then it was Ringwood Primary School. For me, it was just a short walk up to the end of the street, a right turn, and the classic old brick building was down at the end. School was great—particularly the playground, which boasted a slide, a rocker, and monkey bars. I had never seen these sorts of things before. The school was large, with many grades split into different levels. I made several good friends, most of whom lived just around the corner from us. We often played on the street and visited one another's places after school. The street was home to many team games; depending on the season, there would always be boys playing football or cricket on Wilana Street. Since few houses could boast a motorcar, traffic wasn't a problem on the sealed road.

The first highlight after our big move to Ringwood was to attend a Guy Fawkes night, more commonly called 'firecracker night'. Over a period of weeks, locals would arrive with barrow-loads of wood and branches from gardens, and dump them just down the end of Wilana Street on a vacant block. The odd truck would also stop by with a tray load of off-cuts. Then, with all of this combustible material piled into a big heap called a bonfire, come the fifth of November, the entire street celebrated beside this blazing inferno. There were firecrackers, skyrockets, jumping jacks, penny bungers, tom thumbs, sparklers, double bungers, and Catherine wheels, just to name a few. It was better than any New Year's Eve I have ever seen—except for a nasty accident.

It happened at my second Guy Fawkes night: the same street, the same vacant block, and a bigger bonfire. A young girl had a skyrocket aimed at her, she ducked, it landed in her hair, and she was rushed off to hospital. It was frightening. Quickly, the adults got into a blaming game. The girl, in my grade at school, wore a turban-like top for the rest of the year.

Just one block away from our street was a large park on Greenwood Avenue. Again, it was full of kids with footballs or cricket bats, with makeshift teams playing a game. Another craze at that time was kite-flying. A windy day would see half a dozen kites flying. Some kids were quite skilled, and their kite could swoop and dive. The kites were all hand-made with the help of parents or friends. Kids appeared to have few individual toys, and playing with friends occupied most of our time. Robbie and I shared an old, three-wheeled bike, and that was about it. Then someone made a billycart for Ian, and we all shared rides in it down Greenwood Avenue.

Every year, there were annual billycart races held in Ringwood. I cannot recall where, but I remember them being keenly supported, and many races were run before a winner was announced. One time, my brother Ian won, I believe.

Every day after school we went over to our grandparents, on my mother's side. As mentioned, they lived right next door.

There was a convenient hole in the paling fence. Nan was wonderful—she gave us gifts and surprises that my mother was unable to afford. Nan's second husband, Pop, or 'Uncle Jock' as he preferred, was the typical doting grandfather. He worked at a brickyard. At home, he devoted most of his time to his two passions: the vegie garden and we three wee boys.

By 1950, I had a half-brother, John, and the following year Jeff was born. My stepfather, who I now called 'Dad', drove an old ute. Now, that was exciting. The privilege of riding in a car was something we bragged about at school. He also had a Pommy bloke called Duncan work with him in his plumbing business. He was a kind man who joked all the time.

Time just seemed to rush by in those early years at Ringwood. Nothing much happened until, umm … some men may want to skip the next two paragraphs.

About halfway through Year Two at school, my mother kept me at home one day. I was dressed up in a grey coat with grey shorts and tie. Next, she walked me to the station. Once on the platform, Mum changed into her cat-cleaning-a-kitten role. One of her habits that always bugged me was when she pulled out her hanky, liberally licked it, and then vigorously rubbed it over my face. This seemed to happen every time we went near that damn station. Suitably cleaned, we caught the train and got off in Melbourne.

Then, via a rattly tram, we arrived at a very large building that Mum said was a hospital. We went inside. Told nothing, the next thing I remember vividly was lying on a large table, surrounded by people in white uniforms with masks on. It was very scary, with a bright light over my head and with no one around who appeared interested in my welfare. The people in the room all seemed to be talking at once, until someone put a washer, or flannel, with horrible, smelly stuff over my face. A head with glasses and a white mask told me to count to ten, and the next thing I heard was, 'Wake him up now.' This really frightened me, as I was already awake. I remember being wheeled to a room and spending the night in hospital.

The next day, my parents arrived and took me home—in a pram. I couldn't walk. Believe me, circumcision is a very frightening thing for a young boy.

The next week was agony, particularly the act of trying to have a pee. The end of my willy was covered in gauze of some kind, which allowed me to piddle without having to take the dressing off. This meant my wee splashed and sprayed in many directions—mainly over me. The ordeal was alarming, I had no idea why it was done. Not until years later was I told that the same thing happened to many boys during that era, because circumcision had suddenly become fashionable. I was simply thankful that my sausage regained its original colour after a week. I don't think I could have faced life with a purple willy wearing a lace bonnet.

For some reason, Nan and Uncle Jock then moved to Warrandyte. It was during my second year at school and, initially, we boys were very upset. However, it turned out that there was no need for us to worry as it simply meant a trip to Warrandyte every school holiday and on many weekends.

Every break, we three older boys would catch the bus at Ringwood Station, hand over our ticket, and enjoy the adventure of seeing some countryside while riding on the Warrandyte bus. I would kneel on the back seat with my nose against the big window. It was a 20-minute trip.

The driver would drop us off at Selby's store, just a five-minute walk from Nan's along a narrow, dusty roadway. They lived in a tiny miner's cottage perched on the side of a hill. Their block was at least two acres, and one side of the property bordered the bush. The bellbirds sang their normal rowdy welcome every time we ran along the narrow dirt track to the wooden front gate. After waving to our grandparents on the veranda, the next thing we would notice would be Uncle

Jock's garden. It was huge: there were rows of potatoes, and mounds of pumpkins and melons. He must have spent ages in that garden. After rushing through the creaky front gate, we would tear up the narrow path and jump the front steps two at a time, straight into the warm arms of Nana Roy. Sitting on their veranda, they would have been watching us since we'd got off the bus at the store. We always hoped this greeting would be as brief as possible, as we had another agenda on our tiny little minds—feasting on Nan's cooking.

She was a tireless cook, and she would have all the baking tins full with fresh paddy cakes, butterfly cakes, biscuits, and jam drops. It was wonderful—I suppose partly because our mother was never a cook. Meals at home, while always plentiful, were simple, and rarely would a cake or pudding hit the meal table. At Nan's we would pig out on cakes and the like, with every meal except breakfast. Then would come the final treat—a supper of pancakes with treacle and cream. Is there a better way to satisfy the taste buds? We loved the evening. There we all were, around a warm, open fire after tea. Uncle Jock would start to tell yarns in his broad Scottish accent. One of us sat on his knee, and another at his feet or on the arm of the chair. He'd been a soldier during World War I, and he could tell amazing stories, mostly army tales. They were wonderful recollections about the horses, the trip on the ship, the mischief, and pranks that seemed to follow the soldiers wherever they roamed.

Quietly, Nan would put a subtle stop to these seemingly endless adventures by setting up the card table and producing a crib board. Then we boys became spectators to a ritual that happened every night for as long as we visited Nan's. I had no idea about how the game worked. Nevertheless, I recall a chanting of numbers, and matches being moved along a board full of holes. The highlight of the game was watching Nan shuffle and then deal the cards. They would snap in her fingers and float through the air as she dealt. Uncle Jock reckoned she was lightning fast.

Come bedtime, there would be a warm cocoa, another biscuit, and then bed. We slept in the sleep-out on the veranda, beside the small lounge-room.

Uncle Jock used to work Saturday mornings. He would be home by 1.00 p.m. with a packet of Allens barley sugar in his sports-coat pocket. After making us a scrumptious meal of hearty sandwiches, Nan would don her best apron for the kitchen. Saturday was her cake day, and we would be in the care of Uncle Jock. It was always an adventure of some sort, mostly down at the Yarra River, a quick 20-minute walk away. He wouldn't produce the Allens sweets until we were around the corner and out of sight of the house. It was our secret.

Just getting to the river was an adventure. The swampy, lush bush, the odd snake, the trees with their flaky barks, and the dense canopy made it like a walk through a rainforest. Then we would emerge on a sandy bank near a bend in the river.

That first summer, Uncle Jock taught us how to swim in the muddy Yarra River at Warrandyte. It was great fun, and many kids gathered at the local waterhole for a dip. When we returned to Ringwood after those holidays, we would be full of stories of our adventures about the snakes, the flimsy rafts on the river made from bulrush reeds, and the remarkable amount of wildlife in the bush around Warrandyte, particularly the birds.

DURING MY THIRD YEAR at school, I joined the Cubs. Most of the boys in my grade were in the local pack. We learnt to 'dib, dib, dib' and 'dob, dob, dob' together. I gained my first star, to be worn on the Cubs' cap. The star meant that, as a young wolf cub, I now had one eye open.

At the baths, I gained my Herald swimming certificate,

which hung proudly in our bedroom. It seemed I was never home; I have little recollection of our house.

Life was an adventure.

I had a mate around the corner called John Gray. We spent time exploring the nearby pine forest and the Ringwood Lake together. By the age of seven, we had started to go to the Saturday-afternoon movies with my older brother and some mates.

The movies, called 'the matinees', were held in the town hall in the centre of Ringwood. They were a treasure, featuring characters like Superman, Hopalong Cassidy, Roy Rogers, the Lone Ranger, and many others. Every week, there was a serial. If we missed an episode, the kids at the school kept us up to date.

The move to Ringwood was great. My enjoyable memories of Smith Street, Collingwood, soon faded now that we had more freedom, choices of entertainment, good grandparents, bigger meals, and then, of course, school. It all seemed to agree with us three boys.

Then, suddenly, our family changed again. First it had been a new father; now I had no older brother. I often asked my mother, many years later, what happened to him. To me, he just seemed to completely disappear. Mum was reluctant to talk about him—I guess it was too painful for her. In years to come, other extended family members spoke about him in glowing terms. They said he was very energetic, had a paper run before school, and other errands as well. However, the one thing they all emphasised was his role as the older brother. Apparently, he devoted a lot of time to being a good eldest brother, and Robbie and I adored him.

Ian was born in 1942. In July 1952, he was killed in a hit-and-run accident one afternoon. He was riding his pushbike home, having just finished his weekend job. It was his pocket money that he would use to take us to the matinees. All I recall about what happened is a phone call that my parents received at a friend's house, telling them the sad news. My Uncle Cliff said there was a very moving funeral down Whitehorse Road in Ringwood. The Boy Scouts and Cubs apparently formed a guard of honour along the road in his memory, yet I remember nothing of it.

For me, something changed. I can't describe exactly what, but even at that young age I sensed that a difference had come over our family. We must have coped somehow by not mentioning his name, or the accident, but I just didn't understand. Perhaps the only way Mum managed was to never talk about him at all. As for me, I remember nothing of my lost brother.

About fourteen months after his death, we left Ringwood, and Melbourne suburbia, for the wilderness. It was just before Christmas 1954—the year that Queen Elizabeth II visited Victoria. I caught a glimpse of her at the rear of a special train as it moved slowly through Ringwood.

It was another move for us. At first, I thought we were going on a holiday or the like, as Mum said nothing about a move—just about us going on a 'big trip'. Having travelled little in a motorcar, I thought Warrandyte was a really big trip, but this turned out to be a seven-hour drive from Melbourne. It was a very long day. Robbie and I were in the back of the Chevy ute, so we couldn't ask, 'Are we there yet?'

The final stretch of the trip from Bairnsdale to Tongio was mainly gravel—dusty, and heavily corrugated. It was dreadful. It was a winding, rumbling trip that, even a decade later, I never mastered. I got carsick every time I went on that road until I finally got my driver's licence.

chapter three
Entering the wilderness

NO MATTER HOW I TRY TO DEPICT IT, I ALWAYS RETURN TO THIS description: our move to the bush in late 1954 was a shock. Overnight, my world changed to a district 20 times bigger in size than the entire Ringwood area, and 10,000 times bigger than Wilana Street.

We moved to a shire—not a town, a street, or a road, and not really a home, but a district. Every house had a name. For instance, we'd say, 'That's the Giltrap's joint', or 'That's the Harding's joint'. Families were 'bloody Micks', 'Methos', or 'Pressies'. Every man of the house had a label: 'bloody good footballer', 'top shearer', 'lazy bugger', 'womaniser', 'likes his hops', 'tight as a fish's arse', and so on.

Compared to the city, where I'd had my family and a couple of schoolmates for company, at Tongio we were completely on our own. Standing on the front veranda of our new house, the only indication that other humans inhabited this open, wide area was a chimney in the distance. Yet, quickly, I realised that the local people all knew one another. It was very different from Ringwood, where even my schoolteacher was a stranger outside the classroom. Who knew where she lived, whether she was a Catholic, or what sport, if any, she played? We may have known our neighbours and a few families who lived in Wilana Street but, outside that small world, I knew no one much. Very quickly, I discovered that in the country it was the complete opposite.

Tongio was in the Omeo Shire, in East Gippsland, Victoria. It was an isolated farming district commonly called 'the high country'. It turned out that my mother had grown up there as a young child. Swifts Creek was the nearest town from our place, four miles down the road.

This tiny, timber town had a pub, a post office, and a number of shops. The nearest school, in the opposite direction, was at Tongio. It was an hour's walk for Robbie and me. In fact, it was more than a walk; it was like travelling through a war zone. Plovers—very mean-looking birds that, at first, we thought were seagulls—would screech and charge at us when they were breeding. The kids at our new school said these birds had poisonous barbs on their wings, and were capable of slaying us. To avoid them swooping, we would cut across paddocks that contained cattle, sheep, and big bulls. That was really scary.

Being the eldest and expected to lead this expedition, I was petrified. I believed that every bull was a candidate for the ring, and I would try to put a fence between the animals and us whenever possible.

The Tongio school was tiny, like a shed. The country kids viewed us warily—all thirteen of them. They were a tight-knit bunch. One became very inquisitive about my one and only jumper, a Cub jumper with badges that indicated I could swim and had been invested. They had never heard of, or seen, a Cub before. Straight off, the kids viewed us with suspicion.

The teacher was a young man with thick glasses who continually pushed them against the bridge of his nose. More importantly, he used the strap freely. This was different from Ringwood, where no one got the cuts—or no one that I saw. However, after a couple of days attending this tiny, one-roomed school, I could see why the teacher wielded his strap. Two of the boys were a handful, and continually disobeyed his instructions. Their entire time at school seemed to be an endless adventure involving ways to distract the teacher. Their most common prank was to find, and then hide, his strap. Their best effort was a gem.

It was lunchtime. The teacher rang the hand bell and let us out into the playground, or paddock. Raucous laughter replaced giggles when the two boys pointed to the strap, high up, dangling from the top of the flagpole. It had replaced the Australian flag. The teacher's reaction was amazing. Quickly, he rounded us up and marched us back into class. With the large blackboard ruler tapping his open palm, he grilled us collectively. Obviously, he hoped to find the guilty party, but he had no such luck. He then disappeared into the storeroom at the rear of the school for a while. Quickly, he lined us up and, one at a time, we had to march into a narrow passage, where he asked for a confession. Again, he got nothing from us. After another grilling, he disappeared back into the storeroom, fiddled with something for a while, and re-appeared with a most bizarre request. Yet again, we formed a single file. One at a time, he called us into the small room. Once inside, we had to place the palm of our left hand into a bowl that contained a white, milky fluid and had two wires coming from it. The teacher said it was a lie-detector device. Cripes, it took a lot of courage to put my hand in there, I can assure you. However, our schoolmaster must have rigged the thing up the wrong way, as he could detect no culprits.

The whole school went quiet for the remainder of the day. That interrogation method certainly put the wind up us kids. I must admit I admired the fact that none of us owned up. We all knew who had hoisted that damn strap in place of our holy Australian flag.

I've often wondered afterwards what our parents would have thought if we'd told them about the interrogation—I assumed it was a school secret.

Unfortunately for the teacher, the pranks didn't stop. About halfway through my first year at the Tongio school, he bought a new car, a grey Ford Prefect sedan. I guess it was his first car, and he proudly announced his purchase to the school one morning just before the first bell. Lined up outside, we were marched down the steep driveway to admire the vehicle.

Admittedly, a new car was something very special at the time; the only people who drove cars, or new cars, were farmers. We circled it, looking inside as he explained the whiz-bang extras that came with the vehicle. Finally, he showed us the inside.

Back in the classroom, he announced that he would have to go to the township of Swifts Creek at lunchtime, and we would be on our own.

Come recess, I didn't notice anything unusual happen. However, after the lunch bell, the two larrikin boys said we all had to gather around the teacher's car, real quick—to wave him off, or something, they said. The teacher, quite chuffed, started the car up and headed down the road. Admittedly, it was making a sound that I had never heard a car make before—a sort of loud, hissing squeak. Most vehicles I knew made a rumbling sort of noise. About 100 yards down the road, the hiss changed to a loud blurt and then a huge bang. Hell—we all looked at one another. The two boys with the reputation for mischief were giggling. The teacher stopped, got out, scratched his head, pushed his glasses against his nose, looked back at us kids, and then drove off to Swifts Creek. The car sounded like a Harley Davidson motorbike. When he disappeared around the first bend, the story came out.

The lads had snuck across the road at recess, pinched a couple of spuds from the farmer's paddock, and managed to thump three spuds up the new car's exhaust and return to school undetected. I don't think the teacher ever worked it out.

The school at Tongio was completely different from the one at Ringwood. As I mentioned, the kids were a very tight-knit bunch. It was soon obvious to my younger brother and me that our days of fun and playing after school at Ringwood were gone. There were no shops just around the corner, no deliveries of milk or ice—nothing. It was the backwoods, the wilderness. Consequently, for the first few weeks in my new home at Tongio I faced nothing but continuing demands to learn more skills, complete numerous chores, and be in bed at dark. It was like a labour camp.

I would rise at 6.00 a.m. in the morning and milk the cow. Have you ever tried that? No one explained the knack to me. The poor cow nearly got mastitis while I worked out how to milk her. She would swish her tail, and thump the back of my head with disgust as I massaged her teats with not a drop of milk coming out the bottom. You would think that just squeezing the teat and pointing it in the direction of the milk bucket would work. No, the secret is to squeeze with the top finger, then the second top, and so on—a sort of rolling squeeze, like strumming your fingers on a tabletop.

Once I got the hang of it, I became quite quick, so Mum got a separator and I had to separate the milk as well. This meant we had an abundance of cream. It was great on my Weeties. All up, this would take about 45 minutes.

Then Mum got a butter churn, and I had to make the damn butter. It was only once a week, admittedly, but—what with feeding chooks and then giving the milker a biscuit of hay, to mention just a few of my chores—the demands on my time before and after school were increasing. By now, I was rising at 5.00 a.m. every day.

The first really positive change came about when Mum arrived home with a poddy lamb. She'd got it from a farmer somewhere. It was a female, and we called her Mary-Anne. Bottle-feeding this bundle of fluff with its vibrating tail was a sheer joy. Robbie, little brother John, and I would fight over whose turn it was. The confidence I gained from handling this tiny sheep encouraged me to befriend the milker's calf. We called him 'Sooky'. In no time, this gorgeous little fellow became a pet. We smothered him in pats and hugs, then soon found ourselves perched up on his back and taken for rides. Over the next few weeks, we adopted another poddy lamb, and then another. We were farmers.

But I have left the darkest part of our move to last. It was our new house at Tongio. Well, it wasn't new. It was a fallen-down, creaky, leaky, cobwebby bloody hovel that Robbie and I reckoned was haunted. It was a rented house that had no power, hot water, heating, or any other familiar city conveniences.

The lavatory was horrific. It had a new name—the dunny. It was way out the back, and built over a hole that disappeared into the bowels of the earth—the sort of place where a monster or hobgoblin would live. Down in this deep cavern, where one day I finally had the courage to glance, I saw a pinnacle of poop at least six feet high. It tapered like an upside-down ice cream cone, with tufts of pages from an old telephone directory poking out all over it. Blowflies, at great risk to the person about to lower themselves over the hole, buzzed in and out when you opened the creaky lid. However, that was nothing. The kids at school told us to check under the dunny lid for red-back spiders. They said that, after a bite from one of them, 'Y'are dead in no time.' God, had I died and gone to hell?

It was torture going to that dunny. The lavatory paper was an old Melbourne telephone directory. Admittedly, I became fascinated with the strange names and accompanying phone number before I smeared them and dropped the page into oblivion. What's more, the smell around the dunny was putrid. Have you ever tried doing a number two while holding your breath? Both Robbie and I reckoned this was the best method.

Everyone kept on complaining until an enterprising local told Mum the secret of killing the smell, the blowflies, and the spiders. It was a thick liquid called 'Phenyle' that came in a dark-brown triangular bottle. A disinfectant of some kind, its smell reminded me of warm tar. More importantly, it worked.

Inside the house was also a worry. For starters, Mum didn't have her radio, so there were no serials to listen to. There was also no electricity for lights or anything else, and we had to be in bed by dark as there were only two lamps. They were tall, glass lamps filled with kerosene, and lit with a match. If they smoked, the wick had to be trimmed. Mum continually reminded us, 'If you knock it over, you'll burn the jolly house down.'

It fascinated me that a small flame could produce such a strong, soft light. As for the rooms, there were no curtains, so someone gave Mum some hessian. At least that meant we had a bit of privacy, even though we had no neighbours. The only water tap in the entire house was over the sink, and new rules now applied to water use—we were to bathe once a week in a large, galvanised tub. The water wasn't changed as we each had a turn. Daily, we got constant reminders about turning off the tap and saving water, as we only had one tank.

For me, the changes required to adapt to this different life seemed endless. Thankfully, my best source of information for learning about my household and farm jobs—or so I thought—was the kids at the school. They were great, and offered endless advice. This was helpful when it came to unusual chores, such as which axe to use to cut and split firewood and kindling, how to put a cow in the bale, how to hold the bucket between your legs and, finally, how to strip the cow's teat to get the most milk.

But with the new churn, working out how to make the butter edible took some experimentation. How much salt should I add? Initially, even though I followed advice, I used too much. However, over a period of months, I mastered a fit-for-human-consumption square lump of butter, shaped with serrated butter pats, or bats.

Finally, how was I to wash the separator and then reassemble this complicated machine? That took even longer. In fact, as a city kid, I had arrived in the bush with almost no practical skills. Added to this, the kids at school were forever leading me up the garden path when I asked them how to do things. They suggested that, to get the cow to let the milk down before I tried milk it, I should recite a poem to it—preferably an Australian one. Mum frowned when I asked her if we had a poetry book; she told me to ask at school.

They also told me that new poddy lambs could freeze at night, and that most farmers took them to bed. I got into big trouble for that one, as Mary-Anne left her calling card on the sheets.

They also recommended that I use two cupfuls of salt for the first pound of butter I ever made. Mum reckoned the resulting batch would almost make you vomit.

It wasn't just with chores that these country larrikins took the mickey out of us. They advised Robbie and me that all the animals in the area, particularly the wild ones, were dangerous, man-eating, or poisonous—particularly kangaroos, wombats, and emus. Fortunately, we only ever saw a few of them. However, the biggies were kookaburras and magpies, which they called 'tossle snatchers'. The kids at the Tongio school unanimously agreed on this one. Never, ever have a piddle out in the open, they said—always use the dunny. They added that they knew of some boys from somewhere 'above the Gap', who had had their little willies severed from their torsos while peeing in the open. Magpies—the main tossle-snatchers—were particularly savage. That's why they swooped, apparently. My God, that sounded scary. Consequently, some days we found it really hard to hang on during the hour's walk to or from school. The changes and new challenges never seemed to go away.

After a month, I thought I'd seen and heard it all. But there was a final revulsion I had to deal with — Mum introduced me to rabbit traps. How could I use such a thing? What a dreadful contraption. They were dangerous-looking gadgets with a powerful spring and a nasty pair of jaws.

In time, I learned that many poorer people lived off the rabbits. They were plentiful, or 'in plague proportions', according to the kids at school. Not only were they a good source of food, but their skins helped to pay for the groceries.

There was a buyer for them, who travelled once a month to Bairnsdale. Many people sold him gutted rabbits or skins, and Mum hinted that we might use him — which meant we were poor.

Setting the rabbit traps cost me many a bruised finger. Damn things; they would snap shut as I tried to cover them with a fine layer of dirt to conceal their whereabouts. But that was the easy bit. The rabbit — a beautiful, fluffy, brown-eyed little creature — was killed, gutted, and skinned. That didn't seem right. I thought meat came from a butcher's shop. Consequently, my attempts at killing those first poor bunnies, with their mutilated feet, were pathetic. Most managed to get away. Then the kids at school showed me how to give them a 'rabbit killer'. You had to flatten your palm, hold it rigid, and administer a severe chop behind the poor animal's head. Now I was a rabbit murderer.

I was just about to jack up and tell Mum that this was the last straw when I met an old bloke across the road. Well, it wasn't quite across the road. It was quite a walk, through a paddock, some light bush, and just behind the cattle yards.

He was a really old man—maybe 40 or a bit more. Our first meeting was a coincidence. My brother and I had ventured outside our house paddock, for the first time, to find the Tambo River. Apparently, it was about half a mile away. We had to walk through a couple of paddocks and some tangled low bush. On the way, we spotted a hut or living quarters of some kind behind some cattle yards, and we wandered over for a squiz. It looked deserted, but then we spotted a shrivelled-looking old man in an army overcoat, kneeling near a log. He was setting a rabbit trap. There was a dog nearby; it, too, looked old and scruffy. I called out 'Hello'. The old man roared with fright, and dived behind the log. He frightened the hell out of us, and the dog didn't help. It barked savagely. We turned to run away when the strange bloke called out, 'It's okay, lads. You jist frightened me—eh, shuddup, Croney!'

I guessed Croney was the dog. Cautiously, I turned back. My younger brother Robbie walked right behind me, very close. The old man asked us who we were and where we had come from. I did all the talking—and I didn't do very much. I was scared of this hermit-looking old man who wore mittens with the ends worn off, old hobnailed boots, and funny trousers that had string tied around each leg, just under the knees.

'I'm Les, and me dog here, Croney, does tricks. Let me show you one day, eh?'

We didn't even answer, and our first cautious steps were backwards before we turned and ran, not to the river, but back home.

That night we told our parents, and Mum said, 'That's Les. He's a character—used to be a drover, they say.'

It wasn't until a few weeks later that I saw Les again. I had started trapping rabbits myself, on the flats down near the river. I wasn't having a lot of luck around the paddocks near our house. The kids at school said that near the river was the best place, as there were ferns and blackberries—all good cover that rabbits like to hide and play in.

I was searching for fresh burrows when I noticed that one hole had a trap sprung with just the rabbit's paw in the jaws. It was fresh. Maybe I had ventured into old Les's territory. This could be dangerous, as I wouldn't know where the traps had been set. I guessed I had better go and see Les. That was a worry. The kids at school reckoned he was a strange one.

I ventured across the flats, headed towards the river, and turned up near the cattle yards. I found Les sitting outside his hut on a log, clutching a beer. He was shaking and weeping softly. He reminded me of Uncle Jock; he used to do that sometimes. At the time, I assumed this was what must happen to all old men. Stunned at what I saw, I turned to walk away when the damn dog barked and Les spotted me.

'G'day, son. Come over 'ere, mate. Take a seat. Shut up, Croney.'

Hesitantly, I sat and stared at the ground. From the corner of my eye, I could see his right arm shaking. He had trouble getting the bottle to his lips as he sobbed softly.

'Never spills a drop, mate. Not bad, eh? I only has one beer a day. Bloody stuff gives me the shakes.'

I didn't know what to say. We sat in silence for a while when Les said, 'Croney, get me 'baccy, mate.'

The dog, which was busy licking its private parts, jumped to its feet and pushed open the door to the hut. It then emerged with a leather pouch in its mouth, and sat at Les's feet. He took the pouch, patted the dog with affection, gave its neck a good scratch, opened the pouch, and began rolling a cigarette. The dog just sat, looking at Les with panting admiration, alert to any command. When Les finally slid his tongue along the paper and sealed the fag into a tight, neat rollie, he again looked his dog in the eye and said, 'Git the matches, Croney, me boy.'

The dog pranced to his feet, shot back into the hut, and came out with a box of matches in his mouth. The matches were in a metal folder that exposed one side of the box and allowed the ends to open. Les went through the patting and scratching ritual before he lit his fag. He placed the pouch and the matches on the ground, and told Croney to put them both back. The damn dog returned them both to the hut.

'He's a good dog, eh? I used to use him droving cattle with Alan Taylor. We's been here for years now, ain't we, Croney, me old mate?'

My head was bursting with questions. To date, I hadn't said a word, and I didn't know how to bring up the conversation of rabbit traps. Then Les spoke.

'Likes a brew, mate? Time for Marg to puts the billy on I reckon, eh?'

'Yes, sir,' I replied, not really sure what he meant, although I guessed he had a wife inside called Marg—or Mrs Haylock, if ever I spoke to her.

'For Gawd's sake, don't call me sir. Had enough of that crap years ago. Just call me Les. And what brings ya down this way anyhow? Just a stickybeak, or what?'

Gathering that he wanted me to respond, I said, 'My name's Barry. I live up there.' I pointed towards our house, which you couldn't see for the bush.

'You're from the city, eh? I heard a new family moved into the Coffey's house the other month.'

I nodded.

'The old man's a plumber or something. I knew ya mum's dad. What's the matter anyhows, me boy?'

After a lot of stuttering and mumbling from me, Les worked out that I was worried about where he had set his traps or, more importantly, how to set the jolly things. By now we were inside his hut, and his wife had boiled the billy. I was enjoying my first-ever bush brew. It was delightful. Les showed a little pride when I told him so. With that finished, he grabbed a long, crooked stick and we set off around his traps. Looking at me, he asked, 'Where's ya staff, mate?'

Again, I produced a vacant stare that indicated ignorance. He then explained, at length, that I had to have a staff—a long stick. 'For snakes and stuff you know, eh? Either that, or a length of eight-gauge wire, although it's a bugger to walk with, I reckon.'

He may as well have been muttering in Mandarin—what the heck was he on about, eight-gauge something? So we turned back to the hut, and he got his 'good' axe. Then we wandered into the nearby bush, where he selected a strong sapling.

'A stringy-bark, mate. It won't break when ya bash a snake, eh?'

He tapped the stick all over with the back of the axe, and stripped off the bark. Then he handed me my very own staff. With Croney trotting behind our heels, Les showed me where he set his traps. He then suggested where I should set mine. I only had ten and Les had more than thirty. For the first time, I asked him a question.

'Why so many traps, Les?'

Between lots of 'eh's and 'we's, I worked out that Les sold most of the rabbits he caught. Sure, he ate some and gave some to the farmer, but most he sold.

'On the skin, son. They keep for three days, on the skin. I walks into town twice a week and a bloke takes 'em and sells 'em down the mill. You should set some more traps and I'll sell 'em for ya—even jist the skins if ya like, eh?'

I spent two hours with Les. I learnt how to set a trap, then how to skin a rabbit properly, and how to stretch the skin over a wire. It was actually an eight-gauge wire. In future, I would keep the unusual skins—like a ginger or a black one—separate. They brought a penny more per skin. Apparently, once a fortnight, a skin buyer called in and collected Les's skins. He reckoned that most hats were made from rabbit fur.

We returned to the hut. Then he did something I'll always

treasure. He lit a small fire, got a long, thin piece of metal, held it with a leather glove, and heated the end. When it was glowing red, he took my staff and burnt 'Barry' along the side. I was so proud of that staff. I kept it for years.

When I finally returned home, Mum wasn't worried about where I'd been; just why I'd taken so long. When I said I'd been visiting old Les, she said, 'He's a real loner, that one. Used to being on the road. Has a lot of nerve problems—to do with the war, they reckon.'

The kids at school explained what a drover was—someone on a horse who moved cattle along the roads down to the railheads, and camped in the bush as he went along. He had a roll of blankets, a groundsheet, and spare clothes tied together with a rope or strap—it was called a 'swag', apparently, and it hung over the back of the saddle. Hanging off the swag was a billy—for a brew, or a cuppa, or for cooking the odd meal. Now that was as clear as mud. I didn't quite understand it all, but it sounded a lonely sort of life to me. Then again, I guess Les and Croney were a team, and they had one another for company. For me, Les was good company, he told fascinating stories, and I got used to his shakes and tears.

Slowly, probably more out of curiosity than because I needed a new friend, I spent a little more time with Les. He taught me how to plait hay band, and how to make a halter and a strong leg rope, which proved handy when I milked the cow. Over time, my traps caught as many rabbits as Les's did. We caught bigger game, such as hares and foxes, by making a wire snare in the shape of a hangman's noose, which we'd hang over a hole in a wire netting fence and then tie to a post.

I visited Les almost every week. At first, it would be for ten or fifteen minutes, mainly on a weekend. With my chores finished, I'd go down to Les's, swinging my staff along, maybe even hoping for a snake. After a few months, the stopover would last for an hour or so. He'd always answer my queries, provided I stayed away from the subject of his past or where he'd grown up. It was almost as if he didn't have a past.

Then, one day, I had a treat—a thrill, really—because Les invited me for tea. Marg was away and he would be cooking the meal. I rushed home, told Mum, did my chores, and returned to the hut. First, he lit a fire outside in the light bush. Then he produced a big, heavy, cast-iron bowl with a lid, which he called a 'camp oven'. I had never seen a camp oven. As he prepared the meal, he told me stories about droving and some of his 'good' dogs. Finally, we had roast rabbit, potato, onion, and beans. He had cooked the lot together in the camp oven after pouring in a liberal dash of beer. With a wry grin he said, 'That's the secret, son—a dash a beer, eh.'

It was the best meal I'd ever had, and I told him so—it was in the same category as one of Nana Roy's cakes. The juices in the beer-gravy, mixed with the vegies, were delicious. So were the small dumplings: tiny balls of plain flour mixed with milk, rolled into a ball the size of an egg, and cooked in the juices. Although I wasn't seeing him regularly, Les was becoming a special person in my life—my first country friend.

However, back at home, life wasn't good. It was cruel, too busy, too far from my friends in Ringwood, and too cold as winter approached. Although I enjoyed Les's company, it didn't fill the hole created by my treasured family we'd left behind, who seemed beyond reach in Melbourne. There was no Nana and Uncle Jock a 20-minute bus-drive away to Bellbird paradise. Further, I wasn't used to being the new big brother. Although I can't remember my older brother, Ian, he must have been a good eldest child before his death. I'd never imagined being responsible for younger siblings before.

I constantly wished we could go back. I was very homesick for Ringwood, not to mention that I was struggling with the fact that our family had almost doubled. When we left Ringwood, I'd had three brothers: Robbie, a two-year-old half-brother called Jeff, and a four-year-old called John. I was very uncomfortable suddenly being the eldest. Now, when Mum and Dad were out, I was in charge. What were the rules when you were the head of the household?

Then, one day, things changed. Three of us had set off for school—young John had come along, for the first time. He struggled during the very long walk, so Robbie and I took it in turns to piggyback him some of the way. It was early morning. We were almost there when, while crossing a small, low-level bridge that ran over Gap Creek, we stopped and peered over the side as usual. The creek was fast flowing, and only eight feet across.

Suddenly, a magnificent wild mountain duck appeared from under the bridge. It swam along, oblivious to our presence. We didn't move a muscle. Behind it, in a straight line, were six tiny, yellow, fluffy ducklings swimming along. Their heads were swaying as if in tune to a waltz. Suddenly, the mother duck spotted us. She took off and flew down the creek, crudely dipping one wing in the water as if wounded or shot. Wild ducks will do this to protect their young—a hunter's dog would naturally chase the injured bird. The ducklings scattered and disappeared back underneath the bridge, except for one. It went the wrong way, panicked, and found itself swept away by the fast-flowing stream. It quickly slipped into some rapids and swirled around as it rushed downstream. The mother finally flew away, circled, and then flew back under the bridge from the far side, back to her family. Meanwhile, the separated little duckling, quite a distance away, was bobbing swiftly down the stream alone—left to its own devices.

Probably for the first time ever, I donned my eldest-child mantle and rushed down the bank of the creek in the hope of rescuing the tiny bird. My cautious paranoia about snakes, magpies, ticks, red-back spiders, and other wild, attacking vermin disappeared. I dashed, and finally leapt, into the freezing water and lunged at the little bird. It nearly drowned in the tiny tidal wave I caused, and it washed up on the bank. It was too young to fly and could barely walk. I had no trouble catching the little fella, and shoved it down my wet shirtfront.

When I returned the little creature to the bridge some fifteen minutes later, there was no mum or ducklings to be seen. They had disappeared under some low willow trees, or maybe had gone up onto the bank and filtered into some ferns. We looked and looked before we finally gave up. I sensed my brothers were pleased. They were very impressed with my efforts, and maybe hoped for a pet. So, with me clutching the duckling softly in my hands, we continued on to school, where we arrived late and I was growled at for being wet.

The Tongio kids were amazed. In one day, I had gone from a pathetic, outcast city slicker to a dashing animal-saver. All the kids wanted to help this little creature. School for the moment was temporarily abandoned, and we put the duckling in a small box and fed it crumbs, bits of cake, and other good country cooking.

That afternoon, I walked home from school with my new little fluffy friend in a box. Possibly for the first time during that long walk, I looked around. I saw the hills, the beautiful trees, the birds, and the diversity of scenery that abounds in that picturesque area. Somehow, this little mortal seemed to give me courage, or some reason to assume my big-brother role. We walked in a straight line for home, through the paddocks. Damn the cattle, the wild, ferocious bulls, and the annoying sheep—I had a family to protect. I had to look after two brothers and a new member we nicknamed 'Donald'.

chapter four

Settling in

MY FIRST YEAR OF COUNTRY LIVING WAS ENDING. DONALD the big duck had escaped and flown into the wild. He came back twice for a free feed, but probably found a girlfriend, we reckoned, as that was the last we saw of him.

By now I could kill a rabbit efficiently, and had climbed Mount Tongio, the high mountain behind the house. The view from this giant was magnificent. At its highest point, I could see from one end of the valley to the other, a distance of at least 20 miles. Towards Ensay, away in the hazy distance, was Connor's Hill.

Gradually, I got used to every person I met saying hello and asking after me or my family's welfare. I started to venture away from home a bit. During the school holidays I helped cart hay for a farmer down the road—well, not really, as the bales were too heavy for me—and I rode in the front of the truck. Now I could kill and pluck chooks. With the help of old Les, I watched and then helped deliver a calf.

During my walks, two black snakes and one copperhead had fallen victim to the sturdy staff Les had hewn from a stringy-bark tree. I carried it wherever I walked.

My life had changed, and I started to feel settled. I enjoyed school, and mixed easily with these country kids.

It was soon obvious that I had it easy compared to many of the kids at the Tongio school. Some walked or rode pushbikes over long distances to get to school. One family, in particular, did it very hard. They had to rise very early and help hand-milk the dairy herd before school. Then they rode bikes three times as far as we had to walk. As the days got shorter, they would leave school early to be home in time to milk before dark.

However, there was another reason for the change in me—old Les. He was there when the beautiful, shiny, wet calf slid from its new mum. He taught me about the old ways—the 'good old days', as he called them. He talked of such things as the camp oven, how to make a damper, and how to skin an eel. He thoroughly enjoyed reminiscing, once spending ages with me explaining the strange commands used to work a sheepdog. He demonstrated with Croney—'Come here! Go back! Speak up! Steady, steady. Sit! Go way back! Come over here! Come round! Go way out!'

There were many commands. 'However, if you can whistle, Barry, that's the secret,' Les told me seriously. 'Some blokes can whistle, somes can't. If ya can't, ya jist have to shout a lot louder at times.' Les explained that a short, sharp whistle meant 'Sit'. A long whistle was a casting whistle, and an arm would point in the right direction. It was fascinating. Les reckoned the whistle was definitely the best—'Once he gets aways a bit, the dog can still hear a whistle.' He demonstrated this once when Croney was far away on a hill. He gave a short, sharp whistle, and the dog dropped as if shot. I was most impressed.

Then there was their hut, or Margaret's hut, as Les called it. There were bellows for the fire, a poker, a rifle on the wall, and a Coolgardie safe jammed in the corner, right beside the doorway. What's a Coolgardie safe? That was one of my first questions to this funny old man called Les.

'Keeps stuff cool, me lad. Water sorta runs over the hessian here, and stuffs gits cool, eh. Ya gotta leave it near a door or in a hallway ta git tha breeze, eh.'

He taught me to fish, and I recall catching a trout in the Tambo River. The highlight was when Les cooked it in the camp oven. It was delicious.

Sadly, my times with Les ended abruptly. Our school burnt to the ground, which meant we had to move. My parents found another house seven miles away, further down the Omeo Highway. I moved to a bigger school with many more kids, and had a couple of mates in no time. I soon forgot about Les, but not the school fire. It caused a lot of talk in the district.

'Tongio school burnt to the ground!' was the headline in the *Omeo Standard*, our local paper. It was just before the long Christmas break, in November 1955; we had been at Tongio almost two years. Naturally, suspicions and gossip were rife—this is a characteristic of country life. Mind you, I would not have put it past a couple of the boys at the school to have done the deed; they often lit fires around the playground and paddock. Then again, one afternoon I remember the rubbish bin next to the teacher's desk catching fire and being extinguished. The teacher smoked a pipe and regularly emptied it into the bin. Whatever the cause of the fire, the immediate ramifications were frightening.

At home one afternoon, about two weeks after the fire, a shiny black 1953 Plymouth motorcar lurched into our dirt drive, and out stepped some men in trench coats. They wore felt hats, flipped open their notebooks, and removed pencils from their pockets as they crunched their way in their shiny shoes to our front veranda. Robbie and I peered through the hessian curtain in the lounge. They were detectives from Melbourne—heck, did they look important. They spoke to Mum briefly, and then she called out my name.

They asked me to accompany them to the vehicle, where I found myself inside, being grilled by three tough trench coats, one turning and leaning over from the front seat. It was really scary. I was sure someone had dobbed me in, and at the time I believe I would have confessed to anything—yes, I had watched matinees in Ringwood picture theatre featuring wily, square-jawed heroes like the G-Men (who were special American police). I had heard *D24*, a detective serial on the radio. I became very nervous. As one bloke took notes, I had difficulty holding back the tears. However, the trench coats only made a few jottings, and then told me to get out of their car. Then they drove off.

Poor Mum grilled me about what happened, but I couldn't remember much of it. The fact that they hadn't arrested me was a relief.

The Tongio school was never rebuilt.

AS I MENTIONED, after the school fire my parents decided to move to a different location. Called Doctors Flat, it was a short drive of about seven miles to our new home, which was located back down the Omeo Highway, past Swifts Creek. They managed to procure a 99-year lease on a small house and several acres of land, very close to the Tambo River. This new home, roughly three miles from the township of Swifts Creek, meant we would attend the large local school, which had about 120 kids. Our new house was very cramped, as it only had one bedroom. Soon Dad busied himself adding new rooms to accommodate the family.

Then came a giant leap forward for humankind: a new school bus that serviced Ensay, Brookville, Cassilis, and Tongio was commissioned after the Tongio school fire. Great—it meant no more walking. What a wonderful surprise. The bus took fifteen minutes to get to school. So, once again, there were new kids to meet, new pecking orders to sort out, and new teachers to deal with. If Tongio was anything to go by, this was going to be hell.

Fortunately, the new lady teacher was a delight, and such concerns soon disappeared. Swifts Creek was a pleasant school. It had a mixture of kids from farms, and others who were from Ezard's Sawmill just down the road—a big mill that employed almost 100 people. A school bus meant more time on my hands before and after school. I still milked cows and separated milk, made butter, gathered eggs, collected and cut firewood, cut the wild asparagus, and picked blackberries when they came into season. However, for the first time, I could pursue activities that interested me. I spent time with my younger brothers, John and Jeff, and they were delightful. It was great fun having little kids around, and watching them walk, talk, and explore. I found an hour to kick a footy and to discover the Tambo River.

In fact, the river was astonishing. Dad built a small tin boat, and we paddled it along the banks, around small islands, and under low-hanging Weeping Willow trees. With experience, we braved the rapids, were often tossed out, sank, and received many a battering and bruises. Still, it was great fun. A sail rigged to a crude mast allowed us to tack for roughly 100 metres.

The river had small fish in abundance, called 'sand trout'. They were easy to catch. Come summer holidays, we would swim and fool around for hours.

Just up from our house, along the river and around a bend, was Wilson's Water Hole. It was a large pool that had been gouged out in a flood. It was perfect for diving, belly flops, and doing bombies. Parents brought their kids to the hole, and workers would come down after the mill whistle had blown 'knock off' at 5.00 p.m. The waterhole was always crowded.

The banks of the river were open, flat-grassed areas that had the odd Weeping Willow tree standing gracefully upon them. Some of these trees were over 80 feet tall. Swinging on their long, leafy branches out into the middle of the pool and plunging into the water was a treat.

Life was definitely starting to look up. Our new old house was located on a flat, from which it was only a short walk of about 80 feet down a small hill to the river. There was one small fenced paddock. It was too small for our two milkers, called Betty and Goldie, so they roamed the river banks, feeding freely.

The move from Tongio also saw us bringing our mob of sheep along. Yes, we had poddied four lambs since we had left Ringwood. By now, they were family. In no time, we had a new chook house, a cow bale for milking, and a huge shed that Dad built for making water tanks. The river flats, covered in bracken ferns and the odd rivergum tree, added a beauty we hadn't seen at Tongio. These trees were huge, some well over 100 feet tall, and six feet through at the girth.

The soil on these flats was a rich, deep loam. Consequently, Dad decided to clear the flats by hand. A friend lent him a Trewallah tree-puller, and 'Operation Clearing' began. The tree-puller was a hand-cranked winch with a very long cable that rolled out. With the aid of an extension ladder, we climbed as high up the tree as possible and attached the cable. The drum end of the winch was connected by a shorter cable to the base of another large tree about 100 yards away, which provided an anchor. Then, *clickety-clack, clickety-clack*, the handle on the drum swung backwards and forwards.

'It's easy 'til the tension takes up,' Dad said.

The gearing on the winch was so slow that it took an hour to put three feet of cable on the drum. So, every night after school, there I was, *clickety-clack*ing, until, finally, the huge monster of a tree started to shudder and creak, making snapping noises at its base as the roots pulled away and lost their anchorage. You could hear the tree crying out as we slowly ripped it from the ground. The last bit needed two of us to operate the winch. Dad and I took another three nights to finally get it to fall. Then we cut it into lengths about six feet long, with a crosscut saw. After that, with the aid of a crowbar, we rolled the tree away, down onto the river bank. From there, when we had our first flood—usually in early summer—the logs would wash away.

Unfortunately, rivergum is a sour, tight, sappy timber that attracts termites and is good for nothing much, not even firewood. By the end of that year, we'd cleared and sown five acres of lucerne. It was a successful sowing, and we baled thousands of short bales of hay off the paddock over the years.

Within a year, I'd not only settled, but I'd started to really enjoy the country way of life. At school, being tall for my age, I excelled in sports that suited my height: the high jump; hurdles; the hop, step, and jump; and the long jump. They were all a breeze. Yet I couldn't run to save myself—I was too gangly.

At footy, I must have inherited some of the Heard genes, as I captained the school footy team. Both my father and his brother had had distinguished football careers in Victoria. (My father, recruited by Richmond, had played in the seconds as a teenager.) I had good ball skills, but didn't like the rough play. Others who had little ability seemed to take great pleasure in injuring me in whatever way they could. I wasn't very heavy (eight-and-a-half stone), but five feet and ten inches tall.

My brother Robbie was shorter, tougher, and more skilled. He seemed to thrive on black eyes, swollen lips, and bruises—another trait from our father, who was a champion amateur boxer.

At school, I discovered many new games. Most involved groups of kids. Marbles, skipping, British Bulldog, and Poison Ball were common. Skipping was fun. Around April each year, out would come the rope. It was about 30 feet long, and was given to the school by Grinter's Transport. Two of the big kids would hold the ends of the rope and slowly swing it. Dozens of us, young and old, would bounce up and down inside the rope chanting, 'All in together, this fine weather ...'

Then, as it was winter, once everyone was warm the competitions would start. Sally Bock could French skip. It was hard. Two light ropes, pulled very tight, gave the perfect length. Then, with the ropes spinning in opposite directions at the same time, kids would run and then jump through very fast. Sally was the fastest. Then came the one-offs. Some would skip under the big rope and continue skipping with their own rope. It took perfect timing. Bystanders, enthralled by this feat, would clap in rhythm while the skilled ones did crossovers, doubles, and hot peppers. By the time the bell rang, everyone would be warm and glowing.

During those years at Doctors Flat, with the family more settled, Dad's business increased and he hired a labourer named Andy Adams. Mum didn't own or drive a car so, once a week, groceries and bread arrived in a tiny van. Although we didn't get into the town of Swifts Creek very much, it was very exciting if we did—even more so if I had picked up some pocket money.

The Sandys owned the grocery store. Most things in the shop—flour, sugar, honey, crushed oats for porridge, Weeties, and biscuits—were in bulk. A scoop, or a set of scales, were used to measure out most orders. Then a brown paper bag, flipped and twisted tightly, ended up in a cardboard box with your name scrawled on the side. The shopkeeper would then return to the customer's list and tick that item. For threepence, you could buy a large bag of broken mixed biscuits. They were the remains, or leftovers, after the large, square tin was finished. For poorer families, these separated bits of biscuits were a delight. In those days, most people expected unbroken biscuits.

Sandy's store had a long counter with several people serving. There were no shelves where you served yourself, and no packaged rice, dried fruit, or washing powder. Some people brought their own containers, jugs, billies, and hessian bags. For many of the women, it was a social outing. Everyone would be chatting, tutting, and nodding. It was always busy. There were no queues—the assistants knew whose turn it was next, and called them by name to the counter. Before asking what was required, the shopkeeper always had a personal chat, asked after the kids, and finally asked for their list. In the 1950s, there were no packets of anything much, really. There were no rubbish bins ready for re-cycling—there was no rubbish to speak of, and certainly no rubbish collection.

Occasionally, we would head into Swifts Creek to the movies. Every Tuesday we would get off the school bus, and our first wish would be for Dad to come home at a reasonable hour. Then we'd complete our chores in record time, and behave ourselves with perfect manners. Sometimes it worked. The result was a quick tea, a wash, and a hair brush, and we'd pile into the ute.

During my youth, a night at the movies was a great night out. The movies started at 8.00 p.m. with a cartoon, or sometimes two, followed by the Movietone news, and then the first movie would begin. It would be a full-length film. At interval, David Jessup would be ready with his tray of lollies, standing out the front after the lights came on. He sold a variety: Columbines, milkshakes, Jaffas, jellybeans, Violet Crumble bars, barley sugar, and Fags—small cigarette-like candy, which even had a red tip. All the lollies were Australian-made by companies such as MacRobertson, Allens, Hoadleys, and Cadbury.

I recall with excitement when, towards the end of that decade, the local store introduced ice creams in a cone, and milkshakes. From then on, during interval at the Tuesday movies in the Swifts Creek Mechanics Hall, we would dash up the street at interval to the store to order our milkshake and ice cream.

Interval was never at a set time. After the adults had enjoyed their chitchats, and the kids had settled, silence returned. This would be the cue for the projectionist, after which the second half would begin. There would be trailers advertising the next 'Do not miss' movies showing over the following weeks. Then the feature movie would begin. In all, most nights finished between 11.30 p.m. and 12.30 a.m.—usually after four hours of entertainment. Being a big night out, you simply went home to bed afterwards ... so different from today.

DURING THAT FIRST YEAR at Doctors Flat, we started to attend events other than the odd movie—like the footy, the cricket, or the Scouts, and annual events. Due to its isolation, the Omeo Shire had almost no electric power. The townships of Swifts Creek and Omeo had 240-volt electricity, but the rest of the area had almost none, apart from household lighting plants that provided 12-volt or 32-volt power. For most of the shire, this meant no television, and poor radio reception. However, there was always something happening during the year like the Omeo Show, the Omeo Rodeo, or the Boxing Day sports at Swifts Creek, Omeo, and Ensay.

The Swift Creek and Omeo days were for athletics, sheath tossing, mini races, and novelty events like the greasy pig chase, during which a greased pig was given a short head-start in front of a hundred eager teenagers. The winner was the one who caught the pig, and got to keep it.

The Ensay Boxing Day, on the other hand, was mainly for horses and sheepdog trials. There were also annual horse races at Swifts Creek and Benambra, while the annual sheep and cattle sales held at Benambra, Omeo, Swifts Creek, and Ensay were major events, too. Then there were golf, badminton, and tennis tournaments, fishing clubs, and rifle clubs throughout the area.

An hour's drive up from Omeo was Dinner Plain and Mount Hotham, both ski resorts where we visited and tobogganed down the slopes.

However, it was my first visit to the Omeo Show that I recall with wonder. It was a display of all the talent and skills found in the district. There were men in Fletcher Jones Harris tweed sports coats, and wearing squatters' hats, wandering the grounds. Other men wearing dustcoats would be judging sheep, cattle, wool, horses, and cuts of beef and mutton.

In the pavilion, the women displayed their skills in cooking, sewing, weaving, and other homely pursuits. There was a keenly contested competition that decided who was the champion shearer; at times, the winner would be one of the best in Australia. Wood chopping was also a highly sought-after prize and, like Tasmania, East Gippsland boasted world-class axemen.

On the arena were horse events. However, with all this entertainment, only two things appealed to me: the caravans and the sideshows.

The caravans, arrayed in a long line, sold fairy floss, hot-dogs, toffee apples, bags of lollies, and showbags full of wonderful goodies. The other magnets were the numerous sideshows, and the boxing tent. This area was packed. It was the first time I had seen sideshows. There were wooden clowns with heads swivelling, waiting for balls to drop into their mouths. Another tent had a large painting and a sign, which boasted that inside was a person who was half-man and half-woman.

Nearby were a merry-go-round, dodgem cars, and a long walk-through tent that showed snakes. Several times during the day a snake handler performed daring feats outside, to much applause. The man with the snakes was world-class, so the man with the megaphone said. Other tents offered great prizes if you could throw balls, coconuts, and rings accurately. I had never seen anything like this before in my life; it was a real thrill.

To top all of this off, and totally out of character, Dad gave me ten bob (one dollar) to shout us kids to some of the rides, and to buy some sweets. The four of us—Robbie, John, Jeff, and I—were beside ourselves with excitement and expectation. This was a real treat.

We stuck together and headed for the sideshow alley. A kindly man with a pleasant smile invited us to try his game. 'No, thank you,' was my quiet reply. The man then added that we could, with a little luck, make a lot of money. He then explained the game—all I had to do was throw four darts at a board, and score less than twenty-one.

The board was square, quite large, and covered with fine netting, with each number encircled. It was two shillings, or 20 cents, for a throw of four darts. If you got less than 21, you won a pound, which was two dollars. Easy—I could do this. We gathered in a tight little circle, my brothers egging me on. I handed over the orange ten-bob note, and pocketed the eight-bob change. My first three darts registered 21; the last dart was a four.

'Next time, mate,' encouraged the man.

I parted with another two bob. This time I managed 26—I was home and hosed. Quickly I handed over a further two bob. After two darts, I had eleven, then a nine. I looked for a one, then realised I couldn't win even with a one. Okay, I had it worked out—three of six or less, and then the two or the one. But when the first dart hit the two, it bounced off, and my free throw hit a nine. Damn, this time …

I was stunned when it dawned on me that I had parted with the full ten bob. The bloke handed me a card with a photo of Hopalong Cassidy.

I felt terrible, and wondered how I could tell Dad. I didn't but, to make it up, I took the boys to the crowd that had gathered outside Bell's boxing tent. It was truly entertaining. The ringmaster had a group of world-class boxers on a stage about six feet off the ground. It was the front of a large marquee with flags flying on the top. He introduced each of his boxers as a champion in his own right, and stated which country they had come from. This included a 'Red Indian' from America and a 'Negro' from darkest Africa. During the introductions, one of the boxers beat a large drum. Then the ringmaster turned to the crowd. 'Roll up, roll up, welcome to Roy Bell's Boxing Troupe—to the greatest boxing show on earth,' he called out.

The drum-beat got louder and louder. He shouted into a funnel-shaped loudspeaker, encouraging the onlookers. 'Are there any men out there man enough to go three rounds with one of my boxers?' There were rumbles in the crowd, then a man put up his hand and asked what it was worth.

'Two quid a win; five quid a knockout; nothing if ya get done.'

'I'm in,' said the bloke.

'Come on, any other men among ya?'

Several in the crowd nominated blokes who could go a bit or had reputations as pugs. Roy Bell urged the crowd on even more—various men were getting pats on the back as comments abounded about their strength or prowess. It was great fun. However, today, my guess would be that alcohol helped the contestants decide to have a go—sorry, I forgot to mention that the outdoor bar was the most popular place for the men at the Omeo Show. In no time, there were three locals up on the dais on Roy Bell's stage. The crowd, absolutely pumped, pushed towards the entrance as Bell announced 'fight time'.

It was five bob to get in, but I had another plan. I led my brothers around the back and waited until the crowd had entered the tent, and the first bell had sounded. We quietly poked our heads under the tent and tried to have a look. All we could see were a lot of trousers, and hands holding hats behind their owners' backs. Suddenly, there was a bloke tugging at my leg; he wasn't happy, and he swore at us.

Going home later that night, I was very pleased that Dad didn't ask us boys what sort of a day we had had.

THE OTHER THING I really enjoyed attending was the local dances. Mum and Dad could both dance, and we kids, along with many other kids, would sit around the hall watching the adults dance. This happened every Saturday night after the footy or cricket. They were truly old-time dances. At times, there seemed to be a competition between the men as to who was the most suave dancer. With their heads arched, and adopting a look of superiority, they offered themselves and their partner to the crowd, which followed their every move.

One night, a local grazier who considered himself a light-footed dancer was swinging his wife around in a rather risky-looking move when, spinning the wrong way in the wrong direction, up came a schoolteacher who couldn't dance. The teacher zigged when he should have zagged, and all four ended up on the deck. The schoolteacher was slightly primed, and snapped at our local, wealthy grazier. Suddenly, it was on: the two of them were outside, they shaped up, and were ready to biff the hell out of each other. But, as usual, a well-meaning do-gooder stepped in and stopped the fight, and we all went back inside. Pity—it would have been fun.

Alcohol was the cause of many a problem on the dance floor. It was funny but, no matter how inebriated the dancer, he somehow remained upright and able to perform while the music played. Stop the music and, well ...

One night the music stopped, and somebody jumped up on

the stage to make an announcement. However, I'm sure no one was listening, because there was a distraction: old Fred had stopped dancing, and he was swaying slightly as he tried to listen. Mind you, it was well known that when drunk he could only stand still for about five minutes. He always sat on a stool at the bar. The announcement had been going on for about seven minutes when old Fred's legs started to slowly spread apart on the highly polished dance floor. It was fascinating. He just kept sagging until he was almost doing the total splits — something you would only expect from a gymnast or a ballet dancer. Then Fred fell forward very slowly, softly coming to rest on the hard floor. The speaker didn't miss a beat, because suddenly he had everyone's attention — Fred was asleep. People continued listening until the gentleman on the stage announced, in a long-winded way, that there would be a working bee at the footy ground the next day. The Haywood's band started up. A couple of well-built young men grabbed Fred and hauled him to his feet. Poor Fred: he looked around in bewilderment, wondering what had happened. Then he continued dancing.

But local dances had something else of great appeal for kids of our age — supper. It was a true test of endurance when the announcement of 'supper' pierced the air. A drum roll usually heralded it. The adults would saunter into the supper room, have their cup of tea, and stand around holding a plate, which they continually refilled from the abundance of food on the tables. A supper at a country dance was something to behold. It was as if the local ladies would try to outdo each other when they arrived with their plates of goodies. There would be sandwiches of endless varieties, which were normally sampled first, and then came the sponges, lashed with cream and local fruit on top. It was a terrific treat. Fresh scones, along with jam tarts, slices, apple, blackberry, and numerous other pastries were jammed onto a long table. A third table would have cakes of many varieties—fruit, tea, lemon, ginger, marble, orange, and chocolate. Finally, in a corner of the room, was an open window attached to another room that was the kitchen. From there, the women briskly served cups of tea from large teapots—coffee wasn't on the menu, as it was almost unheard of in the Omeo area. The tea-pourers would be chatting merrily. It was truly a banquet.

Finally, the band would start playing again, and the adults would stroll even more slowly back into the hall. At a given signal, it was time for us kids. There would be dozens of us, and nothing—not a crumb or skerrick of food—remained on those tables when we finished. I have very fond memories of those suppers.

The Swifts Creek Hall had many uses: it was the venue for movies, dances, badminton, plays, debutante balls, and amateur evenings that boasted some outstanding singers and musicians—and some pretty ordinary ones as well. There were school break-ups, community meetings, Country Women's Association meetings, and special concerts like Slim Dusty's. It was also the locale of a secret meeting.

Held in the supper room once a month, Bob, my stepfather, used to attend them. It was the lodge meeting of the Royal Antediluvian Order of Buffalo: a very serious and secretive gathering that held mystical rituals and other unusual goings-on. At school, I had heard that those involved dressed strangely, muttered weird sayings, and regularly rode a billygoat. Word had it that the door to the supper room had a guard. Of course, when you waved that sort of information in front of your average country kids we became full of curiosity and simply had to see what was going on in there. With a plan devised, I somehow became the ringleader.

One wall of the supper room had three windows. They were quite high up, well out of reach, so you couldn't just peep in through them. Our plan involved not only a test of courage but also demanded strength. At the designated time, about eight of us turned up. The tall blokes—I was one of them—would stand with their backs to the wall, and hoick a mate up while the others pushed.

The first kid to reach window level was Bloss Higgs. No sooner had he started to sneak a look at the mysteries of the Buffaloes than a noise erupted from inside, and all hell broke loose: someone had spotted Bloss. We took off like rabbits.

The next day at school, Bloss gave us a very vivid description of what he'd briefly seen. There were two goats—one really big. One bloke wore armour and, Bloss reckoned, he wielded a sword or a spear or something. That was damn scary, I thought. However, when Bloss said they were about to behead an intruder—from 'above the Gap'—I lost interest. That was stretching the truth a bit, I reckoned. Still, I never dared ask the old man what went on in there.

AFTER TONGIO, the move to Doctors Flat turned out to be a blessing. I had the river, a school bus, neighbours about half-a-mile away, and the bush. Sheepstation Creek was only 300 yards from our house. It ran into the Tambo River after a short but rapid journey down from the Angora Ranges, a long, high line of mountains to our west. From the mouth of Sheepstation Creek to the bush was a distance of just over two miles.

During that first year, Robbie and I each got a horse. Fizz was Robbie's horse, and mine was Sandy Mac. They were both docile animals, ideal for a first horse. It made me feel normal to get a horse. Every other farm kid in the area had one; the Reid boys even rode their horses to school.

It seemed we had moved to the perfect location—it was like a permanent holiday site, with so much fun to be had up the river, down the river, climbing the high Weeping Willow trees. Then, early in the morning, by sneaking up to the river's bank and peering quietly into the crystal-clear water, we discovered eels, sand trout, platypus, and large frogs. Mum had us cutting a funny-looking, green bushy plant that re-grew very quickly—asparagus—and we loved eating it.

Across the river were paddocks that harboured countless rabbits, which meant that trapping would be easy. Betty and Goldie, our two milking cows, were free to roam the river, as there was no cow paddock. Fortunately, there was an abundance of grass, and they rarely wandered far from home. In fact, I enjoyed getting off the school bus and hunting for them. Although we lived only 100 yards off the Omeo Highway, it fascinates me now that, over the years, our milkers never strayed onto the road—particularly in the mornings after I had finished milking, when there were several timber trucks that used the road daily.

After exploring many of the new places around Doctors Flat, it was Sheepstation Creek and those big mountains that intrigued me. I'm sure I was spurred on by recalling some of the wonderful yarns that Les had told me when we'd lived at Tongio.

The first time I walked to Sheepstation Creek, I decided to explore the bridge. It was a small, wooden structure on the Omeo Highway. Underneath, I found a small grey eel in a rather large pool. It swam away rapidly, and headed upstream. I followed it, and found an old windmill spinning around and pumping water into a rusted water tank. Nearby was an old, small weatherboard house. An old man came out, and I realised that I knew him—it was Mr Dorrington. Mum had known him when she was a child, and he had called into our house at Doctors Flat several times. He wandered over and we talked: he spoke about Mum fondly, and he reminisced about his farm.

That night, at home, I mentioned my visit to the old house and meeting Mr Dorrington. Then, to my surprise, Mum said that we were buying the property Mr Dorrington had talked about. This was exciting—it was a square mile of land up Sheepstation Creek somewhere, through a bush block and an old gate. Apparently, it had a small paddock, and a house or hut.

Suddenly, I became very interested in exploring the bush. No sooner had my parents purchased the block than they named it 'Dorrington's'. Admittedly, it wasn't a farm, as I'd first thought, but a bush property, located behind another timbered property we called 'McCallum's', out on Sheepstation Creek. Both properties, only sparsely cleared, were on the eastern slopes of the Angora Ranges.

The history of Dorrington's went back to the late 1800s. Apart from a few cleared acres, it had no paddocks, no farm buildings, didn't carry any stock, and was generally steep, grassless, stringy-bark bush. The first time I went out with Dad, we followed a narrow dirt road that led to the small paddock. We called it the 'Five Acres'.

There was a log cabin just up from the creek. Around the cabin were the remnants of a yard, a chook house, a garden, and a woodheap. This suggested that the cabin must have been a stopping-off place, or simply a small settlement, at some time in the past. There wasn't enough cleared country to run stock. After our inspection, we could see that even the border fence at Dorrington's had never been completed, and those few fences we found were beyond repair and needed replacing.

Not deterred by this, our first sheep—five ex-poddy lambs—proudly marched out to the property, not long after the signing of certain papers. Well, not quite marched. I walked and they followed. That is exactly what they did at home. Poddies are different in personality from mob sheep. If I went to find the milkers, Mary-Anne and all the other poddy sheep would follow me dutifully. When I got off the school bus, they would run and greet me like a friendly dog would. To be honest, I was sorry to see them moved to Dorrington's.

For me, the acquisition of Dorrington's was like getting a big birthday present. I couldn't wait to go into the bush and explore it. When we lived at Tongio, there was some light bush just below our house; here, at Doctors Flat, it was only just over three miles to the real bush, with large mountains and many things to look for and learn about.

By now I was almost twelve, and I was allowed to use Dad's rifle—a 22 calibre. My first trip up into the bush was on my own, on horseback. A sling held the rifle across my back, and our dog, Darky, came along. It was a very short adventure, though. Sandy Mac, spooked by something, shied, and I ended up thumped against a tree, from where I slid to the ground. Sandy Mac took off. I found him at the first gate, caught him, and returned home.

The next time I headed bush, I decided, I'd ride Sandy Mac to the last paddock, leave him there, and walk into the bush. The old log cabin (the one I called the 'Five Acres') was in that last paddock, and Sheepstation Creek ran right next to it. I would take rabbit traps, a camp oven, some blankets, the rifle, and some food—mainly potatoes and onions. Rabbits were very common throughout eastern Victoria, and I would either trap or shoot a rabbit. My parents were quite happy for me to be away for days at a time—something that seemed natural then, but is virtually unimaginable today.

chapter five

Exploring the bush

DORRINGTON'S WAS THE PLACE FROM WHERE I WANTED TO start my adventures. I had already planned that the log cabin was going to be my base. It had been there since the 1800s, and was possibly 60 to 80 years old. The roof, which was made of stringy-bark, had disintegrated and collapsed. Wombats had dug a huge hole in the floor. Oddly enough, there was a very old iron bed inside—with no mattress—and an open fire with a corrugated chimney at one end.

I filled the hole, put some old canvas over the roof, and generally cleaned up the cabin. It took me several days to make it habitable.

The first time I camped in the cabin was for one night only, on my own. I headed out late on a Friday afternoon, after finishing my yard chores. Sandy Mac wasn't happy with the extra bags and gear I had lashed over his back and neck; his ears were laid back, and it took me several sharp kicks to entice him out the gate. We trotted into Wilson's Paddock and up the Sheepstation Creek track towards the bush, through McCallum's and out to the Five Acres. Darkie and Skipper, however, were beside themselves. Skipper was a black mongrel dog we'd had for a few months. I would use the camp oven to cook chops, along with spuds and onions, and some scraps for the dogs. For brekkie, I had brought along bread and eggs.

That night I lit a big fire outside, and sat for ages poking at the flames, and creating formations of sparks that twirled and twisted to the heavens. There is something about a fire in the open—it always fascinates me, and I can spend hours just staring and fiddling with it as it burns.

After a good night's sleep on the iron bed, I rose early. My plan was to climb up the high mountain behind the log cabin until I reached Mad Lucy's Rock—a very large granite rock near the top that was visible from many parts of the Tambo Valley. There were countless stories and mysteries about that huge rock.

(Legend had it that a local lady, a recluse called Lucy, would wander over this way from Brookville occasionally. Due to her absolute insistence on privacy, she was the subject of many scary stories told to us kids. Some 30 years later, I saw her at her hut near Brookville on several occasions; she was very old, still very wary of passers-by, and she ran inside if a car appeared.)

After a hearty breakfast, only interrupted by two begging dogs trying to give the impression that they were at the point of total starvation, I cleaned up. We started the steep climb to the rock very early—me with a World War II water bottle hanging off my shoulder, and with the staff that old Les had made for me. About halfway up, we startled a small mob of kangaroos. Shortly after that, Skipper fought a losing battle with a large echidna. I'd seen several before, but never in defensive mode. Within seconds of Skipper alerting the echidna, it dug furiously and sunk quickly into the hard, dry soil. Only its long, sharp spikes were showing, and when it rolled forward it presented a very formidable target. Skipper had no chance; he ended up with a bleeding nose.

Then we had visitors—Mary-Anne and her four mates. I hadn't seen them for months. It was exciting. Darkie and I were moving to greet them when Skipper intervened. He had never seen these sheep before and he charged them, barking savagely. Bewildered, the poor sheep, which had never before been confronted by an aggressive dog, turned tail and cleared. That was the last I saw of them for a long time.

After a while, a panting Skipper returned and we continued up the hill. Finally, we reached the large boulder. To my disappointment, it was too tall: I needed something to climb the rock with, like a ladder or a rope. The only thing I had at the cabin was my good axe, so I went all the way back down, returned with the axe, and felled a stringy-bark sapling that was about 30 feet tall. With the fallen tree resting against the boulder, I was able to scale up the furry bark to the top. The view was spectacular. What made it more impressive was the rock. The huge granite rock reached out over the treetops—it was as if I was standing on a tall building, overlooking a city.

After an hour of sitting, turning, and looking in every direction, I slid back down the tree and jogged through the bush back to the cabin. I was on a mission: I wanted to return and photograph a sunset from the rock. Slipping the bridle over Sandy Mac's ears, I cantered bareback to home and grabbed my camera. Actually, it was Dad's camera. He had only had it a few months. It was a Franka, with a Pronto lens and folding bellows—a very good camera. He couldn't follow, or understand, the concept of shutter speeds and aperture settings, so he gave it to me in disgust. I read the book that came with it thoroughly, and had already taken one roll of film successfully.

Armed with the camera in its smart leather case, I rode back to the Five Acres and headed up the mountain again. I struggled to the top of the giant rock and sat until sunset. While I was waiting, I carefully read the booklet that came with the film which recommended the camera settings that I should use to match the time of day. I took a whole roll of film. It was dark by the time I got back home.

At school, I was keen to tell a few mates, and one of my teachers, of my adventures. Mr O'Brien was my science teacher. He was a good man and easy to talk to, even though he was a teacher. He was curious about my interest in the camera, and he was surprised that I understood quite a bit of its workings. He suggested I should try developing my film and printing my own photographs. I didn't realise you could do such things yourself. He gave me a glass tray, and showed me with a strip of heavy, brown paper how I had to slide the film from side to side through the tray. He explained that this had to be in total darkness, for a given time and at a given temperature. Suddenly, I developed an interest in science—or, to be more specific, in chemicals, thermometers, timers, tongs, and the accurate measurement of liquids.

At home that night, in the dark, I removed the film from the camera, rolled away the protective backing paper, hit the timer button, and proceeded to slide the film through the developer in the tray. After the timer sounded, I washed the film in water and then rolled it for four minutes in the fixer. By the final wash, I was beside myself, hoping it had worked out. When the time was up, I turned on the torch that normally lit my pushbike when I rode it in the dark, and there were my first-ever negatives in black and white. Admittedly, I wasn't sure if they were good or even printable. I'd have to wait until I saw Mr O'Brien the next day.

To my relief, he was very complimentary when he saw them. He said I'd done well, adding, 'Only halfway there, Barry. Now you'll have to print them.'

He gave me a book on how to contact-print large negatives. I went home and read the book, and returned the next day eager to try my first prints. There was a catch, though: the process needed electric light, and the one place that had power in those days was the town of Swifts Creek—and even that was only because the local mill had a 240-volt plant that generated enough power to supply the town. Mr O'Brien solved the problem by organising a print-making night at the school, and several kids came along. Like me, they were very keen to see the process. We entered a room carrying a box that contained printing paper, chemicals, a frame to hold the papers, and negatives. He flicked a switch, which turned out the white light, and then he turned on a red safety light. We spent an intriguing night doing test strips in subdued red light, estimating exposure times, and then watching with excitement as an image appeared before our eyes as we rocked the paper to and fro in the chemicals. It was magical. I was hooked. Now, not only did I want to develop and print my own photographs, but I wanted to learn how to take good pictures.

That meant I'd need equipment and books, which meant I needed more pocket money. So out came the traps; rabbits were still two and six a pair. Then I borrowed the good oilstone, sharpened my good knife, and off I went asparagus hunting. It was still in season, growing on the river banks, and the local store bought the small, tied bunches. I also collected empty soft-drink bottles whenever we travelled—after the footy and at school—and then returned the bottles to our local store. They were worth threepence each.

After three months, I had my own darkroom set up. By coincidence, at the same time, Dad put a twelve-volt lighting plant out the back of the house at Doctors Flat, which meant I'd be able to develop and print my film at home. It wasn't really a darkroom; what I had was a kit, which I would set it up in the kitchen after everyone else had gone to bed. No, I didn't have an enlarger; I didn't know such a thing existed, and they required 240 volts. The negatives from the camera I used were so big that they produced a same-size contact print.

In future, this meant that whenever I went on adventures I had two things to shoot with—my camera and my rifle.

Over the years, I didn't get to take all the photographs I had planned during my forays into the bush. My parents, as mentioned, had bought a bush block. Now they were looking at buying a farm at Tongio and another bush block adjoining the one out at Sheepstation Creek. This meant they would have three holdings. Like any country kid, particularly the oldest, I was always working. By the time I was fifteen I could drive a bulldozer, make tanks, roll tank iron, and put in fence posts and strain wire. I regularly killed sheep for meat, and could drive both the Land Rover and a truck. The only time I had a break was during the school holidays, as Dad continued to work in his plumbing business and had his own labourer. It was during these times that I made some memorable treks into the bush—sometimes alone on foot, or at other times with mates. During the long holidays I would take my brother and any relations who came up to camp on the river near our house.

My first long adventure into the bush was on foot, alone, except for the two dogs, Darkie and Skipper. My plan was to set up camp in the log cabin at the Five Acres and to explore the headwaters of Sheepstation Creek. By now I had a haversack, a World War I canvas sleeping bag I used out in the open, and some dixies (square, metal cooking-trays from World War II) for cooking. The cabin was really well set up with a Coolgardie cooler or safe, cupboards, a table and chair, and a Tilley lamp.

It took about two hours to reach the Five Acres. That first night at the cabin, I managed to shoot a small kangaroo. I dressed the two hind legs, which I put in the safe. It made a good meal, cooked in the camp oven. The dogs gorged themselves on the innards and the remainder, and they retired early.

Early the next morning, I packed my haversack and strode off with my trusty staff along the banks of the creek. I left the two dogs tied up—I believed I would see a lot more of the wildlife without them. It was heavy going and steep, and a lot of dogwood and low scrub made getting close to the creek difficult. I tried to walk in the creek itself, but the pools were too deep and the rocks too slippery. I turned and headed up the hill slightly away from the creek, and walked parallel to the stream. Being just above the creek gave me a good view, even though it was heavy bush; the trees were high and some distance apart.

As the sides of the hills became steeper, I used the staff to prop myself up as I shuffled along. About an hour from the cabin, I came across a large tree that had fallen and lodged itself into the fork of another tree further down the steep hill. It was almost horizontal, and it protruded out over the creek. It looked like a long bridge suspended over the water below. I jumped up and crawled along on all fours. Above the gurgle of the creek, I could hear the burble of what could have been a magpie or a mudlark. I knew both calls, but wasn't surprised they would be together. Back at home, two magpie families had adopted us, and I knew they were cheeky birds. They seemed to tolerate mudlarks. I crawled a little further along the grey box tree, and was intrigued when the sound of a rosella pierced the air, shortly followed by that of a bronze-winged pigeon. Stopping, I looked around. Something was different, strange. Then I saw it—below me, about 20 feet away, was a lyrebird. I still recall my first thought: I'd left the damn camera in the haversack, thinking it was too good to bring in case I fell over and damaged it. It was a very expensive camera; Dad reminded me of this many times.

No matter, this was a treat—a very special treat. The bird was plain brown, with no distinguishing features. It continued to mimic other birds, including the whipbird, which would have been difficult as its song is a combination of two birds from the same species. During this performance, the lyrebird bobbed up and down on a crude mound of sticks and leaves. It was about the size of our big leghorn rooster at home. After a time, it strutted in circles around the mound and made a variety of bird calls like those I have mentioned. Suddenly, with its head arched back, it spread its harp-like tail, strutted with stiff, high-legged kicks, and jerked its head as if in time to music. It changed from a dull brown, chook-like bird to a beautiful, elegant bush bird. With its beak wide open, the perfect sound of a kookaburra laugh throbbed from its mouth. I closed my eyes. It was a perfect imitation. Like a rap dancer, its head jerked and twitched in a rhythmic motion as if it was performing a sophisticated street dance in a ghetto. Glancing around the immediate area, I was hoping I would see a hen—let's face it, this was a command performance. I turned slightly to look around the other side, when a lump of bark dislodged and fell. The bird scampered away, and there was a long silence.

What a privilege. Even at my age, I knew I'd witnessed something unique. I swung my legs over the tree, as if I was sitting on a horse, and sat for ages. Slowly, I turned and crawled back along the fallen tree, and returned to ground level. I was elated and wanted to tell someone, so I threw on my pack and headed back to the cabin. In a straight line, it was only a 40-minute hike. Letting both the dogs off the chain, I explained to them with excitement what I had just witnessed—well, I had to tell someone. After a steak sandwich, cooked to perfection, it was time to head off again. This was great fun. In a moment of weakness, I took both dogs and headed straight back towards the fallen tree by cutting over a ridge and heading down a spur. The lyrebird's mound was there, but it was missing. Again, I told the dogs what happened and where—I thought they were interested.

Turning, I headed slightly up the hill again and proceeded to follow the creek towards its headwaters. After a time, I could hear the sound of rushing water. As it got louder, I headed back down towards the creek and decided to bash my way along the bank. As if I had opened a secret door, a beautiful waterfall suddenly appeared. It was probably 40 feet high, and it had a big pool at the bottom. A large goanna was having a drink, and was quite surprised when I appeared—it stood and stared at me for ages. The waterfall was a sheer drop over a giant slab of granite. There was quite a volume of water cascading over the lip and then dropping into the wide pool.

This time, I had the camera. I took several photographs, and named the waterfall the 'First Waterfall' as it was the first large one I had ever seen. As I slowly moved around the pool, carefully looking for trout or other water life, I heard a splash and thought I saw the end of a platypus tail disappear into the water. I went and inspected the bank and, sure enough, there were tiny webbed imprints in the mud—definitely a platypus's.

Quietly, I walked back into the low scrub and sat, waiting. It would only have been a matter of time before I'd see more creatures but, to my disappointment, Darkie decided just then to have a swim. Great—thanks, mate! This meant that any wildlife were certain to quickly hide under rocks, banks, and the like. Whose damn stupid idea was it to bring those dogs along?

I climbed to the top of the fall, and admired the orange and brown stains caused by the water. There was moss and lichen all over the huge rocks, and several well-worn tracks that wound down around the waterfall towards the pool. On inspection, I could see that lots of footprints had been left by wombats, emus, kangaroos, and goannas. Then there were occasional prints of a fox, a dog, or a dingo. Obviously, it was a favourite watering hole, although I was surprised to find no rabbit prints. Years later, I learnt that rabbits obtain most of their water needs from dew.

By mid-afternoon I was quite high up in the mountains. After a time I again headed upstream, this time walking along the creek. It was now quite narrow, and I found it easy to jump from rock to rock. About 300 yards up from the waterfall, the land around the creek was open and flat and looked partially cleared, as if it had been a camp many years ago. Venturing to my left and slightly up a ridge, I found a track—a heavily rutted narrow track that hadn't been used for a long time. It went almost straight up the ridge, and turned to the right towards the top of the Angora Range. It was narrow—about six feet across. Just before the track reached the top of the main ridge, I found a very old fence. It had almost fallen down. Most of the wires were broken and twisted, and the posts were covered in moss.

What had I found? Surely it wasn't a vehicle track; it was too steep and narrow for that. I doubted it was even a stagecoach road, for the same reasons. I backtracked to the creek, and discovered that an area had been partly cleared for something to cross the creek. I noticed that several large boulders had been pushed to one side—a long time ago, as they were covered in lichen and moss. It was one of the few flat areas along the stream. As I moved out from the creek, across the other side, I began to guess that it had been a camp site at some time in the past.

I discovered a flat, semi-cleared area, which was now overgrown, dug into the hill. The track continued on from this clearing. It went steeply up a small ridge, along the spur, and came out at the back of the mountain, overlooking Brookville.

It was late afternoon when I decided to head back to the log cabin. Although the dogs had had a wonderful time exploring and barking at things in the distance that I couldn't see, I decided I wouldn't take them exploring in future.

That night, I sat for ages thinking about the waterfall and the track. I decided that I had to find out its history when I got home. The following morning, between the sounds of the dogs, the kookaburras, and the cockatoos, I was awake by 5.00 a.m.

After a hearty breakfast of toast and vegemite, I grabbed my sharpening stone and honed up my good axe. Today was an entirely different challenge. Old Gator Lambourne had told me how to repair the roof on the log cabin by using stringy-bark. Several days before, I'd already earmarked a couple of suitable trees. The first tree had a girth of about ten feet. I lent a small ladder against the tree, and climbed up about ten feet. At that height, I cut a ring completely around the tree. At the bottom, I repeated the same process. Then I cut a vertical line straight down the tree, joining the two rings. Slowly, with the axe and a couple of sticks, I prised the bark away from the tree. At the start, it was difficult peeling the tight, thick bark away. Then, with a crack, like an apple snapping in half, the bark popped off the tree. I rolled the length of bark along, and then up on to, two strong saplings I'd laid on the ground. Lifting up each pole one at a time, I managed to slide several large rocks underneath. Finally, with the roll of stringy-bark about eighteen inches off the ground, it was ready for the next stage. Using dry leaves and small twigs, I lit a wide, low fire underneath the bark. Then, with the white, sappy side of the bark facing the fire, the large slab of stringy-bark started to spread—just as old Gator said it would. An hour later, I had a perfectly flat piece of bark ready to nail on top of the log cabin. I doused the fire and left everything to cool down. I had to leave the bark there until next time, when I'd return with some help—it was too heavy for me to lift on my own. Four trees later, I'd prepared enough bark to cover the log-cabin roof.

On the last day, I spent most of the time blocking the cracks between the logs of the cabin. I did this by soaking some newspaper in the creek, and jamming it between the draughty gaps. I finished that night. It only needed a door to complete the cabin.

The next morning, I packed up and tramped back through the bush out into the open country, following the creek until I reached the bridge with the sign 'Sheepstation Creek'. That was where old Charlie Dorrington lived. Turning left, I headed for home.

At school, a week later, several of our neighbours' kids were curious about my discovery of the falls. I showed them the photographs I'd developed, and we decided that during the next holiday break we would venture out to the cabin camp and find the First Waterfall, and maybe do some more exploring ... and they would help me put up the roof.

Some time later, when I told old Gator Lambourne about the steep, rutted track I'd found that crossed the creek and continued on to Brookville, he spoke at length about it. It was an old bullock-wagon track, he reckoned, used to haul farming produce to Port Albert in bygone times; he added that, at other times, mine machinery and other engineering equipment was lugged through the bush on large wagons hauled by dozens of bullocks. Since the bullocks travelled so slowly, Gator wasn't surprised that I'd found what I thought was a camp site. He reckoned there was one about every ten or twelve miles. Good. I slotted that comment away, and planned for an expedition to find more camp sites ... and who knew what else?

chapter six

'You're disgusting, Heard.'

BY NOW, I HAD SPENT TWO YEARS IN SECONDARY SCHOOL. The teachers rotated for each subject, which was quite different from primary school. I had no interest in English, History, Geography, French, Art, and Religious Studies—the latter, drilled into us by the local minister, was received with fear and trepidation. I could list on one hand the books I'd read at school—under duress from teachers—and, being a slow reader, I would continually lose track of the story. But give me numbers, and I was happy.

Subjects like Arithmetic, Geometry, and Algebra were straightforward and logical, compared to the written word. I found it a delight to do equations and long division, or to decipher a difficult algebraic problem. Science I enjoyed, mainly because of Mr O'Brien—he was a good teacher. Yes, I was an 'odd bod', which is what Miss Foster, my Art teacher said one day. Most times, when riding my horse or bike, or even walking, I would calculate the best way to multiply 37 by fifty-eight. To be honest, apart from sport or the odd game like marbles, or the subjects I mentioned, school was boring. Away from that place, there were many other adventures awaiting me as a young teenager.

The year 1959 was my second-last year at school, and it was the first year I noticed the opposite sex. Some enterprising teachers and one of the parents had set up dancing classes at the local Church of England hall. I desperately wanted to go, as most of the kids in my class at school went and constantly talked about the fun they were having. I begged my parents to take me, but it was a no-go. I arranged to stay at a mate's place—again, a no-go. I did extra chores at home and helped wherever I could—still a no-go. I was getting quite desperate, because my parents offered no explanations or reasons as to why I couldn't attend. The dances were chaperoned, they ended at 10.00 p.m., and only cordial and sandwiches were served. Now, what was wrong with that?

On one particular Saturday night—dance night—Dad, who'd played footy that day for Swifts Creek, was visiting a mate's place in the town of Swifts Creek, with Mum and us kids in tow. His team had won and he was in good spirits. Again, I asked if I could go, as the dance was on just up the road; once more, it was a no-go. Did I spit the dummy? No, I said nothing; I just walked outside, planning the hour-long walk home. I was going to pack my bags and leave ... for somewhere.

Outside, it was freezing cold, with a razor-like wind slicing the air. Pausing, about to trudge home, I abruptly changed my mind. *Damn going home*, I thought. The devil in me decided to go to the dance instead. But I had one big problem—no money. It was sixpence to get in. I also had no suitable clothes. I never wore good clothes to the footy because we would always have a kick at half-time and I would get my clothes dirty. So that ruled out the dance. I wasn't happy. I wanted to get back at my oldies somehow.

Next plan: I would hide on the floor, behind the front seat of the new Holden. No one would find me, and this would get right up my parents' noses, as dinner was about to be served.

Come teatime, there were calls in and around the house, but I remained put. Then, with everyone outside spreading out and still no sign of Barry, Dad lost the plot completely. This led to name-calling and threats, followed by panic—mother became worried. After half an hour of shouting, I decided to make an appearance. This wasn't a good move. Dad threatened to impose the death penalty when I emerged all guilty from the floor of the Holden.

However, my misdemeanour soon faded into the background. The adults started arguing about when a kid should be allowed go out, at what age, and what about hooligans, etcetera. Mum won. She took me home, where I put on a fresh set of our shared good clothes. I didn't have a bath, though—we only had them on a Friday. Then I was taken to the dance.

It was very late, and it only had about half an hour to run. So I just stood in the corner and looked at the girls—with no eye contact. Apparently, that was what you were supposed to do.

Quite pleased, I walked home afterwards. During the crisp stroll, an owl hooted, and rabbits scurried under bushes. Other night birds called their mates, and several horses came up to the fence out of curiosity, snorting a wary welcome. In all, for my part it was a good night, although admittedly I snuck into bed when I finally got home.

My pathetic, rebellious behaviour at least had one good outcome, if not two: I attended these dances most Saturday nights and, over time, learnt how to ballroom dance. I enjoyed using this skill for years.

Another benefit from going to the dances was the lessons I learned about the opposite sex. They stirred up something inside me that I enjoyed. The opposite sex: what a curious subject. They were definitely from Venus.

For me, there was no question that Miss O'Farrell was my first love. She was a dark-haired, attractive female with a soft, kind smile and a perfect manner; at the time, I was besotted. She was my Grade Three teacher at Ringwood Primary School. Her affection towards me was affirmed by remarks she uttered for my benefit alone. She said that I sat up straight, tried hard, was a nice boy, and always had clean fingernails. The fact that she said this to the other 40 students at different times was irrelevant. I was her favourite. The twinkle in her eye gave it away. It enabled me to realise that I had a rare attribute: I had a way of both charming and winning over the opposite sex. I didn't flout this gift like a Casanova or womaniser; I remained humble and unassuming, and only plied my skills when needed, with absolute care and aplomb.

Armed with this self-confidence, and having forgotten all about Miss O'Farrell, I asked Curls for my first date when I was almost fourteen. We both went to the school at Swifts Creek. There were seven boys and only four females my age at the school, and competition for the hand of one of these mountain maids was an endless battle—as Roy, one of the older boys, was heard to say, 'And we like mount'n women.'

However, at school, my charisma and other natural gifts only got me so far with the opposite sex. Curls, for some reason, didn't respond to my charm. So I asked one of the older kids—again, Roy—who'd grown up in the city, for some advice.

'Money,' he said, 'the evil of a good root.'

No doubt this was another of Roy's pearls of wisdom that I couldn't quite follow, but I gathered that money was a necessity when attempting to court a mountain maid. So, armed with this knowledge, I looked for a job, got an offer, and then wagged school for a brief time just before school holidays. In all, I worked a full three weeks—two of them in the holidays.

Now armed with several quid, I discovered that Roy was right. Suddenly, back at school, I had a lot of kudos and the perfect drawcard to ask Curls to the movies. Yes, money put the male contestants at the top of the popularity queue. Just as well, as, despite my magnetism, I was turning into an ugly bugger, really. With pimples, growth spurts, bum-fluff, and freckles on my face, it was quite a challenge to win a female heart.

But let's go back to earning my pocket money. To be honest, the three weeks' work away from school was a lot of fun. I was the rouseabout in Wilson's two-stand shed, just up the road from home. There were two shearers—both good, neat craftsmen, and I admired their skill. However, I was amazed at the effort required to shear a sheep. Both shearers were capable of shearing one hundred or more sheep a day, and they lost a large amount of sweat in the process. A rouseabout is a busy job. There were fleeces to be picked up and thrown, the floor to be swept clean, and catching pens to be filled up every time a shearer called, 'Sheep-oh!'

This particular year it had been a good season, and the fleeces were heavy and full of thistles—an annoying plant with needle-sharp prongs that stick into your hands. This is doubly a problem if you work in a woolshed, as your hands become very soft because of the lanolin in the wool. Within two days, my hands were very sore, and I had trouble milking the cows early in the morning before work. Then one of the workers in the shed noticed my problem and kindly took me to one side.

'Not to worry,' said the wool classer, Tom—Tom Cook from Ensay.

'I know a good way to harden ya hands. Just pee on 'em, Baz. Rub it in well, and do it every time ya have a leak.'

Three times he explained the procedure until, a little confused, I headed for a catching pen to have a piddle. Tom was a good bloke, so the shearers reckoned, so I was grateful to him, and appreciated the advice. In fact, I was pleased that he almost treated me like an adult. So I began the daily ritual. Every time I snuck out into the catching pens to have a pee, I would liberally smother my hands. Boy, did they sting. I continued with this procedure, even when I went home for weekends, but the sore hands remained a problem. However, I was encouraged, as Tom said they'd be a lot worse if I stopped the pee routine. Nice bloke, Tom—he always had a smile on his face when he spoke to me. It was funny but, at home, Mum complained that there was a foul smell most nights at tea. I never determined until years later that it had been me.

Then the woolshed job finished and I was back at school with twelve quid in my pocket for three weeks' work. Curls was mine. Within a day, I had a date to the movies arranged. I rode my pushbike into the town and picked her up. Fortunately, she only lived around the corner from the hall. It was Tuesday night and we headed for the Town Hall.

A bloke from Buchan, a town just over the hill, ran the movies. He was deaf, the poor blighter. Once the movies started, you could hear the noise that blasted around the hall from half a mile away. This meant that if I wanted to say something really special to Curls, I had to get in early, or shout once the flicks got underway.

We sat in the back row—the 'cool row'. The lights went out, and we all stood for the national anthem. The Queen's head appeared, in the middle of a waving flag. The men and boys all stood to attention. Then it was the Movietone news, cartoons, and trailers. Finally, the first feature started. It was a Doris Day epic; someone had told me that the trailer the week before suggested it was a cool movie with a lot of 'smooching and flapping eyelashes'—very suitable for my first date. Ten minutes after it started, I made my first move. With the grace of a good-looking male goanna, I slid my arm around Curls's shoulders, tickled her chin, and stared at her like a hooting owl.

'What's that awful pong?' she asked, with her nose in the air.

Those around us sniggered. Then bloody Shinga—Tom Wilson, a schoolmate—burst out laughing, the rotten blighter.

'Pardon?' I asked (this was a really bad mistake).

'Ya hands stink. Don't ya wash, ya dirty beggar?'

By now, the back third of the hall was in uproar—this was better than any Doris Day movie. Devastated, I rose to my feet and said I needed a pee (without the hand-washing). Then I snuck out the back and cleared off.

The three-mile bike ride back home was a long one. There were no damn horses wandering up to the fence, or owls hooting. I knew that at school the next day there'd be questions. Not about 'how'd ya git on with Curls?' but about where my hands had been. God, it was embarrassing—everyone in the hall had heard Curls's comment. She'd had to shout above the booming sound from the movies. How would I explain it to the parents, since the word would have reached her mum and mine by the next day? So I learnt my first lesson about dating: take a bit of time before you make your first move.

The next day at school, I lay low. After the movies fiasco, it was best if I steered clear of the girls for the week, I reckoned. Naturally, after pondering on the entire incident, with the hindsight of a typical vacant adolescent, I changed my ways. Well, let's just say I wasn't deterred, and I gave Curls the shove; she chewed her fingernails, anyway.

Meg was my next target. This time I didn't ask Roy for advice or guidance; I simply took my time and waited for the right moment. Meg was a bit of all right: she had long hair and she barracked for the Bombers. As I mentioned, timing was important, and here I had an opportunity. I needed a date for a special occasion—a party for Jacko's girlfriend, Rosie, who was turning fifteen.

I approached Meg, real cool-like, and enticed her for a date with a comment about her beauty. Now *that* was a downright lie because, in reality, Curls was the only good-looker in the school. But Meg had charm and was a goer, according to Roy. Did that mean she was good at netball? (Roy had offered me his opinion anyway, and that was good enough for me.) The main thing was that Meg accepted my invitation, which was great. I begged Mum to let me have a bath on the night in question, and she obliged. I polished my shoes and put on some of Dad's hair oil and a pair of his pants, since I was now taller than he was.

The evening's entertainment was at Rosie's family home. They lived in a mill-house in the town. It was a typical 1950s' country party: some twelve of us in attendance, the boys in one corner with their plastic-looking hair slicked down with Californian poppy, looking smooth and pretending to ignore the girls—a well-honed Aussie ritual. Meanwhile, the mountain maids, even though they were our dates, were over in the far corner, giggling, fluttering, and whispering.

Then, of course, there was Jacko. What a hero. He was fourteen going on fifteen, and he was holding hands *in public* with his girl already—boy, did I envy that. Word had it that they'd been going steady for 22 days.

Naturally, at a bush party, several mothers were there, and they had a nice supper prepared.

We did a rough barn dance to a wind-up 78 record player, followed by the Mexican Hat dance. Then we played some games: Pass the Parcel, and Postman's Knock were usually the first. Both were games that were regularly played at teenage birthday celebrations.

Then we played a new game called Over the Water. Two broomsticks were placed parallel on the floor about seven feet apart while Mrs Buckland leapt around the room in a big circle, giving a brief explanation of the rules. We boys were fascinated by the way her boobs flopped about. The game sounded great—at some stage we had to pick up our partner and carry her between the two brooms. I vividly recall glancing briefly at Meg and wincing. This would test me.

'Let's give it a try,' announced Mrs Jackson, as she wound up the gramophone and carefully placed the needle in the groove. The music started up, and we held hands and skipped around the room in twos to the tune of Pat Boone's hit, *Silvery Moon*. Then it was time for the broomsticks: 'Time to pick up your partner in your arms and carry her over the water,' said Mrs Boucher. 'And remember, if the music stops while you are in between the sticks, you are out.'

Now, to be honest, I wasn't sure if Meg and I were a good match for this game. You see, she was a bit on the heavy side; sort of plump, or pretty solid, is how I would put it. On the farm, you would call her a good doer, in prime condition. The game continued. We were approaching the broomsticks as Pat Boone—the bloke on the 78 record—got to the bit 'on Moonlight Bay', when Mrs Jackson reefed up the needle. Terry and Linda, caught between the sticks, were out. Down went the needle again. We'd done about two rounds, and my poor old arms were stuffed. Then, as I rounded the bend, the broomsticks came into calculation. I bent down, went to lift Meg up, fell backwards slightly, and my hand shot up the back of her legs and got tangled in some clips or something. *Twang!* A shriek rang out, and Meg took a back-hander at me as her stocking separated from its suspender belt, and shot down to her ankles. Her leg was very white.

Holy smoke, cripes, and hell—the party turned into a riot. The girls all ran off to another room screaming and squealing. Jacko turned to me, winked and said, 'Brilliant move, ya cunning bugger. You'll 'ave ta show me that one, mate.'

What one? I didn't know if I should run and hide, or maybe pretend that nothing had happened—or perhaps, in an act of total foolhardiness, look real cool in my new status as a womaniser. It didn't matter. Meg's Aunt Muriel, the evil-eyed old magpie, came out, looked at me with utter disgust, and then *tutted*. Now that put a damper on things.

Then a girl's head appeared around the door. 'You're disgusting, Heard,' she said.

Not long after, the party ended and I rode my bike home, very confused. Again, I did learn something: never date a girl heavier than yourself.

Back at school, both Curls and Meg now avoided me. School holidays couldn't come quickly enough. I'd already planned my next bush venture.

chapter seven

Back in the bush

I SPENT ANY SPARE TIME I HAD IN THE BUSH AT DORRINGTON'S. But this rarely happened, as I usually went out with Dad and Gator Lambourne to work. Gator had been born and bred in the bush, and he enjoyed chatting away about the old days while he helped us with fencing, clearing, and burning off. Our first job had been to fence the Five Acres. We put in three gates, and wire netting all the way around to make it rabbit-proof. This particular year had been very dry: the Tambo had dropped to half its normal flow, and Sheepstation Creek was only a trickle, with just the odd pool. It was the start of the Christmas holidays. For me, it meant fun in the bush—I couldn't wait.

At school, I talked excitedly to the other kids about what I'd found in the bush. Some were keen to explore and help me finish the log cabin. This time, there'd be four of us. We'd take enough flour, spuds, onions, and the like to last at least a week. We had the added advantage of a horse and cart: we had Morrison's half-draught called Dolly, and a heavy, two-wheeled cart available. The Morrisons lived down the road a bit from us, in the same house that my mum had grown up in as a young girl—Boonabirrah Hill.

After school on the Friday, we were packed and ready to go. Two hours later, we were unhitching Dolly at the Five Acres and organising a camp fire outside the log cabin. Now, I have a confession to make after all these years. We had a packet of Turf cigarettes with us, hidden away with the food. They were cork-tipped—though I wasn't sure what that meant—and there were ten of them in the packet. The highlight of our first night, as you might have guessed, was the cigarettes. Pud was sick, I got the staggers and ended up walking backwards, and the other two gave up after a couple of drags. Naturally, we all tried to do the 'drawback'.

In all, it was a very quiet, early night. We didn't even cook ourselves any tea. The idea of smoking got the thumbs down. First thing on the Saturday morning, we put up the stringy-bark sheets and waterproofed the cabin. For a door, I'd brought along a sheet of canvas with a board nailed to the bottom, to stop it flapping too much. By now, the cabin was quite comfortable and clean—although I didn't tell the others that I'd scared off a black snake in there a couple of weeks earlier.

We wandered down to the creek below the cabin, and I was surprised to find almost no flow. More fascinating was the fact that the large pool of water, which was about five feet across and only about a few inches deep, was full of trout. There must have been hundreds of them: tiny trout, about six or seven inches long, with a bright red dot behind their gills. We scooped up a small bucketful, and fried them for lunch. It was a delightful meal. Satisfied, we headed on foot for the First Waterfall.

An hour later, we were there. The three boys reacted almost the same way I did—they just went quiet. The fall remained completely hidden until the last moment, and then, there it was—what a sight. After 20 minutes of just looking and hoping to see some wildlife, we decided to have a swim in the large pool. This was a bad idea—it was freezing. Quickly, we were back on dry land, dressed, and ready to venture further up into the headwaters.

Briefly, I showed them the bullock track I'd found. By now, other locals, as well as Gator, had explained to me that it was a bullock track used in the late 1800s for both the small township of Brookville and the gold mine at Cassilis. My find had created a lot of local interest.

Back to the creek we walked—or, I should say, jumped—from rock to rock, as we moved up the stream. The banks were quite steep and the flow was almost nothing—just a dribble, but certainly more than at the Five Acres. Even in good times, it would have been only two to three feet wide. The water trickled quietly around large rocks and made little noise. As we climbed higher, we noticed the bush change from stringy-bark trees to grey box. Suddenly, the stream flattened again; there was a lot more water. The area became more open and, looking ahead, we spotted a huge waterfall—the 'Second Waterfall'.

It was much higher than the first, and it was in two stages, or steps. Simply, it was awesome. Again, it was a formation of gigantic granite rocks. The first stage was a drop of roughly 25 feet, and the second was even bigger. We all just sat, talking about how stunning it would be after a good rain—even a flood. The surrounding area was different, too. Being higher up in the mountain, there were tree ferns and small reeds. The waterfall was 50 feet wide, and seemed way out of proportion to the small amount of water that cascaded over the top.

My camera quickly appeared, and I ended up running out of film; everyone wanted to be in a photograph. Fortunately, the camera had a self-timer.

After exploring the fall for more than an hour, we headed

up Sheepstation Creek. After all our spectacular finds, the further we went up from Second Waterfall, the narrower the creek became, dividing itself into several gullies and then almost disappearing. We'd found the headwaters. By now, we were a very long way from the cabin, and decided to climb to the top of the nearest spur and get our bearings. It took two hours to trek back to the cabin.

I'd decided to cook a large stew in the camp oven. Pud wandered off with the rifle to get a rabbit, and I went down to the creek to get some water. As I was about to leap the fence, something caught my eye—a snake. It was dead. My guess was that it had been there several days. However, the way it had died was amazing. It was a huge, black snake, probably five or six feet long—it might even have been the one I'd scared out of the cabin weeks earlier. It was stuck in the wire netting fence, facing towards the log cabin. The poor thing must have gone down through the fence earlier, ventured to the creek, maybe, for a drink—who knows? Obviously, it discovered the trout and must have had a ball catching and eating them. In fact, its body was the size of a small football when I found it. When we cut the snake open, it had twelve trout inside its belly. It had managed to get its head and about ten inches of its body through the wire netting, and then it became stuck—its scales, which faced to the rear, wouldn't allow it to go backwards ... it was one dead snake. I said it was probably five feet long as, already, a fox or a dingo had eaten part of its tail. Several battalions of sugar ants had already made a well-worn tiny path from the snake to their ant hill. Within a week it would be nothing but a skeleton.

The remainder of our holiday around the Five Acres was a lot of fun. We climbed Mad Lucy's Rock, trekked to the top of Mount Flagstaff overlooking Swifts Creek, and panned for gold, managing to get a few small specks. We set traps and caught rabbits, shot a kangaroo, and managed to scalp three wombats. In those days, the government paid ten shillings and sixpence a scalp. In fact, we devised a cunning way of catching them. After lighting a good fire slightly inside the mouth of their burrow, and then stuffing green leaves on top of the flames, we would quickly cover the entire opening with dirt. Invariably, when we returned several hours later and dug open the mouth of the burrow, the wombat would be there, dead, having suffocated.

We were away ten days, and it was a great holiday.

I FIND IT CURIOUS, now, to look back and consider my connection with nature then. In those days, I wouldn't hesitate to shoot almost any bush animal I came across. When walking in the bush with my staff, I killed many a black snake—the most common animal I'd encounter—and I never gave this a second thought. For bush meals in the camp oven, I sampled snake, wombat, kangaroo, cockatoo, and emu. I found none of them objectionable. Yet give me a lyrebird dancing, a platypus, an early-morning dawn with kangaroos standing on a ridge, or two snakes curled around each other mating, and I would be struck by the splendour and wonder of nature. Never would I interrupt, or even consider ruining the scene with a rifle shot.

To add to the confusion, how do I explain that I shot dead many a wedge-tailed eagle, and then hung them on the fence facing the Omeo Highway to show passers-by that we were helping to get rid of such vermin—when, at other times, particularly when climbing the steep ridge on our Tongio farm, I had admired the splendour of the eagle? I would stand perfectly still and watch as it dropped out of a tree towards the ground, which it touched lightly, flailing its ungainly legs before jumping, several times, into the air and running until airborne. The transformation to complete beauty is almost instantaneous; this magnificent bird would simply float down off the ridge with such elegance and grace that I could only slowly shake my head in awe. It was a remarkable sight.

In those days, seeing nature, and any animal, as friend and then foe is difficult to explain. To the average country kid, there was no shock in beheading a chook or in drowning kittens. When your best farm dog had pups, maybe six or eight of them, the only decision that counted was picking which one had the most potential; the remainder were destroyed without a second thought. Mind you, this culture of considering almost any bush animal as vermin, and therefore likely to be culled, didn't stop there. It was the same with the bush. Clearing virgin bush on our Fowler Marshall bulldozer, or burning the windrows of trees after they had dried sufficiently, was a source of great satisfaction. Clear felling was very common, and I enjoyed looking back over a day's work because, suddenly, there was a paddock where there used to be a thicket of trees and undergrowth. Not only was this the way of life in those days; it was also the accepted way of life, and people on the land were admired for their farming practices.

GROWING UP on the beautiful Tambo River was a great experience. It had clear water and well-grassed banks, and dotted along the sides of the river were Weeping Willow trees and giant rivergums.

In the banks of the Tambo, I could find, if I was careful, a fascinating gathering of Australian animals. Nowadays, most people only see a platypus on the back of a coin or enclosed in some pool—the poor little blighters. But they were quite common along the river in the 1950s.

As it is a very timid little creature, you had to be very quiet and tread softly as you approached its known territory. Then, lying down on the grass near the edge of the river in the early morning, with the sun in your face so as not to cast a shadow on the water, it was simply a matter of waiting until the show began. Usually, they would only venture out one at a time. On occasions, I saw two or more frolicking about, but I think these were youngsters. I say 'youngsters', as I never saw a small platypus. They must have stayed in their burrowed little cave in the bank until fully grown. However, once they ventured out it was a great show.

They are vigorous animals, although I've always felt that grace and the platypus are at odds. With their strange, duck-like bill, they don't just delve into the sand looking for food; they charge it like a bulldozer. They tackle large stones almost as big as themselves, and viciously push and shove from every angle until the rock is dislodged or rolled over. If the bottom of the creek is dirty, or is coated with a sticky black sludge, they hunt with such enthusiasm that a dirty cloud of milky water hides these little battlers for ages. Then, as if to defy all this energy, a platypus will casually cruise to the surface and lull about, snapping its beak and scratching its belly in delight. Casually, it will turn this way and then that, checking things out with its beady little eyes.

Other little creatures shared this watery home. Sand trout, eels, waterjacks, ducks, water rats, and the odd snake were neighbours. About once a week a snake would slither off the bank and then swim to the other side. Naturally, it would only happen in the warmer summer months, and it was usually a brown or copperhead snake. I rarely, if ever, saw a black snake swimming. The black, which was the biggest of all the snakes, is very timid.

Sand trout were the opposite of the black snake. In broad daylight, they would lie on the bottom in the open water, facing upstream and wagging their tail fins slowly, soaking up the sun, oblivious to strangers. You could walk quite close to them in the crotch-high water before they would dart off at great speed. When bored, I would occasionally get my bamboo rod and catch a sand trout. With worm for bait, it was simply a matter of casting several yards out from the fish and then winding in the bait until it was in front of the trout's mouth. Every now and then it would casually swim forward a little and swallow the bait. It gave little or no fight after I'd reeled it in, and Mum would have it cooked that day. Only two or three small fish were needed for a tasty meal.

The platypus and the sand trout would ignore each other. Other neighbours quite common along the banks in those days were waterjacks, which are like small goannas—large, lizard-like, native Australian reptiles. The moment they spotted you or heard you walking along the river bank, they would make a dash for the river, and would belly-flop into the stream and swim at great speed, their heads above the water. Once they reached the other bank, they bolted away to find some cover. They had a most ungainly way of running, their little legs flailing into the air in a circular motion, while their heads remained rigid, still, and erect, displaying the glare of an army sergeant-major.

The sand trout and the platypus both ignored this dashing reptile, but the little grey eel was a different matter. From what I could see, every time a grey eel ventured into a platypus's territory, the platypus's only aim seemed to be to kill the invader. The eel was too quick for the freakish-looking, duck-like beaver, and I never saw an eel attacked, captured, or killed, but it was full-on war by the platypus battalion. Perhaps the eels stole the eggs or ate the babies. Certainly, while most eels were only eighteen inches to two feet long, and appeared harmless, they were meat eaters.

I recall vividly, as a kid, seeing this demonstrated one evening at a barbecue at the Swifts Creek Gun and Angling Club, when a competition was held for the biggest eel caught. As usual, the proceeds raised on the night would go to a worthwhile cause like the local kindergarten or the bush-nurse clinic. The barbecues were set up on the banks of the Tambo. Earlier that day, Fitzy, the 'creek butcher', had filled a large sock with offal and congealed blood. The sock—lowered into the river just out from the bank near the barbecue area—leaked blood, and this trailed downstream. By the evening, there were hundreds of eels trying to attack the sock. Then, by means of handlines that were fitted with a wire trace and swivel (because eels would bite through a normal fishing line), and a chunk of meat fed onto the hook, numerous eels were caught, measured, and weighed.

By late evening, the contestants—full of sausages, amber fluid (either tea or beer), and endless recitations of *The Man from Snowy River* and the like from a local poet laureate, Kanga Miles—had almost forgotten about the competition. Still, the judge's results were announced and prizes were given. The winning catch would always be a massive congo or spotted eel. Although rare, these monsters were huge: they were more than three feet long and could weigh well over fifteen pounds, and the head was as big as an adult's sandshoe. Over the years, I would have seen only a dozen of them. They swam close to the river bank; their main source of food was the little sand trout.

I always wanted to catch myself a congo eel. It would have been something to brag about at school—maybe I'd even try to eat one, but that would have depended on Mum, since she would be cooking it.

One day I finally got my chance. It was a hot summer's day, and I was dressed and ready for cricket. My brother John had been down near the river, but he ran back up to the house and, pulling my arm, pointed to the Tambo River. I ran down, and found what had distressed young John: it was a huge congo, cruising the river directly below our house.

As it happens, I'd just turned thirteen, and one of my birthday presents was a beauty—a rifle. Well, it wasn't exactly a present: I'd been lent a rifle. With teenage bravado and stupidity, I thought I would use it to stop one of these giants.

When I spotted it, the eel was lazily folding its way slowly along the bank about two feet under the water. I'd shot many harmless water creatures with Dad's 22-calibre rifle. It was simple—by poking the barrel just under the water and then pulling the trigger, I'd concuss them. Mostly, I shot at trout and grey eels. After the explosion, they became stunned and floated to the top. However, the congo eel was a big target, and it required formidable firepower. I had just the thing to deal with it: a big rifle.

Vic Antinoff had decided that I was old enough—and, let us say, mature enough—to borrow his special rifle, a fine-looking, sporting .303 rifle, for my birthday. This was exciting. It was a beautiful-looking weapon with a polished wooden butt. To be honest, the rifle was more than a loan but less than a present—it was more in the way of a bribe to entice me to shoot kangaroos, which were becoming a problem on the farm.

For the uninitiated, the .303 takes a very big bullet, much larger than a 22-calibre. The .303 rifle had been used in World War II; when fired, it has a kick like a mule. It would simply blast a rabbit to bits. It is a very scary weapon.

Back to the congo eel … I rushed back up to the house, removed the .303 rifle from its pouch, and pocketed a couple of bullets. Armed with the cannon-like weapon, I then dashed back to the river. The eel, which appeared asleep, was gracefully and slowly swinging its tail while stationary—great. I poked the barrel down into the water just above its head, so that only the trigger and butt were out of the water. With Davy Crockett-like coolness, I gently squeezed the trigger—remember, this was my first-ever shot with it—when, holy smoke, Jesus, and strike me pink! There I was, flying through the air backwards at bullet speed. I was crunched against a gate some 25 yards back from the river, before a huge but brief shower of water fell on me. Finally, I slid down the wire netting into a sitting position, the rifle still in my hands. Boy, was I in pain. My damn shoulder throbbed, and my neck and jaw felt like I'd done ten rounds with Les Darcy. However, all that pain soon paled into insignificance when I looked at the .303 still clutched in my right hand. The barrel, split wide open and bent at an angle, looked more like a bluster gun. Hell, the old man would kill me. This rifle was like Mum's good scissors—sacred stuff.

Stunned and leaning on the gate, I didn't have to linger for too long. Attracted by the sonic boom—and maybe by water falling on the roof, and the fact that my brother John had cleared back to the house screaming blue murder—the oldies appeared.

I quickly got to my feet, looking very sheepish and pretending that nothing had happened. As you might guess, my parents weren't impressed. There was no, 'Jeez, what happened?' or, 'Are you okay, Baz?' Instead, Dad yelled, 'What the hell happened to the rifle, ya dopey prick? Shit. Victor will kill me.'

Then Mum said, 'You're soaked. How'd ya get so wet, you stupid, stupid boy?'

Now, like most youngsters in this kind of predicament, my mind was racing trying to invent a white lie that would save my hide. Telling a white lie is, in fact, easy; it's whether it has any credibility that's the problem. Consequently, flashing rapidly through my mind were obvious excuses: one of those 'above the Gap' beggars had been trying to steal our milker ... there'd been a huge kangaroo, or maybe a dingo, at our back door ... I'd found an old World War II unexploded bomb ...

However, before I could even open my mouth, my little brother spotted a somewhat stunned, but alive and healthy, congo eel rolling and swimming its way up the river in a peculiar fashion.

'Are you a complete moron?' asked Dad.

The answer was obvious, so I didn't reply.

'Bloody Vic will spew when he sees this,' he said, pointing to the .303, which now looked like an eighteenth-century scattergun.

I didn't go to the cricket, and managed to survive to the next day. I say this because when I gingerly got out of bed and inspected myself in the bathroom mirror the following morning, I got a shock. Bruises ran from the base of my neck, all over my ribs, and down to my tummy on the right side. Worse still, I had to keep this to myself; no way was I going to seek any of the sympathy that normally helps many a healing process. That was too risky. I decided my best move for the day was to avoid any human contact—particularly with the old man.

Victor had his rifle returned, and nothing was ever said to me.

What had happened? On pulling the trigger, the water blocked the bullet from leaving the barrel, and the force of the explosion had reversed backwards through the rifle butt, injuring my shoulder and my ego, and also causing me to get yelled at for minor misdemeanours for the next month. To put it simply, the bullet didn't move—I *became* the bullet. Like I said, it was pretty stupid, but I'd had no idea that this would happen.

THE TAMBO RIVER carried trout, but it paled in comparison to some of the mountain streams in the high country. Narrow creeks, only several feet across, were home to some of the nicest trout I have ever eaten. One such good stream for fishing was the Mitta Mitta River.

For the novice trout fisherperson, there were many tricks of the trade to learn: the bait, the need to be very quiet, to mind your shadow and the time of day—these are just a few of the many I could list.

Now, I admit, I wasn't very keen on fishing. However, my younger brother John begged me to take him with us the next time we ventured out to the Blue Duck on the Mitta Mitta River.

So, when we managed on our next trip to get a lift with Don Walker, a bloke from Swifts Creek, there were five of us, and John. Unfortunately, on the two-hour drive to the camp, John vomited for most of the trip; it was a very winding road. We'd taken grasshoppers and fresh earthworms with us for bait. Ignoring John's distressed condition, the on-board experts on the art of trout fishing and fly-fishing plied him with endless advice. Repeatedly, he was told that when fishing for trout, the slightest noise or shadow over the water would guarantee there'd be no fish to catch.

We arrived after the very arduous trip along a rutted dirt road—possibly the worst road in Victoria at the time. We jumped out of the car, baited up and, keen to start, set off individually in different directions on both sides of the river. In places, dense, low, entangled bush covered the rive rbank. This made it hard to cast our lines. Although we decided to head off on our own, I knew that John was nearby, somewhere to my left. After half an hour, I guessed, most had found their fishing spots. All was quiet when I heard something that sounded like, 'Marby ... mifmup ... millmoo.'

What an unusual noise. I worked out that it came from a human, but what the heck was going on? So much for the quiet ... and it was getting louder.

'Mwarry ... moep ... melp ... millya.'

I thought, *It must be my little brother. The little rotter ... so much for quiet fishing. I'll drown the little blighter. What's his problem anyhow?*

I crashed along the bank, getting angrier every step.

The little hound. I'll fix him, I thought. Then I found my brother—his head was pointing to the heavens, his back to me. With difficulty, he turned to face me. Hell's bells! I could see the reason for the strange mumbled noises. Poor little Bonkeye (his nickname) had tried to cast his grasshopper out into the river. The line had struck a branch above his head, spun in a circle, and on the way up the hook had lodged itself in his bottom lip. He couldn't even lower his head. What a sight. I rushed off and got the other blokes to have a look before I cut the hook.

Poor Bonkeye ... peels of laughter initially greeted him, and then we removed the hook, and continued fishing. Over the years, John was to become an excellent fly and trout angler.

As I said, the Tambo River had a poor reputation when it came to fishing. In fact, the Tambo River's story is a sad one. Over a period of only a decade, it changed markedly for the worse. From the 1950s to the late 1960s, on the river banks, the once odd willow tree became a jungle of both Basket and Weeping Willows. The platypus disappeared rapidly—so much so that I have never seen one since I left school. The bottom of the river, once yellow sand, or a delightful rainbow of many coloured rocks, became a thin slime of green. The water became undrinkable. The flow dropped by roughly two-thirds. There were no more sand trout or waterjacks; just the odd grey eel. The Tambo turned into a low-flowing creek.

This dramatic change wasn't caused by a new dam, or by irrigators or town water-suppliers siphoning off more water. My guess was that it was due to a change in farming practices. The use of superphosphate as a fertiliser boomed in that decade and beyond. Tractors pulling super spreaders, and light aircraft spreading the familiar, white, crushed phosphate rock from Nauru, were now a common practice on every farm. The positive results for farmers showed in increased stocking rates, bigger wool clips, fatter calves, and more hay. Once considered marginal farming country, the very steep and hilly land became country that ran one-and-a-half sheep to the acre. Droughts, although still arriving regularly, were now handled much better: farmers were more prepared, with their haysheds full, and more money to spend on dams, water storage, and pipes to troughs all over the farm. The increased income allowed farmers to sow down more pasture, to experiment with a variety of sheep and cattle breeds and, finally, to clear more land. Many farmers could now afford to own or hire large equipment such as bulldozers.

Times were good. Government agencies like the Lands Department, the Forestry Commission, and the government veterinarian and agricultural departments all expanded, and they encouraged the hard-working farmers to continue to intensify their farming methods. The farmers were the community leaders, the shire councillors, and the heads of committees, and they accumulated the wealth of the district.

Meanwhile, the Tambo River slowed, struggled, and stagnated into pools in the summer, and the numbers of willows along its banks were so dense that the river was no longer visible from the roads.

Then there were the local timber mills. As a young boy, I remember the two trucks that headed off into the bush and returned with their logs twice a day. They were slow and noisy, and were part of a small congregation of trucks that travelled the local roads. Laurie Boucher and Gordon Lucas were the two drivers. Between them, they carted enough logs for the mill to be able to operate and employ roughly 100 men.

I went for a ride with Gordon Lucas one day, up into the Nunyong Mountains. It was a slow, steep, winding road. At the landing, I sat and watched as Gordon's truck was loaded from a landing like a railway station platform. It took a lot of skill for the dozer driver to push the logs onto the trailer. Then we headed back down the mountain. A 44-gallon drum-full of water had been tied onto the rear of the load, which had a hose that allowed water to run onto the rear brakes of the trailer to stop them overheating. Looking out the window, all I could see was a cloud of steam rising above the trailer. Very slowly, the truck crawled back down to the open country.

Those two log trucks operated throughout the year unless they were snowed-out, or threatened by bushfires, or the roads became unusable due to the weather.

Then, almost overnight, towards the end of the 1950s there were bigger trucks, better equipment, and the industry not only felled more and more trees, but it became very mechanised. Technology not only saw the mill reduce its workforce dramatically; it found another demanding market called woodchips. The pristine bush I had enjoyed exploring in every direction as a youngster was now being logged at a very increased rate. The bush altered to a point where re-growth dominated the better logging areas. (On a recent drive up the Omeo Highway—now called the Great Alpine Way, I counted seventeen log trucks in the two-hour drive … All of us are accountable.)

I saw the beautiful Tambo River enter old age rapidly. There was to be no more paddling of boats in it, no swimming in large waterholes, no charging down the rapids. The Tambo was due for a pension.

chapter eight
Finding our way

DURING THE FIRST SCHOOL HOLIDAYS OF MY FINAL YEAR, I faced a challenge. A fellow classmate, Tom Wilson (Shinga), and I were going to try to get our first-class Scout badge. I'd already passed the first-aid requirements, organised a Scout camp, learnt to navigate without a compass in both night and day, completed a 46-mile trek over Mount Nunyong, and passed three proficiency badges. All up, it had taken me two years to get to this stage. We were ready for the last step—a testing three-day trek, starting from a point in the bush that would most likely be unfamiliar to us. I say this because we would be blindfolded and then taken to an area several hours from Swifts Creek. On arrival at this spot, we'd be given minimal directions. Finally, left with a compass and an unmarked map, we'd be given three days to find our way back to a designated point. It would be a difficult test. Once started, along the way, we had to keep a journal describing the local bush and sightings of interest, and assessing how we were managing the journey. Both Shinga and I were really looking forward to the undertaking.

It was a Thursday night, just on dark. We met up outside the forestry building in Swifts Creek. An officer was going to take us … somewhere. With both of us blindfolded, we hopped into his Land Rover and he drove off. Roughly an hour-and-a-half, maybe two hours, later, we stopped. It was dark when we removed our blindfolds and looked about. We were on a narrow dirt road in bush that hosted tall mountain-ash trees, or maybe woolly-butt trees—I couldn't tell in the dark. It wasn't that important … I thought I'd check it out in the morning.

The area was open bush, and the moon was just up. I looked in every direction, but couldn't recognise where we were. The forestry bloke gave us a scant map. It simply had a thin, black line that indicated where we had to trek. Along this line was the odd circle, which indicated knolls. Two short, parallel lines showed saddles. A circle inside a circle marked other prominent features. A cross in a circle indicated water locations. There was a small legend on the bottom of the tracing paper that explained the symbols and showed due north, but that was it.

The Land Rover's engine was still running, its headlights indicating a fork in the road about 50 yards further up. There was an old, yellow 44-gallon drum on the side of the road with a green BP symbol painted on the side. I was keen to get going. The forestry officer took out his compass, put the map on the vehicle bonnet, and orientated the map. He indicated where we were and the direction we would be going if, or when, we set off. He suggested we might want to walk a bit, as the night was still early and the moon would give us enough light to walk through the bush. We both agreed, and he indicated the mountain top we should head for. 'Once you get up there, you'll be able to orientate the map and head off from there. It will take you a good three days to get out,' he added.

The bloke turned the Land Rover around and drove off. I folded the map and put it in my pocket. We headed directly for this mountain. It was high, and it would be easy to locate;

roughly an hour, even quicker, we reckoned. That night, after a cuppa and a good yak, Shinga and I slept under our canvas sheets. Next morning we rose, had some bikkies and an orange for brekky, and packed up, ready to head off.

Then something happened that will always be out of the ordinary in my life. We spread out the map and positioned it using a compass. It was the first time we'd looked at it since the Land Rover had driven off. We started to plan our journey, but nothing was making sense. To the south there was supposed to be a long ridge with a high feature about two miles away — but there was no ridge. The predominant mountains marked were missing. This was confusing.

After 20 minutes, it became obvious that we had no idea where we were. Fortunately, we didn't panic. Shinga was a town kid — his parents owned the Caltex service station, and he wasn't a bushy like me. The only time he went into the bush was on Scout camps. But, like me, he'd passed all the necessary tests to get this far ... except he'd done first aid, advanced knot tying, and cooking. None of this made me feel like a leader, or made Shinga feel inadequate — we simply sat and talked about what we should do. Our first plan was to get up as high as we could and see if there was anything we recognised, like a fire tower or a patch of cleared land. We set off, marking our trail. Half an hour later, we found what we thought was the highest point on the mountain, and we climbed a tree — but we recognised nothing. We returned to our camp site. No one had told us what to do if we were ever lost. All I knew was: stay where you are and light a fire; or, if you do head off, walk downhill, which will finally lead to a creek, meaning fresh water. Then light a fire and cover it with green branches. This would produce a lot of dense smoke. Or, alternatively, continue along the creek downstream — naturally, you'd eventually find a river, and most rivers are crossed by a road, which would have traffic ...

Neither of these ideas I learnt in the Scouts—it was simply local knowledge. I shared this with Shinga, and, like me, he reckoned it all sounded a bit daunting. I didn't share with him the fact that up until I was about nine or ten I'd believed that getting into trouble, or getting lost while in the bush, could be solved simply by calling the Phantom. (For those who have no idea what I'm referring to, *The Phantom* was a comic book my father subscribed to for years; in it, the hero would magically appear whenever or wherever you called his name in the jungle.)

I repeat: remarkably, we didn't panic. We thought about returning to where we'd been dropped off on the road the night before; mind you, it was a narrow dirt road, and seemed to have been rarely used. We weren't even really sure where it was located. Nothing was making sense. Last night we'd both watched as the officer aligned the map and pointed which way we should head.

After a time we decided to try to find the road. Both of us roughly agreed on the direction we'd come up from the night before. If that failed, we'd head downhill until we found water, and light a fire on a high point somewhere. To our relief, we found a road. But was it the right road? Splitting up, we decided to walk along the road for half an hour each in the opposite direction, and then turn back and meet up.

Shinga found the 44-gallon drum about 20 minutes down the road. Almost three hours later, there we were, back where we started, trying to take back-bearings with a compass that matched the map. Thank God, the start-point on the map lined up with the major peaks that surrounded us. By now it was mid-afternoon, and it would be a long walk through the bush to our first guaranteed water. The other thing that we didn't talk about much, but I believe we both felt, was … what the hell had happened? What was going on? Was it safe to follow this map?

I had no idea where we were and, if asked, I would have guessed we were out behind the high plains in between Tom Groggin and Suggan Buggan—a vast area of country northeast of Swifts Creek, where the Murray River starts as the Indi, in the area of the Victoria–New South Wales border. It was more a hunch than a guess. This area was popular for its beauty, wilderness camping, and brumbies, or wild horses. I reckoned we could walk out in three, maybe four days, and probably be picked up at Bindi Station, where there was a phone. As it turned out, I couldn't have been more wrong—we were heading in the completely opposite direction and area. But I am way ahead of myself.

After leaving the road near the 44-gallon drum, we tramped off, a little dejected, and reached our first long ridge line by late afternoon. It was just on dark when we found the small creek. So far, so good—the map was correct. With our spirits lifted, we made a camp for the night and built a large camp fire. After a couple of hours, we were chatting away and starting to make fun of what had happened. We treated ourselves to twisters, which are a damper mix, rolled out on the canvas, twisted like a long snake around a stick, and toasted over coals. Once browned, we'd cover them with honey, which came in a tube ... good stuff.

Looking at the map on the morning of the second day, we realised that we still had a very long way to go. We decided we would walk all day with little breaks, and try to reach a point that would get us back home late, we hoped, on the third day. We didn't want to have people worry about us, even though we knew we weren't lost—if the map was okay. It was apparent that we would be high up on a long mountain range most of the day, until finally dropping into a water point that night. We both wrote up our journals, and tidied our camp area. Then Shinga asked me something unusual: 'Where'd you get the staff, Baz ... with ya name on it, too?'

I enjoyed recalling the story.

About five o'clock, after a long uphill haul, we reached a peak that gave us a good view of the area. I couldn't believe it—we were well east to north-east of Mount Baldhead. The mountain boasts the birth of three streams—the Wentworth River, the Nicholson River, and the Haunted Stream. By reaching the next range of mountains, we would be on the Angoras ... south-south-west of home, where Sheepstation Creek begins its rapid journey to the Tambo River. My guess as to where we were on that first day was completely wrong: I had put us 35 miles north of this point.

We pushed on. I knew that, if needed, we could walk all night and reach Sheepstation Creek. However, that was pointless, as we now believed we would be finished very late on the third day. That night we set up camp in the dark and hit the sack early.

So far, the trip had been through beautiful bush, and we'd seen the odd kangaroo and several echidnas. It was clean, open bush, most of which you could ride a horse through. One section, though, which had possibly been logged ten years earlier, was now nothing but tangled, thick bush and young saplings. This re-growth had replaced the original timber. A bushfire would have loved to get into there—it would be an inferno. However, if asked what the highlight of the trek had been so far, I would have said it was the sound of the birds from dawn to dark. Of an evening, is there anything better than a family of magpies up in a tree talking to one another? They chortle and gab away as if re-living the day's activities.

The other thing was that when I was walking, I just liked looking around me. My eyes were always on a constant scan—first, directly in front of me for snakes and the lie of the ground, and then at the horizon, scanning from left to right. Finally, I'd look up in the trees, where sometimes I'd discover eagle's nests, or see goannas and many types of birds. After that, I'd look back to the ground and so on. Sometimes, one of us would hold up a hand quietly, and the observer would point out the thing he'd spotted—a kangaroo, a deer, a wallaby, or a wombat—wobbling along. We would usually stop until it sensed our presence. It's odd how we thought filling in the journal would be a difficult task, but both of us wrote copious notes about all these kinds of experiences.

Today would be our last day. Already I'd worked out where we would turn left once we descended the Angoras. Then it would be a simple matter to head east along a low ridge, and wander up to Mount Flagstaff, from where you could see the town of Swifts Creek. We would then head for the forestry officer's house. We even talked of taking a short cut. However, Shinga reckoned if we ventured off the indicated track we might miss something that had been planned for us by the forestry officer. The officer would have known we'd cut straight for the finish point once we found our way, so Shinga reckoned he'd test us with the likes of an old bridge, or whatever. How shrewd—he was right.

We packed, and left early. After a steep trek down a sharp ridge, the area flattened out and was quite open. Shinga spotted it first—some stockyards, away to our left. I didn't believe that cattle or sheep grazed this far out. The yards were very old and had sliprails for a gateway, big enough to hold about 40 head of cattle or over 100 sheep.

As we walked around these mystery yards, a small distance away we found the remains of a smaller yard, possibly for a horse or horses. Then, around behind an enormous granite boulder, we found the remnants of an old hut. It was quite small, made of logs, with a single room that had a rock fireplace. We started to search for any other finds when, lying in the grass, we came upon an old bottle. It was made of clear glass, had a top sealed with a marble, and moulded on the front was a scene of a man panning gold. On the bottom of the bottle it said, in its original spelling: 'Made in Ballaarat'. The image of the man was from the era of the mid-1800s.

It was an amazing find. We sat it on a rock and threw stones at it until one of us broke it. Around behind another large boulder, not far away, was a small waterhole—a soak, with many frogs in it croaking all at once. A satisfied big black snake slithered off after we startled him.

I could have explored that spot all day but, after an hour, we pushed on. We crossed the bullock track that led down to just below the Second Waterfall. It was a great day. We arrived late afternoon at Swifts Creek.

Along the way, Shinga and I both reckoned our discovery was a bushranger's hut—probably the Kellys'. They'd been over in our area, so legend had it, on their way to the pub at Tambo Crossing.

We had a cup of tea with the forestry officer and then walked to Shinga's place, where I rang Dad. I proudly read my journal to the family when I got home. The three-day trek had been quite an adventure. Both Shinga and I decided not to mention our false start, and how we'd nearly become horribly lost. Years later, it dawned on me what had probably happened: when the forestry officer had put the map and the compass on the bonnet of his Land Rover, the powerful magnetic fields in the engine had disturbed the compass, and had caused it to turn in another direction.

Later on, I also found out that the old hut had been the home for the Ward family some 40 years before. My mother had gone to school with two of the boys, Fred and Bill. At some stage, Fred Ward had worked on the run, and the hut had become a resting and holding place for stockman who worked a run for Wilson's back in the late 1800s.

We passed our first-class badge. Then, as usual, it was back to school, which by this stage I was finding a waste of time.

chapter nine
Leaving school

BY NOW, THE ONLY THING I ENJOYED AT SCHOOL WAS THE socialising that took place in the playground. Then I had a pleasant surprise. I was now old enough to be allowed to take part in the annual debutante ball, which was a highlight of the year. At every ball, a dignitary attended; his role would be to give a speech and to have the debs presented to him after a special dance. The event required months of rehearsal. Each year, there would be a large group of young women eligible to make their debut. Traditionally, this meant they were now able to attend social events on their own. However, this was almost irrelevant to us. It was simply a night to dress up, engage in a bit of pomp, and have professional photographs taken that would end up in local newspapers and mantelpieces—all in all, it was a wonderful occasion.

On the night, there would be milling crowds of proud, cooing parents. I was fortunate—a fellow classmate asked me to partner her. This meant I had to attend rehearsals for ten to twelve weeks beforehand. At the time, I and a few others in the deb party thought that three months of preparation was a bit much; after all, most of us could already ballroom dance.

The boys had to wear a suit on the night. Like mine, many boys' parents hired a suit for the occasion. White gloves and black shoes—highly polished—completed our outfits. The girls' dresses, similar to a bride's, were not only long; they were a combination of petticoats and flowing, folded material. I'd watched two previous balls and the graduating dance for the debs. At the time, the presentation dance had been an evening three-step—the Pride of Erin or the Palma Waltz. All of us had learnt these dances at the Church of England Hall during the year.

However, after the first night of rehearsals, we soon learnt that there was more to this type of event than just dancing. We had to dance in unison, all turning together in a large, circular formation. After five nights, we'd mastered circular and formation dancing. Then came the complicated process of the presentation to the dignitary for the evening. This required walking hand-in-hand through an archway, up a series of steps, and then bowing, or giving a curtsey, to the honourable gentleman. After that you had to move to the left or right, and then form a semi-circle on the stage. By the tenth night, we had most things sorted out, and the rehearsal went quite well. The last two nights would be full-dress rehearsals.

After being given instructions on how to be prepared, we blokes were pretty well stunned. Surely this was an invasion of our Aussie male privacy? On the nights of our two last rehearsals, they told us to bathe or shower. Then our fingernails were inspected—our hands had to be spotless to avoid soiling the white gloves. Each boy had to be clean-shaven, and had to liberally apply aftershave, underarm deodorant, and powder in private places. My father thought this was hilarious, ridiculous, and a bit 'queer'. However, 'them were the rules', and we turned up smelling sweet, and sparkling clean. The girls, rapt and excited, actually offered us compliments. The last two rehearsals were great fun. It was obvious we were ready ... nerves might be the only problem.

In preparation for the last night, a haircut and neck-shave added the final touch.

The evening was a most memorable occasion. The girls looked superb—just beautiful. When we'd formed the semi-circle on stage, after presenting our partners to the high official, the crowd gave us a standing ovation. After that, we escorted the girls back down to the dance floor and led the audience in a slow foxtrot. Quickly, others joined in, continually swapping partners as the smiles of proud mums and dads beamed out over the floor. It was a great night.

From that evening onwards, tradition had it that the debs could then attend any public dance without a chaperone. Back at school, we now saw these girls quite differently. They became great mates, and we talked about the debutante ball for weeks.

However, apart from such highlights, I had no regrets about leaving when I finally finished Form Four at Swifts Creek Higher Elementary School. My results were poor; I'd failed all written expression subjects, and had only passed those related to numbers. I failed that year's exams for what was known as the Intermediate Certificate. As I expected, though, these results didn't worry my parents. They simply saw school as a place to learn to read and write. Like most parents in the shire, they were waiting for me to reach school-leaving age, to get a job, and to do my bit. Having decided that schooling and I were not compatible, my parents made me leave.

I thought it was a good decision to leave school, too. What a waste it would have been to stay, you know what I mean, keeping a fit young lad like me—who was capable of doing a man's job—locked up in a classroom staring at a blackboard, or wading through some damn yarn about a share-market dealer called 'Shylock' who had worked in Venice hundreds of years ago. The spelling in that book was atrocious: hath, thou, doest, and so on. No wonder I didn't master English.

Consequently, during that last year, I started to lose interest in school rapidly. During all my years at school, I never thought of myself as having any academic talents. In fact, only two people ever made comments about my abilities that were positive. One was my Science teacher, Mr O'Brien, who told me that he believed I had the potential to do tertiary studies. He based this on the ease with which I'd mastered the photographic process and learnt to handle a sophisticated camera. Consequently, he encouraged me to work harder at school, to do my homework, and to get better marks. But his opinion had no influence whatsoever. I had little time for homework or reading. Once I stepped off the bus, I was only interested in having a snack, doing my chores, having a kick of the footy, and reading comics. Also, my parents, like most at that time, believed that school—not home—was the place to learn. Homework was frowned upon, and I never dared ask for help with it.

The other person who encouraged me to pursue further studies was someone who only met me a couple of times. Our first meeting was unusual. My parents had just purchased a second bush block we called the 'top block'. Like most properties in those times, it was a square mile in area—640 acres. It was a better block than Dorrington's or Sheepstation Creek; it had some undulating, open country suitable for both sheep and cattle. The initial problem was that there was no boundary fence; we had no real idea where the block was located. Admittedly, some of the better land had been fenced at some time, but those fences were no longer stock-proof, and needed replacing.

Through a series of indirect coincidences, I met a man by the name of Bruce Nicholson. He worked for one of the government departments, most likely Agriculture. One Saturday morning, as I was preparing to go to the bush block, he arrived at Doctors Flat early. Admittedly, Dad had mentioned that I would be helping a bloke do something on the property, but I didn't understand or hadn't listened, and I was simply prepared to help out in some vague way.

My guess now is that this happened in 1960. Over a cup of tea, Dad again explained what was going on. Earlier, there'd been an arrangement made between Bruce and Dad for Bruce to help locate the top block's boundary. He was going to use a detailed map, the original title, a prismatic compass, and me. I would hold a stick, like a surveyor's assistant, and we would peg out the boundary roughly. Only Mr Nicholson and I would be going out into the bush. Initially, I had to get him to the block and locate the only bit of boundary fence that existed. Fortunately, it was a corner, which meant that we'd have a start-point. We drove out in the four-wheel drive, and it quickly became obvious to me that this man loved the bush. He made comments about the trees, the rock formations, the grass types, the soil, and the general geology of the area. When we arrived at the top block, he showed me the map and told me what the plan was.

I have always been a questioning, curious person. With this in mind, when Mr Nicholson started to explain how we would use his map, I indicated I could read a map, and could use a compass. With that, it started. We discussed the map and its scale, and its added features that I hadn't seen before. Then he produced his prismatic compass; it was a superb piece of craftsmanship with an eye-sighting mechanism that located the bearing. It was very accurate. I was fascinated, and we spent an hour studying the map in detail. Immediately, I had a deep respect for the man because he treated me as if he valued my intellect, and that was foreign to me. He teased out my comprehension and my thirst for knowledge, and complimented me on my enthusiasm and interest. The result was that, after a couple of tries, he let me trace the boundary, and he held the stick. I was so proud. During our time together we had brews and snacks, we sat and told yarns, and we did all those things people associate with the bush. More importantly, he told me about his youth, his studies, his job—and I was fascinated. I had never met anyone like this before. It really got me thinking … in a confused way.

Finally, with the top block completely pegged out, we returned home to Doctors Flat. It had been a big job. During tea, Mr Nicholson brought up a conversation that not only embarrassed me, but I also knew would be taken the wrong way by my parents. Earlier, out in the bush, while sitting and enjoying a cuppa, Mr Nicholson had asked me about my schooling—about subjects I did, and what I liked. So I spoke, probably for the first time in my life, about Arithmetic, Algebra, and Geometry. I cherished these subjects. I explained how sometimes I solved problems a different way to the teacher, but we ended up with the same answer. I informed him of how I liked playing with numbers in my head, and I showed him how quickly I could mentally decipher a difficult multiplication. As Mr Nicholson was an academic and had a degree, I guess I felt comfortable sharing details of the quirky habits I possessed. Then he asked me something that, for me, had always been a secret: if I could do exactly what I wanted, what would that be? I answered that I wanted to be a veterinarian—an animal doctor. His response was that I should tell my parents, and pursue the idea, and that it would be hard work. 'You could do it, Barry,' he said. At the time, that was like telling me to grow wings and fly away. I don't think I even responded to him.

Nevertheless, the topic came up again at the tea table at Doctors Flat. Mr Nicholson was quite glowing and enthusiastic. Dad glared at me, Mum smiled and shook her head, and very quickly they dropped the subject. Later, after Mr Nicholson had left, my parents suggested I mind my own business, try not to be smart with people, and to stop exaggerating. As it happened, my average marks for my last three years in the subjects I'd mentioned were 96 per cent, 92 per cent, and 97 per cent.

It was a brief and confusing moment in my life, that meeting with Mr Nicholson. To be truthful, it's important I point out that I totally agreed with my parents. I thought he misread my secret ambition. In fact, it was only a dream. I had no desire other than to leave school … the quicker the better.

In 1960, with only three weeks to go until the Christmas holidays began, many kids in my class were starting to leave school. Some kids went to work in the timber mill, while others were going to continue their senior years of education at major private schools in Melbourne and Geelong. Other boys went to the technical school in Bairnsdale to learn trade skills. By third term, my parents said I would be leaving at the end of the year to work with Dad in his plumbing business.

Just before my school days ended, there was a lot of excitement in the air. Our Scout troop would be going to a jamboree in Sydney, in January 1961. The only problem with it for many parents was the cost. It was £30 ($60), which was a large amount of money—about two weeks' wages. As a result, many working bees and the like were set up to help pay the expenses. The community decided it would raise half of each boy's expenses. Robbie and I would both be going, and we decided to try to find our own money by taking on part-time work and other jobs.

I approached several neighbouring farmers and asked if I could pick the wool off their dead sheep. It wasn't an idea I was keen on; in fact, I only did it because I knew I could get about one pound (two dollars) a bag. Finding dead sheep in paddocks was common. Many had died from fly-strike, during lambing, or from worms and other diseases. Few farmers could be bothered gathering the carcasses or burning them, so they were happy to take up my offer. Consequently, after finishing my chores on most afternoons and on every free weekend during my last weeks, I walked the paddocks collecting wool. It was a disgusting job. There were rotting carcasses, bloated stomachs, armies of maggots, and blowflies in plague proportions. I lugged the potato bag over my shoulder, and in my pocket I kept a handful of eucalyptus leaves. By continually rubbing the leaves between my palms, I managed to endure the dead-sheep smell. After four weeks of this, I had enough money.

My brother Robbie, though, had no such luck. He got a job on a local farm every afternoon after school for two hours a day. After two weeks, he asked for his pay, and the farmer gave him five bob (50 cents). Poor Robbie thought that was for one day's work. But no, that was it—two weeks' income. With haste, we came up with another plan: stripping wattlebark.

That first weekend, we sharpened our tomahawks, loaded up our horses with supplies, and headed for the log cabin on Sheepstation Creek. For the next three weekends we camped out from Friday night until early Monday morning, worked tirelessly, and comfortably made the required income. It was hard work, and fun. We collected the bark from the bush block and sold it to the tannery at Bairnsdale. However, one night during our time stripping the wattlebark we had an eerie experience. It was just on dark, and we were preparing tea when we heard the sharp, piercing squeal of an animal—a dingo. It was the first time I'd ever heard this animal, and yet I knew it was a dingo. I'd heard others describe its howl so many times as sounding like the bloodthirsty scream of a woman, or something similar. Unfortunately, we didn't have a dog with us. The dingo circled us several times, repeating its scary call. At first, we thought we should catch the horses in the Five Acres paddock and ride home. Then I decided to get the rifle and fire a few shots in its general direction. This worked, but we were still frightened. After tea, we built up the camp fire until it was like a bonfire. This produced a lot of light, and I sat for hours hoping to get a shot at the dingo … but that came to nothing. Next morning we quickly bundled up the wattlebark, loaded up the horses, and led them home.

The Scout jamboree attracted thousands of Scouts from all over the world. We drove to where it was being held, on the outskirts of Sydney, in two vehicles. The first thrill was simply driving into New South Wales—that was a first for everyone on board. The site for the jamboree was in a huge park. It rained quite heavily while we were there, but we were one of the very few groups that wasn't washed out. Yes, we were bushies. Our tent was pitched on high ground. We spent the first day digging a drain around the tent, and had ourselves off the ground with palliasses. The highlight for me, though, was collecting badges. Every day, there was a place in the centre of the large jamboree grounds where Scouts would gather and swap their badges. The First Swifts Creek Troop badge was a very rare badge, and many Scouts from overseas tried to collect it. It was good fun. After two weeks' camping with thousands of others, we headed back to Swifts Creek.

BY NOW, after almost seven years in the area, I was quite familiar with the bush, snakes, biting ants, and numerous other problems and experiences that face newcomers to this type of environment. I now considered myself a country lad. I could shoot or trap rabbits, skin a fox, and scalp a wombat—that was very rewarding, as we still got ten shillings and sixpence for the two ears from the Lands Department.

On Mum and Dad's bush block, I'd found it easy to fell trees with an axe, and I'd learnt to mark calves and crutch sheep. I was also developing the larrikin streak typical of bush kids. One time at home, while our parents were away, Robbie and I laced some wheat with whisky, spread it on the ground around our cherry tree, and watched with amusement as the parrots not only got very drunk, but had trouble flying and then couldn't land properly. Many kept falling over as they walked. Funniest of all, many hung in the trees upside-down like fruit bats, hanging off one leg. In fact, we reckoned we heard some of them laugh.

Once a fortnight, I would cut a sheep's throat and skin it, gut it, hang it on a gamble, and have it in the meat bag in less than 30 minutes. This didn't make me exceptionally skilled. Most farm kids were capable of such tasks, and more. By now I'd experienced both city life and country life, and I was in no doubt that, for all its chores and demands, country life was better.

Apart from going to the debutante ball and getting my first-class Scouts badge, about the only exciting thing that happened to me in my last school year took place at home. It involved our jersey milker, Betty, who wandered in one day when she found the gate to the house paddock open. There were several fruit trees in this paddock, one of which was a quince tree that produced enormous fruit. They were too big for the horses or cows to eat, so I would dice them up into edible pieces while the animals stood at the fence watching me in anticipation. They loved quinces. However, on this occasion, having snuck into the house paddock, Betty decided to gorge herself on the quinces.

The first indication that something was wrong was when I heard a low honking noise, like the sound a tugboat makes. It was that damn milker. Not only had she gotten a large quince in her mouth, she was having difficulty swallowing the big, green fruit. It was huge—about as big as a grapefruit. It moved into her neck and then, unfortunately, it got stuck halfway down. Both my parents were out; what could I do? The cow was very distressed, cross-eyed, down on her knees, and groaning. Hmmm ... I tried to put my arm down her neck and dislodge it—no luck. I pushed a hose down the poor cow's neck and tried to wash it down. Betty started to roll her eyes ... I knew she was going to die, as she couldn't breathe. I rushed inside, grabbed Mum's mop, shoved the handle down the cow's throat, and thumped several times. It worked—the quince moved slowly down into her stomach. Phew, that was a relief. The cow took a very big breath.

In fact, it was a very traumatic experience for the cow and yet, somehow, I managed. Maybe life in the country gives kids a sense of independence, even maturity.

By the time I was ready to leave school I was content, and eager to move into the next phase of growing up. There was no question of continuing schooling, or of where I would find a job. There were always jobs about, and I never knew of any person unable to obtain work. Life was simple, and I looked forward to living in and around Swifts Creek, playing footy with the local team, maybe working on a farm, and then probably marrying a farmer's daughter—who knows? That wasn't too much to ask, surely? Life was a treat. Tomorrow couldn't come quickly enough.

WITH SCHOOLING FINISHED, I was about to start work with my stepfather. At sixteen, I was keen to learn how to thread pipes, flare copper-tubing, solder, and the numerous other skills I'd watched him perform with ease. I was eager to start. Dad's surname was Richards, and mine Heard, which used to confuse some people. When asked to explain this, I would mumble a vague explanation, only adding to the problem. In those early months, the highlight of the work with Dad—who I will now call Bob—was travelling throughout the district and meeting people. I recall once going to a farm at Benambra to help Bob put in a slow-combustion stove. We arrived at the homestead, where I met two ladies in the kitchen. After we'd only been there a short while, Bob sent me out to the truck to fetch some tools. When I returned, the older of the two ladies stopped me at the back door, demanding to know who I was. Startled, I introduced myself, thinking she must have been the twin sister of the other old lady. I entered. Not long afterwards, I found myself back at the truck again and, yes, again I faced a challenge at the back door. What was going on? Finally, the other lady, noticing my distress, said that this dear old lady had 'lost her mind', whatever that meant.

Because Bob was the only plumber in the entire shire, we found ourselves in places with wonderful Australian names like The Blue Duck, Bindi, Bingo, Reedy Flat, Uplands, Shannon Vale, Cobungra, Mount Hotham, Dinner Plain, Tambo Crossing, Dargo, Glenn Wills, and the Omeo Valley. Some days it would take hours to get there. At places like Dargo, we would camp with the people, and we'd stay there until the job was finished. If not, we returned home only at weekends. The people were always friendly and welcoming, and they served up some enormous meals. Rarely would Mum have to make us a lunch as we headed out to a job. Always on arrival there'd be prolonged lunchtimes or morning teas. Sometimes, I'd see Bob spend ages talking with our hosts.

The plumbing work was unusual. Not that I'd worked with Bob in Ringwood, but not too many places in Melbourne had windmills, water troughs, septic tanks, and slow-combustion stoves, or wanted us to make their water tanks. Making the tanks was okay, but getting them up onto wobbling tank stands, or high stands like the one at the back of the Swifts Creek police station, was damn scary. I recall we'd made a couple of very long skids, and hauled the 2000-gallon tank up with a rope. When it finally reached the top, and was tilted and plopped down into place, all I had to stand on was a small space that was half as big as a doormat. Looking down, I was 25 feet off the ground. New septic tanks required a hole almost six feet deep. Sometimes, the ground was so hard that even with a pick or crowbar I could only dig down an inch at a time.

I learnt a lot of practical skills over those first months — a little about plumbing, and a lot about improvising. All too often, Bob had to invent ways of solving problems that required certain materials or fittings. There was no hardware store just down the road when we were out the back of Benambra. This meant he devised ways around problems. He was a good plumber, but plumbing didn't suit me. Perhaps if I'd worked as an apprentice I might have seen a future for myself in the job. However, there were times when I found the work frustrating; I would have been happier on a farm. Mind you, I was working weekends on our bush block and enjoyed it, and my parents were about to buy a sheep farm at Tongio. Apart from playing cricket on Saturday afternoon, I was working the other days.

As winter approached, the coach of the Swifts Creek footy club told me that he wanted me to make an effort to get fit, as he felt I could hold down a position in the senior team. I'd been a school captain in my last year and, although I hadn't excelled as a player, we'd beaten those Omeo blighters — which was the ultimate credential for a new footballer for the district.

Then, from out of the blue, I had another job. Dad and I had arrived home, I'd done my chores, and we were at the dinner table. The conversation was about the bush block and things that needed doing when, quite casually, Mum informed me that I'd be working on a farm at Ensay in the next district. It was down the road a bit from Swifts Creek, about fourteen miles away, on the way to Bairnsdale. This was certainly a surprise. However, it was exciting; this would mean my first wage, independence, and work on a farm that I was positive I would really enjoy. I'd have my own bungalow or room; it sounded perfect. It would also mean leaving home and living on the farm from Monday to Friday every week.

chapter ten
Ensay

I WAS VERY EAGER WHEN I RODE OFF ON SANDY MAC, my horse, for the farm job that first Monday morning. Admittedly, I had to ask Mum which house to ride up to. On my back was a haversack with my pyjamas, a spare jumper, a raincoat, and extra socks in case my feet got wet. I also had spare hankies, a toothbrush, a comb, and some comics—Phantom comics. Sandy Mac was despondent about the extra weight when I mounted up. It didn't take much to make this horse unhappy. As payback, he plodded along slowly—unless I was prepared to kick him in the ribs every step of the way. Knowing this would be the case, I'd left very early.

I was really an amateur farm labourer. I didn't have a stockwhip, a dog, an oilskin coat, or a big hat. Although my parents owned two farms and were about to buy another, their farming methods were simple. I always felt that they treated the enterprise more as a hobby than a business. Neither had come from a farming background; and yet, somehow, we managed. For me, what this meant was that, although I'd been hired as a farmhand, I had no experience other than milking cows, killing sheep, putting in fence posts, and making butter.

I arrived at eight o'clock in the morning. I'd met the owner before, but not his wife. The bungalow where I'd be sleeping from Monday to Thursday was a small one-bedroom hut, with a large window. I would return home at weekends. There was another adjoining bungalow, both out the back of the homestead, and each had a single bed and a wardrobe. I threw my haversack in the door, led Sandy Mac over to the saddle shed, and hung his saddle on a rest inside. The shed was clean, and there were a number of beautiful saddles, bridles, halters, and stockwhips hanging on the walls. On a shelf were brushes (or currycombs), cleanly washed saddle blankets, and canvas horse-rugs for the winter. In a corner there were bags of chaff, a barrel full of oats, and a container of molasses. I'd never seen such a shed before.

I led Sandy Mac to the bull paddock, gave him a leaf of hay, and let him go. I bet he thought that was a treat. He walked over to the two other horses, and they sniffed each other. He didn't go near the bulls or the rams. My new boss drove me around the farm in the old Land Rover, then down to his brother, who lived with his mother on the family farm. The two brothers owned the farm where I'd be working. We had morning tea—or, should I say, my first of many sumptuous morning banquets—while we were at the family farm. It was scones, blackberry jam, and cream. Their mother was a dear old lady whom I became very fond of over the years, and not just because of her cooking; that was a bonus.

Although the new job looked exciting, very early on I realised I was lucky to be working on such a well-managed farm. However, I was hesitant about one thing. The boss had another job as a stock-and-station agent. This meant he'd be away for part of the week, and I'd be on my own. However, he allowed for this, and I always had something I could do while he was away. But, after a couple of days, a problem I hadn't anticipated at all became very apparent ...

It was like the feeling I had when we moved from Ringwood. It was a blunt shock; nowadays, we'd probably call it a 'culture shock'. It happened at the end of the first day—a most unexpected problem. No, they didn't speak German at the dinner table, drink blood, or eat raw meat. I believe I could have almost managed that. The trouble was that the people on the farm were completely different in some ways from my parents. For a start, these people didn't swear, whereas Dad had the most colourful Aussie language, which often got him into trouble. Admittedly, I didn't swear either. Ah, if only it had been that simple. This new job took me into a new way of life that I didn't even know existed. It challenged my upbringing in a very embarrassing but unintended way.

It all started when I'd left home with only the clothes I wore on that first Monday morning. The day had been exciting, and I knew very quickly it was going to be a good job. Then something occurred when I went to tea on that first night that I will never forget. Not only was it a three-course meal, but everyone had had a bath, shaved, and got dressed up for tea. I was still in my work clothes, though I had washed my hands thoroughly and had brushed my hair. I sat very quietly in my seat.

An ironed tablecloth covered the table. There were napkin rings, lots of knives and forks, a round spoon called a 'soup spoon', a plate called a 'bread and butter' plate, and a butter knife. My positive feelings about the job took a serious jolt. I was very embarrassed. There were times I felt so nervous that it made me nauseous. What could I do? Suddenly, I had a plan. I would sneak home straight after tea—at least get some other clothes, even if they were not *good ones*.

But after tea, no such luck; we went into the lounge room, sat in beautiful chairs, and listened to 78 r.p.m. records. The boss spent a lot of time on the phone talking to clients. I looked at the carpet. His wife was a beautiful person, in both looks and personality. Several times, she encouraged me to talk, and tried to discover my interests; little did she know that escaping from this scene was the immediate one. About 9.30 p.m., we had a nice supper and retired to bed. It was too late to return home. In fact, looking back, I would have gained very little had I dashed over to Doctors Flat. A change of clothes? There were no good clothes to change into.

I'd had no idea that there was another way of living out there. Certainly, our move to the country had brought about a different way of life for me. The kids at the Tongio school were poles apart when compared to city kids. However, after accepting, and finally adopting, their way of life, I didn't realise I was only seeing a section of the community. At the Swifts Creek school, the kids' parents worked at the mill, on farms as labourers, drove trucks, and struggled on small farms. Like me, most of the kids left school as soon as possible. As young teenagers, any parties, get-togethers, or the like were at mill houses, the Church of England hall, at woolsheds, or club rooms during and after footy. After the Tongio school burnt down, I was quite shocked that a couple of the kids didn't move to the Swifts Creek school like the rest of us: they went to private schools in Melbourne. I didn't know it at the time, but they were going whether the school burnt down or remained standing. Yes, after primary school, if the parents could afford it, their kids went away to finish their education.

When we'd moved from Ringwood, the only things that really stood out and took ages to adjust to were the strange jobs and the open spaces. Certainly, within the household, Mum treated water and basic foodstuffs differently. There was no corner store. If you lived away from town, as we did, then a cow, a vegetable garden, chooks, and trapping rabbits became the norm ... or so I thought.

We had a large pantry in the kitchen. Many foodstuffs

were in large containers. There were constant reminders about turning off taps and conserving water; even so, it took me a long time to break habits that were entrenched from city life. As a plumber, Bob had a good income, but it went initially into a house and a good vehicle, and then a farm. He bought his first new Land Rover in 1960. At Doctors Flat, we were in a very small, old house that had no lounge, two bedrooms, and a kitchen. It only had one water tank—a 1000-gallon tank. Admittedly, we were right next to the Tambo River; but, because of the Weeping Willow trees, its water wasn't really suitable for drinking. As mentioned earlier, Friday night was wash night, when we took it in turns to hop into the large, galvanised tub. I lived this way when I moved to Ensay and the farm in 1961. Although Bob had started to put on new rooms and, finally, installed a new tank that was filled from the river, this was after I'd left. As for good clothes—I had none. There was no use for them. On the odd occasion when I went to a dance or party, there was a jumble of clothes that I shared with my brother Robbie and Bob.

As a result, my first week in the new job at Ensay was turning into a horror story. I was getting more embarrassed every night as I turned up wearing the same clothes. Then, on the Friday, something happened—the boss's wife stepped in. We drove to Bairnsdale, and I came home with a set of good clothes. This included several shirts, a nice sports coat, and shoes. Suddenly, I felt normal. I returned home to Doctors Flat on the Friday night, full of stories about the farm.

During those initial weeks, my first jobs involved a lot of stock work, mainly with sheep. I learnt how to dose, drench, and inoculate sheep. Chemicals like copper sulphate, carbon tetrachloride, and five-in-one became common to me. As well, in the stockyards, I treated flyblown sheep, and removed grass seeds from their eyes. I learnt to mix chemicals such as Kill Ester and 24D, and to spray horehound. It was fun pulling a super spreader around the paddocks with the Fordson tractor. The most difficult thing was to reload the spreader. Each bag of superphosphate weighed about 180 pounds but, with a bit of swivelling and sliding, I could empty its contents into the spreader. The old, blue Fordson Major was the first tractor I'd ever driven.

By the end of that first year, I'd ploughed many paddocks, harrowed them, then sown down grasses like cocksfoot, phalaris, wimmera ryegrass, and a variety of clovers. On the tractor, I operated a mower, a slasher, and a hay rake. Discing was like a test for me. My furrows had to be dead straight. I took great pride when the ploughed paddock looked like a page from a writing pad. Oddly enough, many times while ploughing I would have a visitor. Jack Campbell, the farmer from up the road a bit, would slowly saunter across the turned turf to have a yarn. His company was great. It was as if he'd adopted me, wanted me to understand life and to grow a little wiser. He did this by telling me a dirty yarn every time he visited. Most, I am sure, went straight over my head. Dave and Mabel were his favourite subjects. Once, when I asked him what the yarn implied, he nearly passed out with laughter. Bear with me, and you may understand my enquiry ...

Dave and Mabel had just married. They were on their honeymoon. The topic of children came up. Dave assured Mabel he knew how to make them, as his mum had offered him some advice—'It's simple, so. Jist put your private parts together, and you will know.'

Mabel nodded as Dave explained. He asked, 'What's your private part, Mabel?'

'My bottom,' she replied.

Dave reckoned his was his ear. So there they were, Dave's ear pressed against Mabel's bum, when Mabel asked, 'What do ya reckon, Dave?'

'Aw, they're coming alright, Mabel ... I can hear

them—they're on motorbikes!'

Now, at the time, I reckon that begged some explanation.

MANY JOBS required carting hay, cutting firewood, or working with fencing materials. It meant I had to learn how to back a four-wheeled trailer, which was difficult, as its two front wheels swivelled. However, even though I was learning many new skills, there was one glaring omission—I didn't have a decent sheepdog.

Most mornings or late evenings, even if he was going on the road for work, the boss would muster the sheep into the yards and I would do the sheep work. At home, on Mum and Dad's farm, even though we had a very small mob of sheep and a few cattle, pretending we were the dogs was how we did most sheep or cattle work. I would run this way and that, attempting to muster the stock. It was difficult and frustrating … until I got my friend Rover. After that, when it came to stock work, it was a breeze. However, Rover wasn't the only unique animal I met on Kanangra. Let me tell you about Swanee.

chapter eleven
Swanee

AS I MENTIONED EARLIER, MANY PRACTICAL SKILLS, EQUIPMENT, and attributes are required to be a competent farm labourer: there's stock work, operating machinery, fencing, spraying, hay carting, and woolshed and cattle-yard work, just to mention a few. Then a good horse and dog, and gear such as a whip, saddle, a broad-brimmed hat, and drover's coat are important. A pocketknife is essential. I had some of this equipment and several of these skills, although I hadn't grown up on a farm. I had wagged school and worked as a rouseabout in a woolshed when I was thirteen. (You may recall that, at the time, this allowed me to go on my first date with Curls.) Like most country kids, I could do all the chores around the house and yard, but I brought few real skills to the job.

On this farm, like most, stock work was carried out with a dog and on horseback. This mean there was just one useful skill which I thought I not only possessed, but also had had a lot of experience at developing: horse riding. Little did I realise that I was about to be proven wrong. This may seem confusing, as I'd been riding my first horse, Sandy Mac, for over five years.

Sandy Mac was a ginger gelding with a gentle and tolerant nature—a good, quiet, first horse for a newcomer. I was almost eleven when Mum bought him for the bargain price of five pounds. Quickly, I learnt to ride him, in no time going into the bush exploring, and chasing emus and kangaroos. I admit it was hard to get Sandy Mac interested in any of these earthly pursuits. He would only move in a forward direction if I continually kicked him in the ribs. When I stopped, he stopped. Eventually, it dawned on me why Mum had only had to part with five quid for this good-looking animal. Sandy Mac was slow, lazy, uninterested, and vague. He had the personality of a boiled egg. He didn't walk; he plodded. After a ride, while I'd be exhausted, Sandy Mac would be content. He'd proved to me repeatedly that there was little point in riding him. Still, I could ride a horse.

When I started work at Kanangra I was keen, waiting for an opportunity to show off my horse-riding skills, whether to the boss or any others who cared to watch—I wanted to show I was okay at something.

How foolhardy and naive of me. Little did I know that I was about to meet Swanee, the 'spare' horse on the farm. He was certainly different. In time, after several months and many death-defying feats, I worked Swanee out. This is how I would describe him. Swanee looked like a horse. He was a bay, which meant he was mid-brown, with a black mane and tail. He could walk very fast. Trotting didn't come easily to him, but he had a rocking-horse canter. When it came to a gallop, bolt, call it what you want, Swanee had a burst of speed that almost defied explanation. It was a frenzied, frightening burst of acceleration. This usually terrified anybody who tried to ride him. However, that was only a small part of his arsenal of surprises.

I said Swanee looked like a horse. True, but that's where it ended. He had a spirit the size of a road train, the strength of a diesel locomotive, and the stubborn determination of a donkey not feeling up to a day's work in the paddock. His larrikin demeanour reminded me of a bloke who played footy at Ensay and was continually dressed down by the coach for smiling and having fun. Combine all of these attributes and you have one very powerful animal—Swanee. You didn't ride Swanee; no way. He let you ride him. He was the master, no question. He set the exam. A pass meant you had permission to ride … for the moment. A fail meant—well, it varied. Some trials or exams saw the candidate injured, or sent off with the blood rule. Others who failed displayed facial expressions that I would describe as being like someone who had had a near-death experience. To be allowed to ride him, Swanee demanded more than a good pass—you'd need honours at least, if not a distinction.

As I said at the beginning, I could only speak of this horse, Swanee, after I'd known him for many months. Initially, I had no idea he was a maniacal, bum-biting, flamin' fiend, intent on killing anyone who tried to ride him. Therefore, when I started the job, I was a farm labourer in the true sense of the word. I didn't have a 'real' farm horse, or a dog. I couldn't work a sheepdog, or ride a horse. I could only labour.

I'D BEEN ON THE PROPERTY several weeks, getting to know my way around and the routines to be completed. One afternoon I found myself at the bull paddock. I un-snibbed the gate and went in to catch my horse. Probably for the first time, I stopped and had a long look at the animals. After a cursory glance, I became fixated on an unattractive steed—an ugly, stocky-looking horse. It was Swanee. A funny, rugged part-brumby, with hairy fetlocks and chin, he looked more like a mule than a horse. He was beside Sandy Mac who was standing in the shade, sound asleep, which he did for 20 hours a day. Nearby was a pretty mare—Honey, the boss's horse. On the dam wall stood a handful of merino rams. The four Hereford bulls stood near the far gate.

I was intrigued. To me, Swanee not only looked part-brumby, but also looked to be a very ordinary nag. I recall thinking, *Fancy keeping a horse like that.* Honey, on the other hand, had a bit of class about her—I reckoned she'd be good to ride. I'd patted Honey several times during that week; on this Friday, when I went to catch Sandy Mac, she walked over for her usual pat. Swanee, however, just ignored me. Anyhow, I didn't feel inclined to touch this inbred-looking nag. With Sandy Mac in tow, I led him to the saddle shed, threw on a saddle blanket and my own worn-out saddle, and mounted, ready for the arduous trip back to Doctors Flat.

I returned to work on Monday, not knowing that the following day I was about to face a rather daunting task—riding Swanee. It was an unforgettable day that's etched in my memory forever. I'd milked the cows, had brekkie, and just finished cleaning the butter churn. I made fresh butter every Tuesday. The boss and I were talking about some stock work that needed doing. He'd already asked me to do some minor stock jobs on the farm using Sandy Mac previously, but he was hopeless—Sandy Mac, that is; not the boss. Hence, I was a little surprised this particular day, when I went out the back and noticed Swanee saddled up and hitched to the ring outside the saddle shed. The boss was heading off for the day, as sheep sales were looming. He would be very busy. At the kitchen table earlier, he'd wanted me to open some gates so the stock had access to better water. I assumed I would plod around the paddocks on Sandy Mac, and even get to ride Honey one day. But … 'Take Swanee,' were his parting words.

As mentioned, I'd really hoped it would be Honey, who was a superior-looking animal. Not deterred, I thought I might just try this rough-looking beggar called Swanee and, just maybe, he might turn out to be a bit better than Sandy Mac—though

I doubted that very much. I guessed the boss thought the horse simply needed some exercise. In fact, I would humour the nag; so, with a smile, I walked up to Swanee, said g'day, and patted his neck. If there is such a thing as a horse's glare, I got one. I shrugged my shoulders—oh well, that didn't worry me. I'd show the blighter who was the boss. Then, taking the reins off the ring, I threw them over his head, put my foot in the stirrup, and attempted to swing my leg over. I had a cool swing, like a rodeo rider. Hmmm, that didn't work—the damn inbred, repulsive-looking brumby stepped sideways every time I tried to mount him. *Hello,* I thought. *A smart alec ... I'll teach this nag some manners.*

With authority, I stood him alongside the saddle shed, very close to the wall. After two determined leaps, I managed to get onto his back, and sort of half into the saddle. But, would you believe, I couldn't get my leg down the other side. Crikey, what an ignorant brute. This unsightly, mountain-bred hack had jammed me up against the shed wall. With his ears laid back, he rolled his eyes, and snorting sounds burst from his nostrils.

'Hah! You swine. Take care, mate—I don't take that sort of rubbish from *any* horse,' I told him.

After much pushing, grunting, and shoving by both of us, I managed to get my boot in the stirrup. Frustrated, I reefed the reins and turned him towards the gate.

'Okay, mate, we'll see what happens to smart arses.' I gave him an almighty kick in the ribs.

My God, Jesus, Henry, Jonathon, Christ, and Holy Mary, Mother of God, and Moses! Let me warn you: never, never, ever kick a horse like Swanee in the ribs. This mad-eyed moron of a horse leapt into a gallop as if shot out of a cannon. Suddenly, I found myself groping for reins, mane, saddle, pommel—anything I could hold on to. It was very bloody scary. I had this insane, out-of-control freak under me, racing at break-neck speed. His hooves thundered on the gravel, and his mane flicked in my face. I had no idea what to do. Then, as I was wondering where-oh-where we would end up, unexpectedly, a gate appeared. I thought, *My God, he's going to jump it.*

I hung on for dear life, but no—he went from flat out to stop, in 20 feet. I ended up along this idiot's flamin' neck with my chin between his ears. He put his head down and I fell off, the bugger. For someone who claims he does not swear, all of the above was the extent of my foul language. Some more would have been handy.

I stood up, brushed off the dust, and then noticed we were at the gate to his paddock. The equine swine had decided it was time to knock off. Without a doubt, he was the most bad-mannered, poorly trained, ill-tempered, ugly, inbred, mongrel-dumb horse I'd ever ridden. Someone should shoot the brute or send him to a knackery. You might guess that I was angry.

However, there was something else to add insult to injury. As I led him warily back to the saddle shed, he tried to bite my bum on two occasions. The second time he pulled the seat of my pants so hard that I nearly came off the ground. I turned and walked backwards. Outside the shed, I hooked the reins over the ring. I went inside and sat on a bag of oats ... I'd failed. I hadn't even opened a single gate. The boss would be disappointed. I was at a loss, and thought I might just leave the prat, and go and catch Sandy Mac. Meanwhile, as I sat rather stunned on the bag of oats, Swanee put his head in the door-opening, made a throttling noise with his nostrils, and then, would you believe, I reckoned he smirked. Bad move, ya monster. Just you hang on—I don't give up that easily.

I went outside, reached up to the ring, slid off the reins, and put them over his head. It was like stepping into a boxing ring. We eyeballed each other. After he gave me several dirty looks and a sharp nip on my bum, I spent ages going around in circles as I persisted in my attempts to mount this crazy freak.

Half an hour later, I'd worked out how to get into the saddle. You had to pull both reins very tight, stand beside his head—not too close, or he'd bite your backside—and then swing up. Swanee would walk under the swing.

Ripper. I was up on his back. It was as if I'd at last won a round against him, and was sitting in my corner getting a well-earned towelling down. Now, I ask you, what do you do? I held the reins really tight. No way was I going to loosen them and ignite the fuel tank in this butane-boosted bloody fanatic. I sensed he was angry ... maybe really bloody angry. His eyes had almost turned black. As I planned what my first move might be, Swanee, yet again, took over. He threw a wobbly and started walking backwards ... he was, no doubt, a complete maniac. Great—so much for my horse-riding skills. What was I to do now—open all the gates going backwards through the paddocks? His nostrils flared as he snorted in frustration. I decided to release the reins ever so slightly. Good—he stopped walking backwards, but started dancing sideways. Thank God there was no one watching; this was scary stuff and, for the moment, it was definitely one-up to Swanee. The bout continued. Another gentle release, and he stamped on the spot frantically. His head was jerking up and down violently. By now, there was a strange, throttling noise coming out of his nostrils ... the stupid, damn ogre. I was having doubts ... he continued to stamp ... I waited ... I felt ready ... another tiny release of the reins, and ... he jumped straight into a rocking-horse canter.

It was a perfect canter.

I hung on ever so tightly. He stopped at the first gate and pushed up against the strainer post, which enabled me to reach over and undo the chain. Then he pushed the old wooden gate open with his chest, spun around, and pushed it shut. I'd never seen a horse do that before—usually I would have had to dismount and tug a gate like that to open it. I turned him carefully, gave him another gentle, minute release, and he dropped straight into a canter. His action was as smooth as silk.

We headed for the other gate. Same procedure: he pushed open the gate, then turned and nudged it shut. He was very good. What strange behaviour from a horse with a mad stare, knock-knees, and a gumboot-shaped head. Yet, if you managed to ride him, he had an air of class. You would never guess that by his looks.

We continued. I left open the gates that the boss had indicated. I turned to head back to the house paddock and saddle shed. Swanee seemed to have settled a little. Again, he cantered off. However, by now my arms were aching from holding this unusual horse. I felt like I was hanging over a precipice, too scared to let go. Judging the tension of the reins carefully, I relaxed, just a fraction—whoosh! The wild-eyed thug bolted. Jesus, feeder of fish and bread—he was fast. A dry water-race appeared in front of us: it was fifteen feet across. The mad frigg'n bastard ... he leapt it in one bound, skidding almost to a stop. Christ Almighty! *My God, please*, I thought. Again, I shot up his neck, thumping my precious parts against the pommel of the saddle. Oh, the agony. I wanted to groan and roll around, holding my crotch—which is the accepted ritual for crushed gonads. But I was on this whacko horse. The first thing to do was to get off. Too late—the mad, flamin' mongrel just took off again. Now it was my head bumping on his rump. I'd lost the reins ... suddenly I was upright ... then he skidded to a stop ... *God help me*, I thought.

We'd reached the house paddock gate. I got off very slowly, opened the gate, and led him—with me walking backwards—to the saddle shed. I was walking as though I had a 44-gallon drum between my legs. I reckon cowboys ended up with bowlegs from pommel incidents, not from endless horse riding. Well, that was it. I'd had enough. Battered and bruised with two bite marks on my bum, I slowly took off the saddle, put it in the shed, and returned with a hairbrush, or currycomb. I brushed his back, which he seemed to enjoy. Unhooking his reins, I ever-so-slowly led him to his paddock—backwards, naturally. I opened the gate and undid the chinstrap on his bridle. Thank God, this saga was over. Reaching up, I slid the bridle over his ears. Shit a brick. (I don't like using that word; but, believe me, in this instance it was appropriate.) Suddenly, I was on my stomach, tearing across the grass at water-ski speed, bouncing, jerking, and trying to get onto my knees. There were thistles, and sheep, horse, and cow dung thumping me in the face. The odd clump of phalaris grass lifted me into the air. Too stupid to let go—this is a pig-headed trait I have had all my life—the body-battering continued for ten seconds.

What in the hell had happened? As I lay there exhausted, I worked it out. He'd reared backwards as I'd lifted the bridle over his ears. The bit had become stuck in his mouth, he'd bolted, and I'd ended up dragged across the paddock. God, was I in pain. Quietly, I checked myself out: no broken bones; a very, very sore crotch; no buttons left on my shirt; one boot missing; and my stomach and legs covered with gravel rash. It felt like my arms were six inches longer. However, my mouth was the real problem. It was full of a combination of soil, grass, dung, and other disgusting objects. It must have been an attractive mix, because a blowfly was already circling my head. I struggled to get to my feet; it was going to be a long, painful walk back to the saddle shed. I turned to glare at this four-legged idiot, when—did you know that a horse could smile? I swear on the bushman's book of camp fire prayers that the ugly thug smirked at me.

Game, set, and match to Swanee.

I went to walk off—no good. Even slower, I shuffled back to the saddle shed. On the way I found my boot, but I couldn't find the bloody sock.

'How'd you go today, Barry?' asked the boss later that night at tea. Have you ever been asked one of those questions? I could take half an hour, or tell him a little white lie.

'Okay,' I said with a grim, feeble smile.

'What happened to your chin?' he asked.

Christ! I thought to myself. *My bloody chin! What about the rest of my poor battered body? You should see my family jewels ... they've changed colour for the second time in my life.*

'I slipped, getting some hay out of the shed,' was my pathetic response.

Several days later, the rematch was on. I collected the bridle and headed for the bull paddock. It took me an hour to catch Swanee, the hideous brute. No, he wouldn't be bribed; neither food (I'd taken some oats) nor sweet-talk worked. He had 'you must be kidding' written all over his face. He could have toyed with me all day. This inbred, flaming tyrant had his head in a corner of the paddock, and just kept swinging his rump towards me. If I ventured too far up one side, the lout would turn and canter to another corner. Twice, he tried to nip me with his huge bloody teeth. Finally, in an act of kindness, or sympathy, he let me put the bridle on. I walked backwards to the saddle shed—you just couldn't trust his bloody mouth. At the shed, I got a currycomb and brushed him before I put the saddle blanket on. He liked a brush. Then I threw on the saddle and tightened the girth as much as I could. So far, so good—Swanee stood quietly.

Today, something was different; perhaps he was in a better mood. (If I could have read his mind at that moment, he would have been thinking, *Ha! How gullible, you raw fool, Barry.*) I was ready to mount up. Now, being very tender in the crotch area, this meant it was going to be a delicate manoeuvre. In fact, I knew from an inspection the night before that my private parts had not only changed colour, but the swelling was considerable. However, I also knew I would have to suffer in private. I'd considered visiting the bush nurse about the bruising, but it took raw courage to lower your pants in front of that woman. I didn't have the fortitude, or the ego, to handle the gossip that would have rushed around the district like a bushfire. It was a grin-and-bear-it matter.

Sorry ... got waylaid. We were at the saddle shed; I slid the reins over his head, placed my foot in the stirrup, and took a deep breath. Like an old man of 80, I swung my leg up. Good, Swanee didn't move. But God Almighty, Mary of Magellan County, and Moses the well-known water-parter—the bloody saddle did. I felt like I'd been zapped in the crotch with a cattle prodder.

It slid and almost ended up under his belly. Shit! (My vocabulary was expanding rapidly during my time with this beast.) As usual, with most things I'd had to do with the ill-mannered horse, I ended up sprawled in the dirt.

I looked up. The girth was loose—but I'd tightened the damn thing. I staggered to my feet, and I could have sworn the brute smirked again. I had a flare of anger, but didn't react or do anything. A loose girth—and the saddle hanging upside-down underneath his belly? Not possible. Hang on ... ah-ha! It took me a while to work it out. The cunning, sly bastard ... it was so clever. When I went to tighten the girth after I'd put on the saddle, he must have taken in a very deep, slow breath, swelling his belly considerably. I hadn't noticed. At the time, naturally, I tightened the girth and shook the saddle, which is the habit of most horse riders. Meanwhile, Swanee, with the girth tightened, quietly breathed out. The result? A loose girth, then *crunch!* and me on my backside yet again.

After I'd brushed myself down, I grabbed the saddle and slid it around his stomach and back into place. Slowly, I pretended to tighten the girth. I waited and waited. I could see the ugly, flat-headed, evil fiend struggling as he tried to hold his breath for as long as he could. His eyes started to water—he must have been in agony, the dumb prat—then he started to let air out. Great ... I heaved on the girth and did up the buckle. Swanee laid back his ears, rolled his eyes, and flicked his tail.

Suffer, you four-legged freak. One to me.

After that, the day went by almost without incident. I spent most of the time standing in the saddle to protect my you-know-whats. There were a couple of minor mishaps. The moron almost ripped my leg off as he cunningly cantered too close to a fence. Then the brute tried in vain to dislodge me under trees that had low branches. As well, the flamin' inborn brumby idiot flicked me with his tail whenever I dismounted. Then came the final insult—he chewed a hole in my hat, which I'd hung on a hook near him while I'd gone and had a cuppa.

Over the next few weeks, I rode Swanee regularly. He still appeared to have a sour demeanour and a mad stare about him. Every day and every time we headed off, there would be a new test for me. I was passing them almost bruise-free until one particular day.

It was early morning. I had to ride the crazy freak down to my boss's family farm. It was a pleasant, fifteen-minute canter to their property. Even though I hadn't warmed to this inbred, mad beast called a horse, it was a joy to be on his back as he gently rocked along in a perfect rhythm. I rode alongside the road. It was early—a glorious day. There were parrots arguing in the trees ... they are always arguing, those birds. The magpies' burbles heralded good morning, and a wedge-tail soared on his breakfast run. There was frost still on the ground. It was the start of a beautiful, late-autumn day. Swanee's canter was silky smooth, almost rocking me to sleep, when suddenly—*thump!* I found myself flat on my back with a very sore shoulder. The sly bastard had bided his time. We'd ridden on this track many times in the last fortnight, yet he'd waited until I slipped into a daydream. Then, the swine, he'd lined me up with a support-wire or guy-wire, hadn't he? It ran from the top of a telephone pole to a concrete block in the ground. Luckily, it caught my shoulder and I was wearing a heavy coat.

Rarely do I get angry. However, this time, I got to my feet, walked over to Swanee, and punched him as hard as I could on the head. Hell, did that hurt. I clutched my fist into my stomach with agony. He didn't blink or show any indication I'd even thumped him. Me—I thought I'd maybe broken a few knuckles and strained my wrist. The pain was the only reason I didn't punch him again. So I surveyed the area, looking for a weapon ... a decent log of wood. I might add that, by now, I was one of the walking wounded, and very angry. That's a bad combination for me. Let's face it: I had a suspected broken shoulder, crushed nuts, severe gravel-rash on my stomach, elongated arms, a lost sock, a chewed hat, a shattered hand, and a busted wrist. Why me, Lord? Then, as if to add insult to injury, the stupid nag gave me that smirk.

'Bad move, mate.' I narrowed my eyes, intent on revenge. His wry smile quickly disappeared. I increased my hunt for a lump of wood with which to attack the cruel, ugly creep. I was looking for a really big piece. No luck—fortunately, for both of us. I quickly calmed down. The temptation was high, but I didn't hit him again.

Then something strange happened. He walked towards me, the reins dragging along the ground.

He was giving me permission to hop up on his back. His eyes were soft, his ears forward with concern. He was saying sorry. Yes, that was the day he let me graduate—the day I took a stand.

AFTER THAT, I never had any trouble catching him in the bull paddock. He stopped trying to nip my bum, and he always hinted—after I took the saddle off—that it was a time for a long and vigorous brush. He loved the brush. Over the years, he proved to be an outstanding stock horse. He was brilliant with cattle, and he worked tirelessly. Staying on his back was all I had to do. He would sprint, spin this way then that, forcefully pushing stock with his legs and chest. I worked him in the yards, and drove cattle with him in the days before trucks took over. He was the ideal drover's horse, having boundless energy and being very intelligent. The first time Alan Taylor asked me to do some droving, I knew why. Was there a better team than Swanee and Rover? Once the calves were out in the open, Swanee was a master at controlling them. Rover was a bonus.

However, as I mentioned earlier, when droving there was more to the journey than just droving calves. From the very start, it was a most picturesque trip. Both of my special animals would feel excited every time we set off after that first sale through the high plains, with Lake Omeo on the right and the Benambra footy ground on the left, and then up and along past McMillan's lookout, admiring the view from the high ridge. You could see the picturesque area of the Great Divide with the high mountains of the Alps. Like a perfect oil painting, in the background was a beautiful vista: Mount Hotham, Dinner Plain, Feather Top with its sharp, distinctive ridge, and the bareness of those high, treeless peaks. Then down along the Livingston into Omeo—such a beautiful town. With the blink of an eye you could picture this same scene happening 50 years earlier ... the Omeo yards, right on the edge of the town's main oval would draw a large crowd of locals adorned in big hats, jeans, and riding boots. The auctioneers were loud and colourful. There was always a competition to have the top pen sell for a higher price than the top price that had been paid at Benambra.

I always used Rover in the yards after the sale, while Swanee had a rest in the shade. With the mob now swelled, it would be time to head east, out to the other side of Omeo. Behind us, as we settled the newcomers, was the perfect backdrop: by turning and looking behind, you saw the rolling Omeo Valley. By now the Benambra calves would lead, sauntering along, quite content. In the middle, looking for security, would be the new ones. By the time Mount Stall, the Splitters, and the other far-off ranges came into view, the wide plains started to narrow. We would have time to relax a little before the scenery changed. Almost abruptly, the road went downhill. It was a sudden, steep decline called 'the Gap'. From the top, down to the next flat road was over three miles. Then we were 'below the Gap'.

Mind you, I wasn't sure all the drovers agreed with my description of 'above the Gap'. I recall once, we'd just descended and we were at the bottom, heading towards the Tambo River, when Plugger, one of the drovers, said something like, 'Bloody cold bugger of a place up there ... bloody good to get away from, I reckon.'

From the bottom of the Gap, we would herd the calves into the Tambo Valley, along Sandy's Flats and past Holland's. This was the hilly, undulating sheep-and-cattle country around Tongio, Bald Hills Creek, and then Swifts Creek. High mountains and bush surrounded this lower country; and, already, after only a couple of days on the road, there would be a notable rise in temperature, as we'd dropped more than 1000 feet. Then we'd travel along the Tambo River, past Doctors Flat, and Sheepstation Creek, and then up Connor's Hill and yet another magnificent sight. There is something special about the view from Connor's Hill.

Then Ensay—which was another well-supported annual sale, with more beautiful, sappy calves. Rover and Swanee were home, for the moment at least. Cossie's Little River Pub would have its best weekend sales for the year as well.

After Ensay, we reached the rugged scrub that has always kept this entire area in isolation. In the early times, the bush from Bruthen to Ensay defied road builders; they declared it almost impassable. It's no wonder that the entire Benambra, Omeo, and Swifts Creek areas were settled from the north, down from New South Wales into Benambra, then slowly south and east. The road from Ensay through to Bruthen is very winding, and the drop to the river at times is steep and dangerous—if we lost a calf, the retrieval was like a scene from *The Man from Snowy River*. The bush is dirty, rock-strewn, and dry. Rocks would be dislodged from the high banks, particularly after rain. Many an unwary driver has driven around a corner, only to be faced with a road strewn with rocks. The calves would string slowly along the winding Omeo Highway, which follows the Tambo River for some way, and then we would turn towards the west, arriving at Double Bridges for the evening's camp. Early the next morning it would be up Walsh's cutting, down to the Goat Farm, across Ramrod Creek and then Evan's paddock near Bruthen.

Every evening, and again at dawn, Alan Taylor would count the calves. His reputation for doing this was legendary. Most sheep or cattle sold within the entire area relied on a final count from the man. I never saw a count disputed. He would count sheep in fives as they rushed from the yards to get out.

After Bruthen, it was the final stretch. At the top of the hill, just before the town, it was like opening a door—we would emerge out into the open, flat country. It was the same when we reached the top of Lucknow Hill, coming into Bairnsdale. Many people would venture out to watch the drovers during the last stage of the long trip. Normally, it took ten days to complete the journey. By the time the calves reached their final destination, they were quiet, docile, and easy to handle. This would make them excellent farm stock. All of this was very different to the abrupt journey provided nowadays in a rattling, rushing cattle truck. It's no wonder that calves charge down the ramp from a truck with wild eyes, panting as if they'd run the entire way.

> *As the stock are slowly stringing, Clancy rides behind them*
>   *singing,*
> *For the drover's life has pleasures that the townsfolk never*
>   *know.*
> —from 'Clancy of the Overflow' by Banjo Paterson,
> *The Bulletin*, 21 December 1889

FOR SWANEE, droving was the ultimate. He never tired. Other drovers often commented on his energy and speed. Wisely, I never asked a drover if he would like to have a go on Swanee. I honestly believe we had a special bond, a pact. Whatever it was, I grew to love him and to enjoy his larrikin behaviour. Somehow, we seemed meant for each other (surely I am not that pig-headed?), and he would nudge me with affection at times—admittedly, a little roughly so that he would almost knock me over. He became my mate, my horse and, when appropriate, he would do little favours for me. I would almost swear that he knew what was required of him—like a mind-reader.

For instance, one of the farmers who lived nearby, who often borrowed things or asked for help, never returned the favour. One day he asked to borrow a horse. At the time, we had four horses, including Swanee. The opportunity to have fun with the neighbour was one I couldn't resist. When he arrived I had Swanee saddled up, and slowly brushed his neck and sides. He loved the brush. I put my arm around his neck, gave him a warm hug, and said, 'Do us a favour, mate? Frighten the crap outta this bloke if ya can.'

Swanee nodded, and I'm sure he winked at me. The

neighbour came over, and I had a brief chat to him and then held the reins as I legged him into the saddle. Quietly patting Swanee on the neck, I offered some advice to our neighbour.

'He's a bit lazy, this horse, mate. Let him know who's the boss,' I suggested, trying not to smile. Swanee glanced at me; again, I'm sure he winked.

Rip ... The neighbour tugged the reins, seesawing poor Swanee's mouth and then spinning him tightly. He then kicked him savagely in the ribs. Jesus! I cringed with fear. I could just picture what was about to happen in Swanee's head—sure enough, bloody Swanee arrived at the first gate at blistering speed. It was like a car at a drag race. Our neighbour had his arms wrapped around the horse's neck, muttering obscenities. Closing the gate, he reefed the reins again and—believe me—he kicked Swanee again, even harder. There was a noise like a mini sonic boom, followed by a large cloud of dust, and the sort of high-pitched wail one hears in a Dracula film. The neighbour's hat flew off as he grasped at Swanee's mane, saddle, and neck. They disappeared down the dirt track like a fighter jet on take-off.

Our neighbour returned an hour later, walking backwards, leading Swanee very slowly. The poor bloke looked like he'd had some pommel treatment—maybe his gonads had changed colour. His legs were very bowed. His face looked like it had spent an hour in the school dentist's chair. Swanee? He had a smirk on his face. I loved that smirk, then that cunning wink ... I loved him dearly at times, the bloody rogue.

Naturally, I asked the neighbour if he'd prefer one of the other horses, one with a bit more life, or sting, in it. He mumbled something, something you wouldn't hear in church, gave me a new pedigree, and left. I took the saddle off Swanee and gave him an extra long brush. He loved it. He'd done well. The neighbour never came back looking to borrow a horse.

FEAR WAS SOMETHING I thought Swanee would never display. However, one day I found him standing, shuddering, with fear in his eyes. Caught up in some loose wire, he was extremely distressed and standing still like a statue. No way was he moving. I have seen other horses in similar situations — if they panic, particularly if they bolt, they end up not only entangled completely, but also the wire tears into the skin and results in terrible wounds. A smart horse will stand still, and Swanee was rigid, like concrete.

Slowly I unthreaded the wire from around his legs, crawling under his belly and hindquarters. I had some wire cutters, but the loud 'click' as I cut the wire really frightened him. It took ages, but Swanee remained frozen to the spot. After I finished, he was wet with sweat and looked exhausted. I left him standing there, walked to the saddle shed, and returned with a currycomb. After a long brush, I talked to him quietly, patted him for quite a while, and then led him by the mane back to his paddock, away from the wire. He stood there solemnly after I let him go, then he turned and gave me a quiet and friendly nudge. We were mates.

chapter twelve

'What's that horrible smell, Barry?'

DURING THOSE EARLY MONTHS AT MY NEW JOB, THERE WERE quite a few changes at home. We now had a new water tank on a high stand, which enabled Mum to change the way she did many of her domestic duties. A pump, located on the Tambo River, filled the tank. This led to a hot-water service being put in, as well as a shower in the bathroom, and a flushing toilet at the back of the house that replaced the long drop found over the bank.

The long drop had a proud history; I was sad to see it pulled down. Dad had erected it in 1956, and it was a vast improvement on the dunny we'd had at Tongio. The other added luxury in the new toilet was proper paper. However, the toilet was in for a shock. In 1959 the Tambo River experienced a major flood. The river rose rapidly and levelled off just two inches below the floorboards of the house at Doctors Flat.

The two things I remember vividly involved Mum and the outside lavatory. At the time of the flood, Mum was heavily pregnant with my youngest brother, Peter. On the night that the river peaked, I recall lying in bed and listening to the roar, and the snapping and crashing of the large trees and debris that were charging down the swift-flowing river. The dogs barked all night. We got up at dawn and couldn't believe our eyes: the river was at the back door. It was several hundred yards across, and moving speedily, with small, swirling eddies and whirlpools in the brown, murky water.

Next thing, we could hear voices calling out and car horns tooting. We went out onto the front veranda and, to our surprise, there was a group of people with a boat, organising to rescue us—well, to have Mum and the younger kids rescued, really, as the water around the house was only, at the most, three feet deep, and we were able to move around if we were careful. The small outboard motorboat was moored to the veranda post, and Mum got in and carefully sat in the middle. It putted back to the Omeo Highway, about 100 yards away, and she waved to us, indicating that everything was okay. Then my smaller brothers were also ferried away.

That left Dad; Darky and Skipper, the dogs; and me. Meanwhile, back at the house, we were quickly working out what had washed away and what needed saving. Would you believe, the first job given to me was to swim out to the outside lavatory? Then I had to lash a rope around it. Finally, I followed Dad's shouted orders, anchoring it to the sizable, old, dead tree nearby. It must have been in part of Dad's plumbing training manual—save the dunny first. Having completed that, Dad seemed to breathe easier. Then we let the horses and cows out of their paddocks, and moved them onto the road, as it was the highest ground available. The chooks, whose pen was two feet deep in water, simply sat on their roost as if it was bedtime. The river, which was lapping under the veranda and sloshing up against the stumps and bearers under the house, stayed at the same level for the rest of the day.

That night, we waited. It stayed the same. Slowly, the following morning, it subsided. Call it luck or whatever you want but, the following day, it continued to go down. When it finally returned to its original course, mud covered most of the fences, paddocks, and yards. It was six inches deep in some places. The water had also caused a lot of damage.

At the time, another two inches and it would have entered the house; another two feet, and who knows what would have happened? Noticing the size of some of the huge trees floating down the river, we had no doubt that this large volume of water had had a tremendous force. The outside lavatory did survive—although it ended up at an unusual angle. If Dad had his way, that leaning lavatory would still be there to this day.

Over the next couple of years, the house was modernised with a gas fridge, a gas stove, a hand basin in the bathroom to replace the outside trough, and a shower. And then, most importantly of all, Mum bought a new—and her first-ever—washing machine. It had a two-stroke engine that operated the water pump, the agitator, and a wringer on top of the machine. To get it operating required a kick-start like a motorbike. Few people in the district had one. For once, Mum was able to get ahead with her washing. Between a new baby daughter, five boys, and Dad there was always a mountain of washing to do. The new washing machine was a hit.

After several trial runs during that first week, Mum had it mastered … until one unfortunate day. She got up early, put on a load, and was inside attending to breakfast. The machine, when it had finished the washing cycle, would automatically stop and turn itself off. To do the wringing, it had to be re-started. It was a Saturday. Most of the family were inside when we heard a blast from the .410 shotgun, right at the back door. We all rushed out, and there was Mum, standing with a proud smirk. She had just shot a sizable tiger snake that had wrapped itself around the warm engine of the washing machine. Let's face it—it was winter, probably between one and three degrees. Was there a warmer place for a snake to snuggle up in than a washing machine that had cooled slightly? The result: one very mutilated snake, and one wrecked washing machine. I can't imagine what Mum was thinking. Our local mechanic told Dad that the machine was beyond repair, so Mum went back to the scrubbing board and the hand-wringer until electricity arrived in 1967.

THERE WAS another incident around the same time that I'll reluctantly share with you. Not long after I'd started the farm job, the boss invited a niece up to the farm to stay for school holidays. It was quite a thrill to learn that she was my age, a city girl, and that she was really looking forward to living on the farm for the holidays.

What with my new good clothes, my newly acquired table manners, and my riding abilities, I wasn't only keen to meet her, but I also thought that, if she fitted the bill, I'd attempt to impress her. Sadly, this didn't run to plan. Let's just say that my next sortie into the female fold taught me something I've never attempted again: do not wear gumboots when attempting to impress the fairer sex.

Let me explain. After leaving school, I worked a seven-day week, either on the farm or with Dad. This meant I had little spare time for courting. Nevertheless, my mind was continually clicking into overdrive with thoughts about women—like, how I would court them, speak to them, or tell them about myself, and even about what to do if it came to a bit of smooching.

The day came, and she arrived. She wore a very pretty dress and was quite a looker. Her name was Irene, and she was from Melbourne. It was her first visit to both the bush and a farm. As I expected, she took a shine to me straight away. Well, she smiled in my direction ... and I took the hint. Let's face it: I could drive a tractor and milk a cow, not to mention separate the cream, and so on—all earthy, man-like chores that set a fair maiden's heart on fire, eh?

After lunch on that first day, with the boss away, I offered to take Irene in the Land Rover for a ride up to the hayshed to get some bales for the animals in the bull paddock. She came, and opened the gates as I drove, real cool, with a hand draped over the steering wheel. I bet Irene was impressed. I was only a sixteen-year-old boy. I chewed a bit of straw on the way back to the bull paddock. When we arrived at their gate, the animals were standing, eager for their treat. Irene was apprehensive, and asked if I could open the gate … no worries. Once inside the paddock, I put the Land Rover in low-low, a very slow gear, and told Irene to steer it as I fed out the hay—normally I would feed out, as the Land Rover simply wandered across the paddock with no driver. She was besotted—another tick to me. When I finished feeding, I asked her to jump aside as I took the controls. So far, so good—I could tell she was more than just a little interested in me.

Later that afternoon, like every afternoon, I headed for the milker's paddock, and rounded up the cow and calf. With the calf locked up for the night, I gathered the eggs, split some firewood, and took in an armful of larger logs for the open fire. Irene followed me everywhere and, by now, I believed she was completely head-over-heels—even if we had only spoken eight words for the day.

At the dinner table that night, my manners were impeccable. It was during supper that it happened: the confirmation of my inner thoughts and desires. Irene asked what I did in the morning, when first I got up. I didn't mention that I usually had a pee, but I explained the milking, the separating, and the calf- and lamb-feeding ritual that took up most of the morning before brekkie. She wanted to rise early and come along … wow. The next morning she was there in jeans—another wow—and she was beginning to ask endless questions … about the animals, not me, but I knew that would not be far away. However, of all the highly skilled tasks of mine that she admired or complimented me on, it was feeding the lambs and calves that set Irene's love *haw-moans* pinging.

We had three lambs, all very cute; and when it was the last one's turn, Irene begged me to let her feed the poddy lamb with a bottle. This was no big deal, although there was a preferred angle to hold the vessel, for the uninitiated: bottom end up. With that explained, Irene fed the woolly little lamb with affection and joy; she was really excited. I then returned to the separator room and got a bucket of milk for the poddy calf. Irene walked very quickly behind me as we headed towards the little feller, its tail in the air in anticipation. I could tell she was just trying to get near me—Irene that is, although the calf was keen, too. When it came to feeding the poddy calf, Irene was infatuated. She just sighed with admiration at my casual, but deftly crafted, method of putting my finger in its mouth to induce sucking. Admittedly, she would not have been impressed a week earlier, when I had to biff the little beggar for almost amputating my ring finger. It was a new calf, only five weeks old. Its mum had died during birth.

Perhaps I should explain the method. To feed a new poddy calf, you first let the calf suck your fingers. The calf is always hesitant when you first entice it to suck, but a little cream mixed with honey usually does the trick. Then, once the calf sucks with confidence, you stand behind the little fella, push its head into a bucket of milk, and it drinks by slurping the warm milk through your fingers. I was coolly explaining this to Irene while she just beamed at the way I was carrying out this demanding task involving our fluffy little calf. I bent over the little blighter, my knee behind his rump, and my other hand holding down his head. The calf, a cute little white-faced Hereford, slopped and gulped while Irene gasped with wonder. When it had finished drinking, I ruffled his soft fur and let Irene pat him. By now, I reckoned I had Irene well and truly hooked—I was her man.

With my shoulders back and my chin squared, I calmly picked up the empty bucket and turned to head for the house, when I realised there was a problem ... a really big problem. *Hell*, I was thinking, *Come on ... do something.* So, temporarily, I pretended I was injured. I held my thigh and limped, trying not to stir up the problem, but ... bugger ... that didn't work. Then, just as I was desperately thinking of a way to get Irene to leave my side for a while, I got asked that bloody question again—yes, almost word for word, the same one that Curls had asked me in the Swifts Creek Mechanics Institute Hall at the movies that memorable night. Here we were, walking along, Irene and me—with me limping (I was going to suggest I had a torn bone), when she asked, 'What's that horrible smell, Barry?'

I declared I didn't know, which was a blatant lie. Thankfully, she hadn't noticed I was walking peculiarly. You see, there was a small problem with my right gumboot: it was half full of calf turd. The little blighter, unbeknown to me, had quietly filled my boot with disgusting, yellow, custard-like, stinking calf-crap. I reckon Irene worked it out after a while; she started to drift away from me as we headed back to the house. How embarrassing could life get? Perhaps she thought I never washed, never cleaned my teeth or, worse, never used toilet paper.

Anyhow, a potential blossoming romance with Irene had been nipped in the bud. In fact, for the remainder of the week she just giggled every time she saw me—particularly when I was in gumboots. Unfortunately, I had to put them on every morning. You see, they were the only boots I could wear in the muddy milker's yard. In fact, after the turd incident, I scrubbed that right boot and poured boiling water in it, but the smell lingered for weeks. It was such a small matter, yet it shattered a budding romance. I guessed that was why Irene never visited the farm again.

chapter thirteen

Bob versus Bernie

FOOTBALL WAS VERY IMPORTANT IN THE OMEO SHIRE. THERE were only four teams, and the rivalry was intense, bordering on all-out bloodshed at times. I have seen decent, law-abiding men run across the boundary of the oval, shudder, and turn into mindless morons. Being in the country, most men were used to hard work, which consequently made them quite fit.

The four teams were Omeo, Benambra, Swifts Creek, and Ensay. Ensay was a very small town that harboured the essentials—a pub-come-post office, a small shop, a service station, and a large set of sale yards around the corner. It was just like Benambra, which was another small country town at the other end of the Omeo Shire. The only real difference between the two towns was that Benambra was 'above the Gap'. This was a bit of a worry.

Omeo and Swifts Creek were much larger, and their town populations were measured in the hundreds. Consequently, when it came to a game of football, Benambra and Ensay usually had just enough locals to fill the team, with a few really old, or reluctant, players on the standby.

As it happened, up to the time we moved from Melbourne, I hadn't seen a footy match. The sport didn't appear to interest my mum or my new dad. Speaking of Dad, he was an unusual footballer. He had grown up in Melbourne and had played soccer most of his life. He was a plumber—or 'turd burglar', as they were known in the high country, where it was generally felt that most of their work involved clearing blocked turds from fouled sewerage systems. When we first moved to the area, he continued to work as a plumber. As a tradesman with no reputation, one of the best ways for him to fit in with the local community was to play footy: Aussie Rules, naturally. After proving that he had a high level of fitness and no skills for the game whatsoever, he eventually got a game for Swifts Creek.

The team wasn't low on numbers—just short of handy footballers. An entrenched local law had it that if you possessed above-average skills for the game, you were almost committed for life. The age-range in the team was amazing: the oldest bloke was 48; the youngest, sixteen.

In fact, even though he had a soccer background, Bob had slightly above-average skills. He was nippy and accurate—fast on his feet and a straight kick. The players trained on Tuesdays and Thursdays ... well, they ran around a bit and kicked the footy to one another. However, it was hard to do a lot of ball-handling because, being in the winter, most blokes arrived at the ground well after five o'clock, when darkness had set in. So doing a few laps around the ground was the main mode of training. This suited Bob and a few of the others—those not keen on running long distances. As the players ran around the boundary, Bob and his mates would drop to the back of the pack, jog into the bush, and hide behind trees. The keen ones put in several laps. On the last lap, when most of the keen ones would be buggered, Bob and co. would rejoin the back of the pack, sprint to the front, and win the lap race, naturally, gaining praise from the coach. It was all done in total darkness.

Thursday night was pie night. After an evening of this sophisticated, intensive training, copious amounts of beer and numerous hot pies were the go. They were Fitz's pies, of course, from the local baker—essential food, good for bursts of energy or for keeping regular, they reckoned. The liquid intake—beer—was required to maintain their high level of game awareness, and to encourage more fluid movements when chasing the ball, or something. I was too young to grasp that stuff.

The other thing was that, each Thursday night, the coach announced the team for the following Saturday. I wasn't there when Bob got the nod, but we were thrilled for him when he announced this at home. We couldn't wait; it was going to be really exciting. We would be going to a local footy ground, and watching our first game.

IT WAS A LONG DRIVE up the steep, winding road called 'the Gap' to Omeo and then on to Hinnomunjie. It was my first trip into this area. The views along the way were outstanding. The road from Omeo wandered along the top of rugged mountains, then dropped down towards the broad, flat plains of Hinnomunjie and Benambra. The first thing you noticed was a spectacular lake, Lake Omeo, which was like a scene from a fairy story. It was beautiful and huge. Once down onto the open plains, we encountered the first long, flat road I'd seen since Bairnsdale. About halfway along this strip of sealed road there was a sign: Hinnomunjie Racecourse.

We headed towards what looked like a farm. It turned out that the racecourse was a farm and a footy ground, as well as a place where people played a bit of golf.

Bob's first game in the forward pocket is perhaps best left unmentioned; or, to be polite, let's just say he really struggled.

The club president was kind enough to walk over to him and say, 'Jesus, you're weak, Richards.'

Over the next few years, we made many trips to Benambra. Perhaps the one that stood out most was when we went to watch a regatta on Lake Omeo. It was more than a regatta: there were people water skiing, and sailing boats and motorboats—beautiful, sleek wooden ones.

I really enjoyed going to the footy; I knew most of the kids from seeing them at school sports and the like. It was great to tear out onto the ground before the game and play kick-to-kick. This also happened at half-time. Then came the drama of three-quarter time ... it was like theatre. The players would be in a tight bunch, surrounded by local supporters and kids. The coach's address was always an inspiration; it was one of the few times that you could hear quite foul language—strangely, its use seemed to be condoned.

The coach would start, 'Look men, this is it ... You back men, stick to ya frigg'n men. You forwards, git in frigg'n front. And put ya head over the frigg'n ball, okay? Try and run it out ... look for a lead. Frigg'n Johnno, good on ya—you're doin' okay.'

There would be grunts of approval at this last comment. Then he'd continue, 'Kick it long, okay? Frigg'n long. Now, when we go back out, I want you to hit 'em frigg'n hard, okay? Okay?'

Almost primitively, the team would grunt in unison, 'Yeah!'

'We're not going to win—we're going to frigg'n shit it in, okay?'

'Yeah!'

'Come boys, let's frigg'n go get 'em!'

'Carn the creek' was the common chant from those supporters gathered around. This would bring grunts, cheers, clapping, and a lot of backslapping.

Bob became a permanent member of the Swifts Creek team. Over time, his footy skills never really improved much, except that he was a very accurate kick. But, following the examples set by the men bred in *them thar mountains*, he learnt to limp off the field at the end of the game, even if he had no injuries—this was a local tradition, apparently. His spitting reached the good distance of seven feet, and his nostril-clearing matched the best of them. However, it was his team spirit, or willingness to uphold the code of mateship, and other male-bonding attributes that strengthened. Within two seasons, he was able to perform advanced team skills. For example, he developed that 'Are you look'n at me?' stare, accompanied by a low snarl. He, like most, heaved and tugged at his jockstrap with vigour. Bob never shaved or showered for a week before the game, and refused to brush his hair. So our Bob filled a spot in a team that was short on handy players, and he reached the high level of Aussie honour that involves 'laying ya life down for tha side'. He heroically displayed this at the Hinnomunjie footy-ground-come-racetrack in his third season. Unbeknown to Bob, he'd recently upset a Benambra player in a most unusual way.

It had happened when he was doing a job earlier in the week at Benambra on a farm. It was morning tea, and Bob, the farm labourer Max (or Rowdy, as he was known), Tiger Tomkins, and two old women were present. The women owned the property. As often happened in the winter during that repast, the topic of footy came up. Both Rowdy and Tiger played for Benambra. It is important to add now that Bob was from below the Gap—a bad slur on anyone in the Benambra area (more about that later). The conversation got around to the Benambra team. A bloke played with them called Bernie. Now, Bob had a description for Bernie's type, but he couldn't say this in the presence of ladies. So he referred to Bernie as 'a cad and a bounder', a well-known saying used by Poms that Bob had heard many-a-time in Melbourne. Apparently, everyone just looked blank, not realising it simply meant that Bernie was an undesirable ... whatever. Rowdy, being a typical above-the-Gap gossip and dobber, couldn't get down to the pub quickly enough after work to inform Bernie and the rest of the team what that bastard, Richards the Turd Burglar, had said about their Bernie ... It was on.

So, the next time Swifts Creek were playing Benambra, there we were, stopped at the gate to the entrance to the farm paddock, paying our way into the game. Already, there were about 20 cars parked around the boundary; it being a typical winter's day, there was frost still on the ground at 2.00 p.m. A lazy wind howled across the wide, flat area—the sort of wind that goes straight through you, and not around. Long sleeves and T-shirts were definitely the go. Naturally, like most footy ovals in the district, cake-like dollops of frozen cow-turd covered it from one end to the other. Iced-over puddles and potholes also dotted the oval for, apart from Saturday and the annual horse races, the oval was a paddock—part of a farm.

Before the game, the umpires and Bob's team—known affectionately as 'the Creek'—changed in the jockey's shed. Perhaps, more accurately, they jammed into the small enclosure with a dirt floor that was a bit short on room. This provided a major problem for the players—not the size of the room, mind you, but the fact that they would all be baring their snow-white arses in a very confined area. They all stared at the ceiling as they lowered their dacks, put on their shorts, and pulled on their boots. High-country folklore has it that it's a trip to purgatory if you're caught glancing at another man's arse. Naturally, the home team, Benambra, had a large room with a bloody shower at one end.

The Creek were playing those Benambra bastards for the third time this season, and there were a few paybacks and scores to settle. This was yet another silent tradition that was always carried out after the first bounce. More importantly, Bob was unaware of Bernie's bitter demeanour towards him on the day.

The ump held up the ball and blew his whistle, and the game began. I have to point out here that I received several versions of what then happened. I was only a witness on the sidelines. Unfortunately, both sources of the following yarn were from 'above the Gap', and most of them struggle with putting a sentence together. I hope the next bit makes some sense. So here goes ...

Typical of the Omeo League, the first quarter usually consisted of a bit of footy and a lot of charging shirtfronts, wild arm-swinging, and the biffing of any poor bugger who wore the opposition jumper. The locals loved it. Now, as if it were pre-ordained, our Bob, the Turd Burglar, was on this same tough-nut called Bernie.

To describe Bernie, let's just say that he was a bit thick, slow-talking, and ignorant; nevertheless, he certainly recalled that, the last time they'd met, Bob had given him a bath. Well, not literally—those rugged, mountain men wouldn't be seen dead washing a mountain man.

The fact was, the last time they'd played on each other, Bob had kicked four goals on Bernie. He'd given the cross-eyed bastard from Beloka a hiding. The thing was, our Bob was quick, and Bernie was as slow as a wet week. So now there were several reasons for retribution—it was Bernie's chance for some payback. In the back of Bernie's blank head was a confused thought. It darted around his skull as he wobbled around the windswept, turd-covered oval. Yes, our Bernie was going to take the slack out of Bob; slow him down a bit before the game really got going. In fact, he'd announced as much in the rooms before they jogged out. Later, one bloke was to comment that it was the longest sentence Bernie had ever muttered.

Meanwhile, back at the game, it was only minutes into the first quarter when Bob received a decent biff behind the ear followed by a smack in the chops from Bernie, the cross-eyed, back-pocket bully from Beloka. Now, Bernie was a bad-looking bugger at the best of times. He was missing half his ear'ole. In fact, two blokes played for Benambra with half their ears missing. It had happened the year before — Bernie had half his left flamin' ear bitten off in a minor clash when they played Ensay. It bled profusely; afterwards, most reckoned he deserved the chunk ripped out of his ear and, in fact, it only added to his ugly looks. Mind you, Bernie boasted at the time that he would have bitten the Ensie bastard back, but 'I gots no teeth, you know'. However, for all his ugly looks, Bernie's cross-eyes were what scared off most strangers. This unfortunate disorder had happened after he'd suffered a head injury as a lad. Apparently, a rogue bloody horse had bucked him off, kicked him in the skull, and trod on him several times, which resulted in him going cross-eyed … Bernie, that is. I think the horse was okay. However, the consensus was that it not only improved Bernie's looks, but that he gained some intellect from the incident.

Sorry, got waylaid again — God, they can yak, those Benambra buggers.

Back at the oval …

As it happened, after Bernie smacked Bob in the ear'ole a second time, he glared at Bob and stated, 'Call me a stinking bastard, a shithead, or a low-down mongrel, but never call me a cad and a bounder.'

Bob just smiled, and Bernie took another swipe. Well, that really riled our Bob — it was a bit below the belt, and all that stuff. Too late for Bernie … Bob had a tradition to uphold. He leapt at Bernie like a sumo wrestler, and knocked him flat on his back, *thump*. So there was Bernie, down on the deck, and our intrepid goal-sneak, Bob, sitting on his chest mumbling profanities. Bernie started punching Bob furiously. All this time the game kept going, although I and most of the crowd were riveted on Bob the Turd Burglar, and Bernie, that cross-eyed bastard from Beloka.

Unperturbed by the crowd's adulation, Bob, after focusing on several strategies to enhance his position and move forward in a meaningful way (I have added that sentence for all the CEOs reading this book), decided to shove two of his rarely washed fingers straight up Bernie's nostrils. Hooking them as far as he could, he then proceeded to lift poor frigg'n Bernie's head off the ground. Bernie was stuffed. Nevertheless, so was Bob.

Stalemate. Bob knew that, if he let Bernie up, that Beloka inbred bastard would most likely kill him ... slowly. Suddenly, Bob had another burst of intellect. Choosing his words carefully, he informed Bernie, 'I got worms, ya ugly bastard, and I've been scratching me arse with these two fingers for the last week.'

Bernie dry-retched and tried to get to his flat feet. He was a frightened man. Although I have called this a burst of intellect on Bob's part, and it did have the desired outcome for Bob, he could have taken another tack. Bob, being a plumber, spent many an hour in the belly of septic tanks performing jobs like unblocking huge turds, emptying overflowing bowel movements, and general maintenance. Bob should have simply told Bernie he showered, at the most, once a fortnight, never changed his underwear, and that lice loved his body—a slight exaggeration, but you get my drift. You see, Bob was in fact a walking bacterial time-bomb. Now, that would have frightened the crap out of our Bernie, or any other poor bugger picked to play on this plague-infested plumber. The impasse continued; Bob would not remove his fingers, and although Bernie tried to explain he would not be biffing Bob again, his voice sounded like a duck with a peg in its throat.

'Jeethus christh Richthards! Leth us up, ya basthard, you

farthking ... fucathing, faaarknth (he couldn't get that word out) well win.'

Bob couldn't decipher a single word. Finally, the ump ran over. He had to—the crowd and most of the players were enjoying the Bob-and-Bernie show. It was better than the footy.

'Okay, enough ...' said the ump, with a huge grin on his face.

'Bugger off—I'm busy,' muttered Bob.

Finally, two of the heavies from both teams separated the pair and sent them to either ends of the ground. Bob received whooping cheers and tooting horns as he sauntered to the back pocket. He adjusted his jockstrap, and cleared his left nostril. Yes, he'd done well, and the tradition lived on ... he'd been prepared to put his life on the line for the club.

As for poor Bernie, not only was he pleased to get away from Bob the Turd Burglar but, after that incident, let's just say he remained subdued for the rest of the season. To be honest, poor Bernie walked around with his head bent back for the next month. It wasn't a pretty sight, looking up those hairy nostrils. As you can imagine, no one was game enough to ask him if he had worms.

chapter fourteen
'You're a weak-kneed chicken, Heard.'

THE SUMMER WAS OVER. EVEN THOUGH I WAS WORKING AT Ensay, I had played cricket for Swifts Creek and enjoyed it immensely. I'd started playing for them in my last year at school. Perhaps the highlight of the season was a game against Omeo. I was the wicket-keeper, and I'd watched their early batsmen amass quite a total. Suddenly, their top scorer was out. Admittedly, I had a little forewarning that what was about to happen might be amusing. Several times I'd noticed kids run across the road from the pavilion to grab more beer for the waiting batsman. This meant that Alex, the next batsman in, would be very well primed. Slowly, he wandered across the oval in an S-like weave as he came to face up. After Alex duly took block, the bowler rushed in. Alex waved his bat far too late, wobbled backwards and then sideways, tried to focus on me, fell over on his stumps and, some ten seconds after the ball had been bowled, was given out—hit wicket. He was totally drunk.

In fact, most of the Omeo side were quite merry. This always happened if the opening pair did well. Naturally, after the game, regardless of the result, everyone headed for the Hilltop for a good feed and some serious drinking. One of the players, Ned, drank so much that he collapsed at the bar. Team mates rushed to his aid, carried him outside, and sat him in his blue Austin ute, where he came to. Someone started it up and he drove off. Much later that evening, we were heading home and, just past Holland's, there was Ned in his ute, in the middle of the road. It was upside down. On inspection, Ned was okay. He commented, 'I'm sorta lost. I think I missed the turn-off, mate.'

CRICKET WAS A LOT OF FUN, and was always played with good spirits and a lot of camaraderie. However, footy was a different matter. I was seventeen years old, and the footy season was about to begin. Growing up in both Tongio and Doctors Flat, which were both only a few miles from Swifts Creek, legend had it—some say it was carved in stone—that you played for the local team. The Swifts Creek coach, a schoolteacher who'd watched me play, was keen for me to pull on the jumper the year after I left school. I felt pretty chuffed that he'd spoken to me, and I looked forward to playing with the Creek. My father, Bob, played with them, so I would be following the family tradition, so to speak. Over the years, when I'd watched Bob play, I'd enjoyed the camaraderie that existed in the dressing shed and the huddled groups that got together during breaks on game days.

This particular year, it being at the start of the new season, the community of Swifts Creek naturally thought I'd play for them. At the same time, the Ensay community thought, 'Barry's a local now … he'll play for us.' I'd been on the farm at Ensay for just on ten months.

Even at that young age, I could see I was in a no-win situation. My schoolmates played for Swifts Creek, while both my bosses played for Ensay. Looking back, the Ensay community helped me make up my mind. It was very small, very welcoming and, just like Benambra, very close knit. Everyone was involved in everything. I liked that.

To be honest, I don't think I gave the decision a lot of thought. I simply donned an Ensay jumper, and we played Omeo at Ensay in my first game. I kicked four goals and, afterwards, the umpire voted me best on the ground. Never mind that the bloke I played on was nearly 50, had one bung knee, couldn't run, and enjoyed chatting more than playing footy. After the game, there was a barbecue, and then we all ventured around to Cossie's Little River Inn for celebration drinks. Despite being under-age and not allowed to drink, I was still welcomed into the bar and made to feel at home. This was what life was all about—getting a pat on the back, an 'Onya, mate', and a 'Well done, son'. I was shouted countless sarsaparilla drinks.

After the celebrations, I hitched a ride home with one of the Omeo blokes, and received a traitor's cool reception for the remainder of the weekend at home. Bob wasn't impressed with me. The following week, we would be playing against the Creek. I was to play on the ball, a difficult position that normally requires speed and an ability to turn quickly—neither of which I possessed much skill in. I was to change in the back pocket on my father. He had a reputation as a goal sneak, and was very quick.

After a week's work on the farm, I returned home to Doctors Flat. Come Saturday we got up very early, went out, and worked on our bush block. That was the normal pattern. Bob and I were clearing 640 acres of stringy-bark trees with axes ... I am serious. Then, just before lunch, we returned home and prepared for the footy. Mum, Bob, and the kids drove up to the ground in the new Holden, while I stood on the road out the front of our house and hitched a ride with one of those Ensay mongrels.

After changing into our footy gear, our team got a rousing talk from the coach that offered no intellect or wisdom. I would be playing on my stepfather. He played for Swifts Creek, and from the day I donned the jumper they were definitely the enemy. But there was a bigger worry for me than playing on him ... so help me, who could forget the time when I'd watched him play at Benambra? It was etched in my mind like a brand on a calf's rump. Yes, the way he wrestled that player to the ground, sat on the poor sod's chest, and jammed two fingers right up the bloke's nostrils. The incident had bestowed hero status on Bob.

So, with this recent memory deeply imprinted in the fear-department of my mind, I turned up on Saturday to play the Creek. Now Bob, the old man, hadn't spoken to me on the Friday night when I'd arrived home from work. That was okay—for those who don't follow our sophisticated game of footy, treating your opponent as if he was a carrier of the black plague or smallpox was part of the pre-game ritual. Even Mum and my brothers kept themselves aloof.

Then came the big day. After an inspiring talk from coach Jim, we burst out of the dressing shed and charged onto the ground. Little did I realise what was about to happen.

'You turncoat prick, Heard.'

'You low, Ensie piece of shit.'

'Hope some bloke knocks the crap out of ya.'

Boos and jeers came from every part of the ground. The Creek crowd were disgusted ... fortunately, some of the Ensie supporters told them to 'git stuffed', and so on. After the toss of the coin, I quickly moved to my position ... on my bloody father. No handshake, just a spit on the ground, and then some jumbled words that announced a total dislike for any Ensie bastard. Several Creek supporters I'd known for years gave the old man advice on how to take the slack out of me. The umpire raised the ball, blew his whistle, and it was on.

The crowd faded—game on. I was keen to get a kick. It had been going for ten minutes, and it was exciting even before I got my first kick; cars tooted their horns, and several girls screamed—I loved that.

By the end of the first quarter I'd managed a few more kicks, and coach Jim decided I was to be moved to centre half-forward, which was a key position—boy, that was an honour and, just quietly, I was relieved to get away from Bob's nostril-wrecking fingers.

The second quarter started. I had been in my new position for about two minutes when the football came soaring towards me from a great height—I believe our tiny league has a reputation for kicking a football higher than any other league in Australia. I braced my ten-stone frame for a screamer, then ... *thump*, *crunch*, *wallop*, and *crash*! I ended up pummelled into the ground. I could hear some swearing, and blokes mouthing off to one another. There were others pushing and grunting. My main concern was my lungs—they'd stopped working and I couldn't take in air.

I'd been the only one going for the ball, according to descriptions of the incident I heard after the game. The Creek full-back apparently had me lined up from 20 yards away; he was all of eighteen stone. Their centre half-back, a fifteen-stone thug with a gut like a poisoned pup, had me in his sights, too. Mrs O'Brien reckoned he took ages to gather full speed, but he was at peak acceleration when we collided. At the same time, our playing coach—probably the toughest bloke in the district—had this Creek bastard, who he didn't like, lined up. The bloke back-stepped, and I was hit by all three of them. Hel'ls bells—I'd been crushed to death. Vaguely, I recall several car horns tooting, and many a cheer. Apparently, it took me three goes to get me up on my feet. My only memories were a terrible taste in my mouth like rust, or rotting teeth, and sparkler flashes popping and going off like bursting stars within my vision. Then someone eventually ran out on the ground and put a mixture of dead maggots, sheep urine, one of Bob's fingers, and wombat dung under my nose. They had the gall to call it 'smelling salts'. It cleared my head, burnt my throat, and made my eyes water to the point where I had no vision.

One of the Creek blokes ran past and muttered, 'That's just for starters, ya skinny arsehole.'

Unfortunately my legs, knees, and brain would not cooperate after this near-death experience, and I had to sit down again. I remained on the ground. Suddenly, the umpire and a player pulled me up to my feet and gave me the footy. As I stood there in a haze, I quickly worked out that I hadn't taken a screamer—in fact, I'd been well and truly 'decked', as they call it. At least there was a small compensation; the umpire had awarded me a free kick. No, I didn't spin the ball in my fingers as was customary. I simply staggered backwards, as spots blinked and splashed in front of my eyes; I was in excruciating pain. But, true to male form, I gritted my teeth to hide any sign of agony. Then, just as I went to kick the ball, the umpire blew his whistle. He gestured several times, pointed behind me, and was just about to say 'play on' when Jim Mildenhall, our coach, sprinted past saying, 'Y'are facing the wrong way, ya bloody drongo, Baz.'

My 30-yard kick was pathetic, and shortly afterwards I was told to come off the ground. This was just as well, I guess, because after I'd kicked the ball, I believe I asked the bloke playing on me who I was. I have to admit I was feeling a bit groggy, but to come off the ground in the Omeo League, you had to be almost dead. Then one of our runners turned up and told me to get off, or he would kick my arse. I wearily turned, and plodded for the boundary. Yet again I had to be turned in the right direction, as I was heading for the opposition's bench.

Then there was a miracle. Like Moses parting the sea—with a staff that had his name etched on the side—it was a moment that men would be prepared to die for: the Ensie women cheered me off the ground, while even some of the Creek girls clapped quietly. Wow and strike me lucky; suddenly I was pain-free, and stood taller. However, my nose, unbeknown to the adoring crowd until I lifted my head, was pouring blood like a tap. The mountain women noticed this, and it made them cheer even louder.

Up until this stage in my life, regardless of my rugged ironbark looks and charm, I wasn't having much luck in the field of pulling chicks. Then, like Newton and his falling apple or Archimedes in his bathtub, I had a revelation: the gateway to a woman's heart is to play a *bone-crunching sport*. It was so easy to impress those fair damsels if you were seen to be suffering pain. I could have walked off that ground with two broken legs.

As I sat on the bench, I saw three girls heading in my direction. I adopted a smirk normally reserved for film stars. The girls gathered with adoring looks, and for what seemed like ages—probably 30 seconds—the applause from the Ensie supporters came freely. Many looked in my direction, saying things like 'On ya, mate' and making other familiar heroic mutterings. Suddenly, I realised I'd made it. What exactly I'd made I'm not sure, but I just knew I'd made it. I was a footballer; a local hero, maybe.

As the game went on, the three girls came really close and just looked at me. Then one of them—Susie—hinted that I was *a bit of alright*. Later, the runner reckoned that it meant she wanted to *'ave it off with me*, whatever that meant.

At half-time, Jim, the coach, wanted me to go back on. But just as we were due to trot back out, I vomited all over the floor. Consequently, I donned a dressing gown, had a bucket handed to me, and sat on the players' bench. When you did that, it meant you were finished for the day.

I went home after the game, my head spinning from the pain as well as the attention the girls had bestowed on me. I told my younger brother what Susie had said, and he replied, 'Gawd you're a drip. It means she wants to marry ya, ya dill.'

Cripes, that was a worry. Marriage was a big step. Then, to make matters worse, Mum put her head around the door. 'There's a girl, Susie, just phoned. She's coming down with her mum to see if you're alright.'

Now, this was a serious worry; I certainly wasn't ready to go steady and then to get hitched at the tender age of seventeen. No way was I going to let this Susie get her claws into me. Meanwhile, Bob and the rest of the family were ecstatic. Knowing I was very shy and had been a disaster in the courting field, they couldn't wait for Susie to turn up. I needed a plan. Therefore, ever the master of evasion or lateral thinking—thinking without lying down, that is—I decided to do a runner, and took off like a startled wood duck to the Tambo River.

Sprinting along the bank, I could see that there was a fair bit of low bush I could hide in, and even some big trees I could climb up. But then, on second thoughts, as sure as eggs, I reckoned I would be found in those places. I left the river and headed for the main road. It looked the best option. Quickly, I found a culvert under the road ... perfect. I crawled up inside. It was dark, wet, and smelly. A car arrived some 20 minutes later, and I heard Susie's mum shouting from the window.

My parents would have been horrified—Dad would be in full muttering mode very quickly. In the past, I'd heard him describe Susie's mum as 'a bit wet', 'loose', and 'as thick as a brick' (whatever that meant), so he wouldn't have been impressed. The car doors slammed. Then, as I would have expected, everybody ran around giggling and shouting. I could hear things like, 'Susie's here, lover boy' and, finally, Bob saying, 'I think the bugger's cleared off.'

They headed down towards the river, and I stayed put. After some time, the shouting jibes stopped, and threats took the place of the merriment. But I stayed put.

It was dark when I emerged from the culvert and snuck home. I didn't go inside; I just attended to my chores. Susie and her mum had left in disgust, and the dogs weren't happy about the late feed—I usually fed them just on dusk. Then it was difficult to find the milker's calf in the dark as a light fog had already descended. Finally, with all my chores completed, I went inside. That took courage. I copped a lot of smart-arse comments and snide remarks, but that was how my family handled awkward situations. I put up with the rubbishing but, believe me, it was better than getting married.

Unfortunately, the incident was the highlight of the week when it came to local rumour and hearsay. The local gossips apparently had a ball. Worse was to come. Over the next week, I vomited regularly and had a splitting headache. Naturally, I lined up for footy the following Saturday against Benambra. Looking back, I probably had concussion; but, in those days, smelling salts cured any footy injuries except for multiple broken bones and missing teeth—that required a sniff of the salts and a dash of the cheapest brandy donated from Cossie's Pub.

The next Saturday at the footy, Susie was there. I didn't see her on arrival, but word got round. I hadn't forgotten the culvert incident, but I hoped that Susie had moved on, as it were. However, within five minutes of being on the ground, above all the local cheers and abuse I heard a very high-pitched voice: 'You're a weak-kneed chicken, Heard,' bellowed Susie.

'Yeah!' echoed her squealing mates. They kept up this and similar insults all day. No, I didn't get decked or thumped that day; I managed to get very few kicks, and my efforts resulted in a lot of attention from the opposition footballers, and no cheering from the females. Consequently, although what I am about to say may seem obvious to the average, well-bred Aussie male, to army officers, politicians, and those from other countries, my advice is: gauge the amount of battering you want to receive on the footy field. Whether you get a kick or not is irrelevant. If you want to pull the chicks, get flattened. Remember, they only go stupid over pain ... it took me quite a while to recover from that heavy knock.

Benambra, as I mentioned earlier, was a cold bugger of a place in the winter. After a couple of seasons, I was enjoying playing with Ensay, and I always looked forward to playing against Benambra, even though they were 'above the Gap'. They seemed less savage than the Omeo blokes and perhaps a tad simpler. However, I hated the weather that seemed to pervade that place for eight months of the year. Most days, before the game started, kids would run onto the ground and lift all the dry, frozen cow-pads, leaving the wet or fresh ones. True to form, the Benambra blokes would run onto the ground in sleeveless sweaters. They were either tough or stupid—the latter sounds the most logical.

On one particular day, the game had been going about ten minutes when Big Pete, our rather well-built centre half-back, accidentally ran into a goal post and it snapped off at ground level. A well-meaning Benambra supporter named King slowly strolled over and volunteered to hold the post in position. Admittedly, it was a big post—probably fifteen feet tall and eight inches through at the bottom. Although this appeared a kindly, well-meaning act, in fact it enabled this bloody Benambra supporter bastard to win the game for them single-handed. Let me explain: as the game progressed, every time his team had a shot for goal, King would lean the post outwards to their advantage so that the opening would almost double in size. The umpire, even though he was aware of this foul deed, ignored the bastard. Yes, the ump knew his life would have been in danger from those inbred bushranger mongrels up there in and around Benambra if he'd opened his mouth. It's a well-known fact that the high altitude that one experiences growing up in areas like Benambra causes both intellectual stunting and cannibalism (Bob often muttered about this at home).

Nevertheless, Ensay were playing well, and perhaps our side could have overcome the distinct advantage Benambra had with the broader opening to their goal. But during the next quarter, bloody King would do the opposite when our team kicked towards its goal: he lent the post inwards, to the point where it was almost impossible to score a major, and we lost.

The ump was shouted free grog and a feed after the game that night by the victorious Benambra mob.

chapter *fifteen*

'You'll pay for this ...'

BY MY SECOND YEAR AT THE FARM IN ENSAY, I HAD WELL AND truly settled in, and I loved the job and my life generally. I became involved around the area in many activities, the first of which was with the Scouts. I recall one day after a footy game, Tom Cook came up to me and said that the Scouts needed another leader, and I was their man. Although it appeared I had little or no choice, I wandered down to the Scout Hall on the Friday night, liked what I saw, and attended every Friday night for the next three years. The kids were great—typical country larrikins, full of life, and always into mischief. We regularly went on camps, and these kids were at home in the bush.

The Scout Hall was very old and tiny. Most nights, we would have about ten or twelve kids, and the hall would be at capacity. Apart from school, it was the only thing available for boys around Ensay when it came to entertainment. Every boy attended. The scoutmaster was Big Pete.

As the year wore on, I became increasingly involved in community activities. By 1963, I was on the cricket club committee, the grounds committee, and the football social club committee … we put on a hilarious pantomime that same year. Like all locals, I'd been involved in fighting bushfires; they'd been bad that summer. However, perhaps the most intriguing of all my community involvements came about when an enterprising farmer formed a small group of volunteers to run movies. After organising the equipment, we had to have training, and then work as team, learning to overcome problems immediately—or face the wrath of an engrossed crowd—and, at times, see a bit of the show. It was a first-rate idea, and now we had our own movies at Ensay every other Saturday night in the Ensay Hall. However, the biggest problem I found when operating the projector was that I often became absorbed in the movie that was showing. Yes, I know, you've worked it out already … like the nose on your face, you could have guessed I would blow it one night, and I did. Without a doubt, it was the highlight of my brief career as a projectionist.

It all began one night when, with the lights turned off in the Ensay Hall, the show got underway. I was in charge of the first projector. As usual, there would be a lot of coughing, shuffling, and grunting in the hall during this initial period. The first film was always a short clip of Her Majesty the Queen riding side-saddle along a crowded London street. I'd set this up earlier. Everyone in the hall would stand—this was serious stuff. Up in the projectionist's room, after I had the Queen jogging off down the street, still on her horse, I turned my attention to the other projector, ready to flick it into action following the two-minute royal homage. I didn't notice that my shirt-tail had hooked in the projector as I turned.

The first indication of something going wrong was from coughs inside the hall and someone sprinting up the stairs to our little projection room. Turning, I looked through the small, square hole in the wall that enabled the operator to watch the screen. Oh dear. The Queen was jerking up and down in a way that looked like either she or her horse was having an epileptic fit. Worse, Her Royal Highness suddenly froze, buckled, and then distorted before melting in front of the entire audience ... there were gasps, small squeals, a little laughter, and many tuts. Finally, the screen only showed folds of black smoke. I had murdered Her Majesty.

Actually, the reel had jammed ... poor monarch. There was panic in the tiny room, and it took fifteen minutes to repair the projector. I wonder how many kids had nightmares that night. It's strange but, after that small incident, I was relieved of my projector duties, and instead was asked to work in the hall canteen selling sweets before the movies and at intervals.

I HAD ALSO TURNED EIGHTEEN in 1963. This meant I could get my driver's licence and use the family car. Owning my own car was out of the question; in fact, most young men of my age simply couldn't afford one. However, I did upgrade to other modes of transport during those early years at Ensay. This came about gradually. As mentioned earlier, when I first started work on the farm I rode Sandy Mac. To put it plainly, he was a slack horse. The boss referred to him as 'docile'. To his credit, I always thought that this horse was on a mission: he wanted an early retirement.

Almost six months to the day that I'd started work at Ensay, I made a decision. It was after a tiring, Monday stroll to work with this damn horse demanding a snack every fifteen minutes. It was time to modernise; to speed things up a bit. So I pensioned off Sandy Mac, a good kid's horse, and I got some wheels.

Updating to a gleaming, second-hand pushbike was thrilling. It hummed along the partially sealed road, and I used less energy pedalling it than I did when riding Sandy Mac. The bike was a 28-inch fixed-wheel Malvern Star. Thirty minutes was all that it took to get to work on Monday mornings;

then 20 minutes to come home on Friday afternoons. Going to work was very hard at first. The journey included a long, uphill drudge that made my calf muscles twitch with protest. Connor's Hill added the extra ten minutes to the journey. It wasn't steep, but it was a steadily increasing climb, about a mile and a half long. The hill led you up, out of the Tambo Valley, and into the Ensay area. There were times when I considered dropping off Rover, my dog, and making him run beside the bike. But after I gathered a rhythm by counting to myself, Rover would sit quietly on the bar between the seat and the handlebars, listening to the transistor radio.

Yes, I was now proud to own a pint-sized radio that had taken three weeks' wages to buy. It was my first gift to myself. As a rule, the radio reception would be reasonable as I pedalled to work—until we hit that bloody long climb, that is. The damn radio reception would disappear when I rode into cuttings while climbing Connor's Hill. Rover, annoyed at the loss of sound, would pat my hand firmly with his paw. He enjoyed the radio. However, once out of the cutting, the radio would come back on and he would thump my tummy with his tail as a sign of approval. Then it was downhill all the way to work. However, sometimes I would stop and simply admire the spectacular view from the top of Connor's Hill—it was beautiful.

By comparison, going home on the bike after the week's work on a Friday night was a joy. At the top of Connor's Hill, both Rover and I would lower our heads over the handlebars, narrow our eyes, and then, like a rodeo rider, I would lift my legs in the air to avoid the spinning pedals—the curse of the fixed-wheel bike—and away we'd go. Once we reached full speed, the only complaint I had about this thrilling experience involved Rover's tongue. The bloody thing flapped up and down, and flicked warm drool all over my face. However, that didn't stop the laughter and shouts of, 'Hi-ho Silver! Away!'

and 'Steady big fella, steady.' Both sayings I got from my Lone Ranger 78 r.p.m. vinyl record, which starred my hero, the Lone Ranger, and his Indian friend, Tonto. Silver was the Lone Ranger's trusty horse. I'd also seen movies of them both at the afternoon matinees in Ringwood.

Back to the downhill bike ride ... Occasionally, the bike would get up so much speed it developed the wobbles, particularly if I had to swerve to avoid a pothole or something on the road. I might add that this fixed-wheel bike had no brakes, other than by putting my boot on the tyre at the front—mind you, I rarely used this sophisticated method, as I got a fright one time when smoke started to pour from under my boot. No matter, Rover and I would sool down the hill so fast that at the bottom I wouldn't have to peddle for the next half a mile. I believe we must have got up to speeds of 20 to 30 miles per hour.

This was highlighted one evening on the way home. Rover and I were in our low-profile positions, and the bike was simply humming. We shot through the first cutting and came around the slow curve when I spotted the Lands Department truck inching along. It was returning to the work depot at Swifts Creek after the crew had spent the week spraying weeds on the roadside down Ensay way. The sedate speed of the truck was a compliment to Tom, the driver. It ensured they would arrive at the depot exactly at five o'clock—knock-off time—and, boy, they were really crawling along. This would be fun. Tom, like many country drivers, didn't use the rear-view mirror very much. Traffic was a rare thing on the road in those days, and overtaking was almost unheard of. Therefore, the habit of checking out what was behind you as you were driving was never a required skill.

On this particular evening, with the bike hurtling along at just below wobble-inducing speed, I explained the plan to Rover. I didn't want balance to become a problem (I'm almost sure the dog understood), so both Rover and I lowered our heads even further. As I approached the vehicle, I tried not to giggle—this would be a real hoot. As I shot past the truck, I shouted, 'Up the mighty Bombers!' followed by, 'Creek bastards!'. That was only fair, as Tom and one of the other occupants in the truck were Swift Creek footballers. Then Rover ... well, naturally, he barked in approval. Tom got a hell of a fright. I could just hear him shouting abuse as I sizzled past on the mighty Malvern Star, my fist punching the air.

The next day at the footy, Bill, an Ensie supporter, told me I'd 'frightened the crap out 'uv 'em'. The story of me roaring past the Lands Department truck became a highlight of the night at the Albion Hotel in Swifts Creek. Apparently, poor Tom had hit the brakes when he'd first heard my yells. With that, the truck jerked and Cliff, in the middle, hit his chin on the dashboard and stubbed out his cigarette. Meanwhile, Les, the other worker, spat out his false teeth in fright. They reckoned I was doing 45 miles per hour ... Come on ... but how slow was the truck going? I loved that pushbike, and so did Rover.

There was no doubt that stepping up to faster transport after Sandy Mac was a bonus. I was home earlier and enjoyed the freedom of the bike. There were some drawbacks, of course. Punctures, loose gravel, and swooping magpies I could tolerate. But one morning I suffered the curse of the fixed-wheel bike ... again.

Be warned: some Aussie men might want to skip the next page.

Like most eager but over-enthusiastic young men of my era, I'd caused myself severe physical pain at times due to having dumb accidents—to this day, my wife reckons nothing's changed. Once, for example, I tried lassoing my first steer, and got dragged 200 yards up the paddock. Then, of course, there was Swanee and his tests of my manhood. However, if you measure pain by how long your eyes water, an incident that occurred while I was riding my Malvern Star to work one morning took the record.

It was Monday. Rover and I had just started to climb Connor's Hill. It was a cold and frosty winter morning, there was a headwind, and I had on a balaclava and a thick jumper. Rising out of the saddle, my skinny legs were pushing the pedals like mad while Rover's head was swaying side to side with the bike. Suddenly, with a jerk, my pants caught in the chain sprocket. The pedal slammed the back of my leg, Rover leapt off, and my family jewels slammed down on the bar. Both my agates shot up into my stomach and dinged around like a pinball machine as I flew off the bike. Rolling around on the dirt clutching my crotch, I wondered if I'd become a eunuch.

When I went to get up, I realised the bike was still a part of me. Gingerly, I wound my pants back through the chain sprocket, then sat on the side of the road while tears softly rolled down my cheeks. This was far worse than the bow-legged pommel treatment. Then it dawned on me, I would be there for quite a while—walking was out of the question. Sitting in gloom, I decided that my days of bike riding were definitely over. Luckily, after a 20-minute wait, Mick Bryce, a local farmer, came along and gave me a lift to work. He flinched when I told him what had happened; then, gritting his teeth, he told me his story. Yes, most men have a story of crushed nuts, which they tell while gritting their teeth.

Later that week, I sold the bike to a schoolkid. 'Good bike, mate,' I assured him, and went back to riding that bloody pensioned-off horse, Sandy Mac—boy, was he browned off when I threw the reins over his head and swung the saddle up onto his back. Rover wasn't happy, either; he had to run to work. Fortunately, the agony of riding Sandy Mac only lasted two weeks.

As luck would have it, there'd been talk around the district about a city bloke who'd had a motorbike accident. It had happened just up the road from us at Reid's Corner. The story went along the lines of: new motorbike, gravel road, inexperienced rider, mug from the big smoke. *Tut, tut* were the comments from the local old bikers, and there were plenty of them.

Our local mechanic, Victor (the owner of the sporting .303 rifle), had repaired the bike and it was now for sale. It was a Super Bantam B.S.A.—quite a classy bike, they reckoned. After a chat with Vic, I was convinced. A fair price was set, and I had just enough money in the bank to pay for it. Vic seemed thrilled to welcome another biker into the fold. I had no idea how to ride the bike but Vic, a good rider, gave me a quick lesson. He pointed out the clutch, the throttle, the brakes, and the kick-start, and everything I needed to know about fuel—it was a two-stroke, and that was the end of the technical lessons. He then did a wheelie, skidded in a circle, and spluttered some riding instructions. This took all of ten minutes. Every other word he uttered cursed the lord, or contained the sort of foul profanities usually saved for the footy … sometimes aimed at me—Vic was one of the Creek's most ardent supporters. I was pleased to get away, assuring him that I would follow all of his instructions carefully when, in fact, I didn't have a bloody clue.

At first, I rode the motorbike very slowly, finding where the brakes, gears, and other essential stuff were located. Gradually I gained a little experience and heaps of confidence. I rode it the whole of that first weekend and then put a very wary Rover on the fuel tank, and headed for work on the Monday. We made it in good time and without a hitch. What an excitement machine. It was such a thrill to ride it. I did even more shouting, laughing, and whooping while Rover barked and howled with enthusiasm. Slowly, I turned into a maniac. It was based on a simple formula, which still applies today—all you need is a

ton of confidence, some skill, and no concept of the potential
dangers you're subjecting yourself to. Naturally, you have to be
male and in your late teens. Then, given an audience, a maniac
turns into a complete, suicidal moron—yes, I was prepared to
jump at any dare with gusto. Just read on ...

By now, about three months after having bought the
motorbike, I considered myself totally skilled in riding it. On
this occasion, I'd ridden home with Rover on a Friday night
from Ensay, in probably a record time, because I was on a
Christmas holiday break.

The next day, a stinking summer's day, I'd just returned
home from the bush block with Bob. In the distance, from the
house at Doctors Flat, I could hear shouting, frivolity, and fun.
It came from just up the road from home; there was a group
of people enjoying the river. I knew there'd be young people
my age who I'd grown up with, adults from the town, and
many local farm kids who rode, or had walked, to the pool.
The swimming hole was a popular spot known as 'Wilson's
Waterhole'. It was quite deep and wide, and probably the best
swimming place in the Tambo River that was close to the small
township of Swifts Creek. Just below Wilson's hole was a river
crossing, 40 yards across and about two feet deep.

After a hard day's work, it took little for me to convince
myself that a swim would be fun. I pocketed my bathers, and
rode my motorbike up to the pool. There was a clump of brush
near the pool we used for changing. Naturally, I couldn't just
ride up, then go behind the dense melaleuca and change. To the
swimmers' delight, I stopped the bike with a cool 360-degree
spinning skid on the green grass near the waterhole. It drew a
crowd, and in no time there was a mob admiring the bike—my
Super Bantam with a 175cc engine, which I kept polished. It
was only four-and-a-bit months old—good as new, apart from
a few repairs. Great, this was it: being one of only two local
youngsters who owned a motorbike (George Gallagher had a

250cc Honda), I was the star for the day.

One of the local girls had a girlfriend up from Melbourne. She said, 'I saw Steve McQueen, you know, in a movie, you know, and he, you know, tore right through this river, you know. Sorta like across just here like.'

I gave that silent, John Wayne pause. 'That'd be easy,' I said, swaggering towards the bike and brushing imaginary dust off my new leather coat. I kick-started the Bantam and went back about 100 yards from the river. Turning and lowering my head, I then started my death-defying feat. Throttling through the gears as fast as I could, I punched my fist in the air and sucked in the cheers and screams of the audience—which was a total of maybe ten people. I reckon I hit the water at 35 miles per hour. *Crunch!* The bike went about four feet into the water and stopped dead as if it had hit a brick wall. I shot over the handlebars and surfed the entire width of the river. My head jammed into the muddy bank on the other side. The gang clapped and yelled, 'Do it again!'

No way—my neck had almost disappeared into my chest. The only sign of the motorbike was a handlebar protruding out of the water. Without a word, I walked through the Tambo River fully clothed, and retrieved the Bantam. By the time I had it on dry land, there were more than a few heckles and wisecrack comments being directed at me. It took me 20 minutes along the side of the road to get home, pushing the poor Bantam, and then hours to get it going again. My parents weren't impressed, and words like 'idiot' and 'complete fool' flowed freely every time they came up to the shed. The only friend I appeared to have was Rover. He sat quietly, looking wisely at the bike. Thank God I hadn't taken him with me.

However, incidents like this soon faded, and they never dented my confidence. As I mentioned, riding to work on Monday was awesome. There was no peddling involved—I'd just hang on. It was always a quick trip, and Rover loved it.

The throttle would be jammed on flat out the whole way. Soon, I started to use the Bantam instead of the horse in the paddock at work. This was difficult if the grass was damp, and I came off a couple of times. The green, wet grass made braking almost impossible and, when mixed with fresh cow manure and a maniacal speed, it made staying on very difficult. True to form, I persisted.

On the farm at Ensay, like on any farm, there were routine jobs to do. For instance, just on dusk, after work, it was time to gather the eggs, feed the chooks and dogs, lock up the milking cow's calf, and throw some hay to the bulls. One evening in April, I set off to do my jobs; by now, the milker's calf was quite big and almost ready to wean. When it came to the milker and her calf, it was a simple routine. Come evening, after opening the gates, I'd cross the paddock, round up the calf and mother on foot, and return to the milking yard. Then, with the calf separated from its mother for the night, I'd return the milker to her paddock. This meant that the next morning the cow would have a full udder and would be milked, and the calf would be released. It wasn't worth catching the horse to muster the cow and calf so, most late afternoons, as I walked up the paddock, the cheeky calf would run away in defiance as soon as it spotted me. That is, save for this one night. As I strolled across the paddock to retrieve the calf, in a burst of welcome intellect I hit upon an idea. *Right*, I thought, *I'll teach ya, ya dopey beggar.*

I went back to the shed and got my mean machine—the Super Bantam. After a single, mighty pump kick, the Bantam roared into action. I did my Steve McQueen 360-degree spin, and headed down the paddock with Rover on the fuel tank as an observer. The cow stared at me in total horror and alarm while her calf took off. He had a look of fear in his eyes. I sizzled and weaved daringly between large lumps of dung. The calf's tail was in the air as he raced off to the far corner while his mother Sarah, the milker, bellowed in fright. Naturally, the calf was no match for the Bantam. Screwing the throttle tightly, I got beside him in no time. Rover let out a short, sharp bark and leapt off. Then I decided to do a 360 in front of the calf. Well, the skid didn't go quite to plan, and things got a bit hairy. The bike slid sideways, and I buried my head straight into the calf's flank—a sort of full-on head butt. The calf went down, and lay on the ground bellowing. I ended up beside it making loud groaning noises. The milker, her tongue out and frothing at the mouth, roared in my ear. The bike did several spins on its side while blowing blue smoke into the air and tearing the paint off the fuel tank. Bloody Rover, who always seemed to go unscathed through many a hair-raising prank with me, sounded off with the bark he had that I was sure was a laugh.

The calf was the first one up, and made a frenzied dash up the paddock. I got up gingerly, undamaged, but the bike was badly wounded: it had a broken throttle, a bent mirror, a twisted foot-brake, and dirt jammed in the engine. It was dark by the time I got everything finished, and the calf was still panting with fear. Thankfully, the boss came home late and had no idea of what a crazy day I'd had. I tried as hard as I could not to limp inside the house at teatime. They couldn't see the huge bruise on my left thigh, and I hoped they wouldn't comment on my shortened neck. However, the next morning the boss was suspicious, as the cow gave no milk.

Over the next year I became a skilled rider, but that's only my opinion. Winter was approaching, and the fun of riding a motorbike was fast fading. Heavy frosts, frozen puddles, and slicing, cold winds were the norm. Even the short ride from home to work made my hands ache, my ears ring, and my nose burn. Wearing gloves made little difference; mind you, they were only knitted ones, and didn't stop the biting wind. To combat the cold, I worked on two alternative approaches:

1. I could ride slowly, but I would end up frozen to the bone. If I putted along at a sedate pace it meant that, once I arrived at work, it would take half an hour of hard physical work to thaw out.

Or

2. I could go as close to flat out as possible, only slowing down for known ice spots or large puddles. This was more to my liking, but I had to put Rover in a sack. It was so bloody cold that, while riding, I would have just enough movement in my hands to apply the brake. As a result, I would arrive at work in no time, but my poor hands would be blue, and aching as if they had a severe burn. I would dismount like an old man of eighty. Then, holding my hands in front of me like a zombie sleepwalking, I would head for the nearest garden tap. Awkwardly, I would turn it on with my elbows and rinse my hands under the cold water; slowly, gradually, I could stretch and squeeze them into some form of movement. The thawing-out process would take fifteen minutes.

You might ask why I didn't go into the warm kitchen in the homestead. To be perfectly honest, I was so damn cold I couldn't have opened the kitchen door or even talked. Further, I knew the boss's wife would have scolded me for being such a bloody idiot.

When both modes of getting to work were analysed, method two was the winner—it was more fun. But I reckoned Rover preferred number one.

AS I'VE MENTIONED several times, growing up in a remote area carried with it certain rituals and obligations. If you were male and could walk without the aid of a white cane, you played footy. If you owned sandshoes, you played cricket. Being able to write meant a stint on one or more committees that ran sporting clubs, and similar organisations. Without such institutionalised conventions, sporting clubs, fire brigades, and the like would not have survived. Becoming involved helped maintain a close-knit community. It was important in the country where I lived, but it appeared to be missing in cities from my experience in later years.

As a result of my obligations to various committees and working bees, the Bantam started to take us—yes, Rover was normally a constant companion—on longer trips. On Friday evenings after work, I would shower and change into my shorts and Scout uniform, and ride to the Scout Hall. Rover would sleep under the bike, or come inside if it was raining. The small, timber Scout Hall was just up the road from the Ensay pub. For most of the young boys in the district, Scouts was the only activity away from school. They came from everywhere, and their dads would deliver them to the hall and then retire to the pub. I was scoutmaster of the Ensay Troop, along with Big Pete Duggan, a local wool-presser-come-handyman-and-fuel-deliveryman. You have never seen a more unlikely pair. I was skinny, young, and a couple of years older than the Scouts. Big Pete was big, had a squeaky voice, and would have preferred this time on Friday spent in the pub. But, like me, he had a duty to perform. Mind you, the cunning blighter would tell his wife that we finished Scouts at 9.30 p.m. when in fact it was 8.30 p.m. This gave Big Pete an extra hour's drinking time, as we would adjourn with haste to the pub after honouring the Queen and lowering the flag.

On arrival at Cossie's bar, most of the dads would be suitably primed, and they usually inquired of their sons, 'Wotdidya learn tonight?' The sons would reply, 'Aw, heaps, like knots'n stuff, you know.' Funny, every Friday night there were the same questions—and the same answers.

Years later, I was well informed that the Scouts had also

learnt how to swear, roll smokes, and swap gossip about girls—and I thought they would have at least learnt some bushcraft. Maybe I failed there. They were typical country larrikins, these young boys. Their main source of entertainment during Scouts was having fun with my damn motorbike. They hid it in a variety of places—behind trees, over the bank—and I believe Rover was party to these shenanigans. Rarely did the little beggars fool me. Most nights it took me only ten minutes or so to locate the bike. Any longer, and Rover would take over and stroll to the Bantam.

However, one night I had to take my hat off to them. Normally, the hideouts for the Bantam were behind the Scout Hall or down near the creek, just over the bank. This particular night, I couldn't find the damn thing. I'd just about given up when, for some reason, I was enticed to look upwards. Maybe it was Rover, turning in a circle, looking up and barking. Perhaps it was the creaking, groaning noise that the bike was making as it swung a good fifteen feet off the ground in the huge gum tree. We all had a laugh and lowered the rope. Two of the lads boasted that the feat had been achieved because of the new knot I'd taught them—the sheepshank. The little blighters.

The first time I rode the Bantam out to Dorrington's farm on Sheepstation Creek was a hoot. With its broken exhaust, the bike sounded like a low-flying jet as I sped through the bush. We arrived at the Five Acres in no time. I'd decided on the Bantam instead of Sandy Mac because, that day, I was on a mission to find our bunch of missing poddies, which hadn't been seen for several years. I think the last time I'd spotted Mary-Anne and her woolly mates was when I'd first ventured up to Mad Lucy's rock, and Skipper the dog had chased them away. The weekend before, I'd found some sheep droppings below the cabin, down near the creek.

On arrival at the Five Acres, I put the bike on its stand in the shade. Over-heating was always a problem on the Bantam — in rough terrain, if I stayed in a low gear for too long, the engine would get so hot that it almost burnt my legs. When I planned this venture, I reckoned I could ride it for roughly 25 minutes in the bush before I'd have to let it cool down, so I wasn't surprised that it was still quite hot from the trip out. Rover and I headed down to the cool of the willows for a drink.

The sheep dung, now a lot dryer, was still there. I showed the droppings to Rover. Now, I admit I had the highest regard for this dog; however, this was a big ask. He sniffed the droppings briefly, looked around for a bit, then had a swim in the small pool just below the Five Acre gate. I decided to cast him out there, somewhere.

'Rover! Here, boy. Go way, away, away out.' I waved my arm in a big circle. He jumped, spun around, looked at me quizzically, and stood still. He didn't know where to go. Neither did I. I repeated the command. This time, he ran off. I sat in the shade and waited. Apart from trying to get Rover to find the poddies, my other plan was to ride around in the bush — that's if he came back without them. I waited.

The bike took my interest. Looking at it, I wondered if I could put a big cog on the back wheel. She could really climb then. But maybe … yeah, not enough air around and through the motor … she'd get really hot. I got up, and went for a walk.

Still no Rover and no poddies. I waited.

In fact, even before I'd headed out on this venture, Gator Lambourne had told me that you couldn't muster poddies. He reckoned they don't act like normal sheep; they just run off in all directions. They were only good for eating — stupid, bloody things. Perhaps the old bloke was right. Over half an hour had passed …

Then there was a bark in the distance. Walking back up the bank, I looked … nothing. Another low bark … and there he was, that beautiful, remarkable dog. He walked quietly towards me. I whistled, but he ignored it. As I went to whistle again, there, about 20 yards behind Rover, who was wandering slowly in my direction, were the poddies. Mary-Anne approached me warily. My God, what a sight. I didn't recognise her. She looked like a huge ball of matted wool with two eyes half-hidden under a large flap. After a pat, she walked down to the creek and had a drink, with the other four following her. Both Rover and I stared at these sheep for ages. They were huge. Apart from the tips of their noses and the bottoms of their feet, enormous bundles of fleece smothered their bodies. If I recall, Mary-Anne had never been shorn. She must have been six years old now. I had to take them home, to Doctors Flat. What was I to do now? I hadn't thought about that.

So, as had happened all that time ago, when I'd first brought Mary-Anne and her mates out to the Five Acres by walking in front and them following me, I walked back home, very slowly. It was like a circus: Rover at my heels, Mary-Anne and co. right behind him. We went back and got the Bantam later on.

It was a lot of trouble to shear them. Their wool was stained and dirty, and their skin was very soft and pink. Try as I did, they still ended up with quite a few cuts. I was worried they'd get sunburnt; but, no, they simply rested, and enjoyed the notoriety and affection as they lay quietly under the willows at Doctors Flat.

BY NOW, I'd been riding the bike for over two years. I'd come off more times than I could remember but, thankfully, it was always on the farm. I admit that I drove flat out on the road, but the mainly sealed surface ensured much better traction, and I never looked like having a spill ... until one particular night.

It was summer. After finishing Scouts and having some fun at Cossie's, I mounted the Bantam ready for the 20-minute trip home. The summers in the mountainous high country of far-eastern Victoria have long days, and it can be twilight until 10.00 p.m. Riding the bike at this time of the year was ecstasy. I often made loud whooping noises at the joy, exhilaration, and freedom that the motorbike seemed to offer. This night, I stopped at my work on the way home and picked up a happy Rover. He'd had a hard day, and wanted a good rest. Like me, my dog appeared to love the warm weather, the thrill of the bike, and my antics as well.

We were about halfway down Connor's Hill, and the bike was flat out when ... *whack!* Someone had shot me with what felt like a twelve-gauge shotgun, front on. There were pellets in my forehead, up my nostrils, in my mouth, and in my neck and ears. My hair was matted with hard lumps of something, and a quick wipe of my face produced a handful of blood. Hell! I veered off the road and crunched to a stop in the dirt gutter. Rover leapt off in disgust, but he seemed to have kept out of the firing line. Badly wounded, I sat and inspected the extent of the damage.

First, though, a small point of clarification: it wasn't a shotgun; it was a swarm of Christmas beetles. These little golden bastards, each about the size of a Mintie, have an outer shell, or body, that is brilliantly coloured and hard—like a lump of steel. They'd been hovering just above the road in a swarm. I'd blasted into them and, in turn, they'd ripped into my body. The result? It looked like a deranged mountain cat had attacked me. On second thoughts, it was worse than that. Half the bloody beetles, still hooked in my body, were wriggling to get out. Covered in minute spurs, their little tough legs had penetrated my face, clothes, and so on. They weren't having much luck escaping. Most were well and truly implanted into my skin. Jesus—that was all I could say, or tried to say, as it dawned on me that I had about a dozen of the little beggars in my mouth. I spat and coughed most of them away, and hooked the rest out with a finger. Rover didn't have a single one on him, but he wasn't impressed with my forced landing.

Half an hour later, with most of the beetles plucked from my body, and with my sanity back, I mounted the Bantam. A very wary sheepdog clambered back onto the fuel tank. We rode at a sedate, sensible speed the remainder of the way home. I wandered into the lounge room still pitted and blood-splattered. Unbeknown to me, I still had some beetles in my hair and clinging to my back. My damn family thought I looked hilarious—it was a bad night all round, really.

However, wisdom comes with age, as farmer Jack Campbell, our old World War I Gallipoli veteran who lived up the road, would say. Whatever the saying, I guess after that incident I gained a little insight into motorbike riding—particularly just on dusk. I slowed to a very moderate speed whenever I rode at that time of night ... for a while anyway. Then, one day, I thought, *This is no damn good ... surely there has to be a solution.* I visited Victor, the .303 man and the mad biker. Within a week, I had a helmet, goggles, and a windscreen attached with U-bolts to the handlebars on the front of the bike. Beauty—that meant we could go flat out again. By the look on Rover's face after my first short trial-run and the length of his tongue dangling out, he approved as well. The only difference I noticed was that the bike went a bit more slowly. Then again, I never wound her right up, either ... I thought I'd do that on the Monday when we returned to work.

That day, after a hearty breakfast, I donned all my safety gear, and we tore off to work early. It was a breeze with a new amour-plated, beetle-proof motorbike purring calmly up Connor's Hill. Then, over the top, I thought, *Now's my chance.* I wound the throttle down hard, and we slowly accelerated to flat out. I was amazed at the amount of wind that the windscreen deflected; I guessed Rover was impressed as well. We were almost flat out when ... *thump.* The U-bolts holding the bloody windscreen had collapsed. It slammed forward and down on my good mate Rover, pushed me onto the rear seat, and lodged itself in my guts. Hell, I could barely reach the handlebars. Stretching, like someone trying to moor a boat at a jetty, I somehow managed to stop the Bantam. Yet again, I was in pain. This was worse than the beetle fiasco … in fact, it almost topped the crushed nuts. Lifting my clothes and inspecting my poor tummy, a bruise appeared there almost immediately—as if someone had painted a long, black band across it. Worse was to come. After I dislodged my poor old mate Rover from under the windscreen … well, let's just say that he spat the dummy completely. He just stood there and barked at me. I apologised, tried the usual warm, fuzzy words and pats, but he was angry—very browned off, to say the least. I just couldn't get him back on the bike.

Decision time. I left the bloody Bantam and we walked to the farm … late again. Slowly, the Bantam started to wear out. No matter. When I rode in the paddocks, prangs—followed by a long, limping walk back to the shed—continued, as did the constant repairs. However, I did slow down considerably on the open road. I guess a change of attitude was required, as Rover was a wary passenger until I convinced him I had gained a little maturity and skill as a driver.

THE FUN AND CAMARADERIE that goes with sport had always been a large part of my youth. Even in a remote country area like Far East Gippsland, there were many different sports to take part in. After I got the Bantam, I was able to travel some distance in the evenings. In the winter, I played footy and badminton. Footy was the best fun; I preferred the forward line, as you had a chance to kick a goal. Badminton was completely different. It was another popular winter sport, usually played in the local hall. On completion of the evening's competition, there would be a generous supper and a cup of tea. This was totally the opposite of the footy, where beer and hot pies were the preferred choice. Also, in the hall on badminton nights, apart from the players, there was no crowd on the sidelines hurling abuse or adoration, no jockstraps for the men to adjust, and rarely, if ever, would you receive a life-threatening injury—although I must admit, one night I came horribly close.

It was mid-winter. We were playing Omeo in the Ensay Hall. Most games consisted of singles, doubles, and mixed doubles. The mixed doubles were my favourite. In those games, the woman played in the centre of the court near the net; the bloke, up the back. Now, unlike footy, badminton players were not required to wear a uniform—just something white, as a rule. Some blokes wore long pants, and the women, short skirts. Of interest were the women's undergarments, or knickers. You always got a good gander at them when they bent over or reached for the shuttle. They were all frilly looking—like a good head of cauliflower. Being a modest bloke, I have to admit I enjoyed glimpsing the fluffy panties of the opposite sex. They lifted the pulse-rate somewhat.

This night I was playing with Ethel Hartman, a local lass. She was a well-proportioned, alluring female of courting age. To put it simply, I had the hots for her. Most nights I could ply my smooth charm and gain a few points, but this night I had to be cool because Ethel's parents were there. I might add that they were there not to barrack, but to keep their eyes on loose-pizzled buggers like me—Fred Hartman said this several times while I was within earshot.

I was on my best behaviour during the first game. Ethel and I were two points up, and it was my serve. I belted the shuttle to the back service-line. The return, just over the net, was fast. I bent over and returned a powerful, low, penetrating shot. It hit poor Ethel fair in the quoit—her rear, backside, rectum, bum, call it what you want. The bloody shuttle not only thwacked into her bum, but the damn thing stuck in her frilly knickers. Not realising this, poor Ethel looked around for the shuttle, while giggles started to arise in the small crowd. Then, trust bloody Gus Krusp, he had to open his stupid bloody mouth. A rough bugger at the best of times, and from above the Gap, his stockman's tongue took over. He turned to Ethel and said, 'It's stuck in ya bloody arse, Ethel.'

Jesus, they're crude blighters, those Omeo buggers. Poor Ethel. She cleared out, and I, like a damn fool, burst out laughing. Most of the others did, too, but Ethel's dad leapt to his feet. He wasn't impressed. He offered to punch my bloody lights out, and he was serious. I should add here that bloody Fred, Ethel's dad, was a cranky bastard at the best of times. He took a swing at me, fell arse overhead—I forgot to mention, he was warmly primed with the amber fluid—and hit the pole that held the net up, which fell and hit Mrs Hartman on the head. She grabbed a racket and smashed poor Fred so hard on the skull it drew blood and bent the racket. Rubbing his scone, silly damn Fred then turned to me and blurted, 'You'll pay for this, you dirty little worm.' Then he staggered out, pushing young Ethel in front of him with Mrs Fred in tow. She glared at me with flame-throwing eyes, and then strutted outside. To top it off, I think those ugly Omeo buggers beat us.

MY LIFE ON THE FARM and at Ensay just seemed to get better. Rarely did I think it was time to spread my horizons—to leave the farm or the district, or to look for a change. To be honest, I was basically very content, although I was always hankering for a girlfriend. Absurdly, whenever I had a rush of blood and tried to impress the opposite sex or put out some vibes, something always went wrong. For some reason, when it came to courting, I could be best described as immature, mindless, and a dill. Sadly, I have even more examples than those I've already quoted. Of all places, it once happened while I was droving cattle with my two mates, Rover and Swanee.

I'd been working on the farm for over a year when, just before the annual cattle sales, I was offered a trip droving cattle from the high country to the railhead at Bairnsdale. Great—this was every young farmhand's dream. I waited eagerly for the sales to begin. Being the early 1960s, the local roads had little traffic. At the end of each sale, the drovers would collect the calves, tightly move them onto the road or track, and head for the next sale. The first sale was always at Benambra, and the first few days would see the calves very edgy, as things were very hectic. There was a lot of demand on the drovers to keep them in tow. As the mob got bigger, the original calves became quite placid and, within a day of the sale, most of the calves started to settle.

This year when I joined the drovers, my job was to tend to the packhorse as well as to escort cars through the mob. Local drivers were no problem. They followed behind my horse and obeyed my instructions. Strangers, though—city people, I guessed—were different. They were often impatient, and tried to force their own way through by tooting their horns or thumping the side of their cars. This would spook the calves and create little stampedes and panic. I have seen a car surrounded by wary-eyed calves that, when the driver tooted, suddenly kicked out, jumped, and put many a minor dint in the car. Then there were those drivers and passengers who were awestruck at witnessing this almost bygone age of droving. They would get out of their cars and want to talk to the drovers, or pat the horse or dog. I often found myself the photographic subject of these people. When it came to me, I would casually push the hat back on my head, and then, without warning, crack the stockwhip for the camera. My only regrets were that I hadn't started shaving and I wasn't a smoker—I would have looked better with a rough bristle, and a rollie hanging from the lip would have set the scene, I reckon … just like in a cowboy western I'd seen at the movies.

That Sunday, I was about to direct a local car through the mob when I noticed a nubile-looking beauty sitting in the front of a car next to Les Copper, who was a bachelor from Reedy Creek. Les stopped the old Austin ute and introduced the stunning beauty.

'Baz, this 'ere's Beryl. She'll be working on tha switchboard at Hensie North, mate. She's me niece.'

Gulping and lifting my Stetson, I made a really dumb reply: 'G'day, I'm a drover.'

Beryl didn't giggle; she gasped with wonder. Great. I found my composure quickly. Pushing my hat back again, I gave my best smirk and lent on the pommel of the saddle as the film stars do.

Beryl then asked, 'Can I please take your photo, Baz?'

'Sure.'

My brain snapped into moron mode and I thought, *Great, she's fallen for me already*. I noticed a steep bank on the other side of the road. I reckoned Swanee could dash up this bank in one stride while I cracked the whip with that charming smirk on my face during the entire manoeuvre. So, naturally, I told Beryl she could get a good snap of me leaping up the bank and cracking my stockwhip at the same time.

Les commented, 'You be careful, Baz. That bank's pretty bloody steep, mate.'

Great—thanks, Les, mate. That puts me into hero-come-dare-devil status, I thought. I beamed with pride, and retained that heart-melting smirk on my dial. I released the reins slightly and, as I expected, Swanee surged effortlessly up the incline. As he did, I flung back my ten-foot plaited stockman's whip and lashed it forward. It normally produced a loud, resounding *crack!*

Next thing I know, *crunch* … I'm on my arse, Swanee's bolted, and Rover's sitting, bewildered, with a bloody curious look on his ugly dial. Later that week, Les told me he reckoned Rover actually smiled while shaking his head. What happened? Well, how was I to notice the bloody telephone lines overhead? The damn whip wrapped itself around the wires, I kept hanging on—as was my pig-headed wont—and, bingo, Baz was on his arse. Meanwhile, Beryl was having a fit of the bloody giggles. Les shook his head, called me 'a bloody rabbit', and drove off.

chapter sixteen
Coming of age

THE BIGGEST CHANGE IN MY SOCIAL LIFE CAME ABOUT WHEN the Young Farmers organisation became popular. It was relatively new. At the time, clubs were forming all over Gippsland. This changed many young people, particularly those from remote areas like the Omeo Shire. At our first formal meeting, one of my bosses became the new president, and I became the secretary. Tambo Valley Young Farmers became our new club name.

The new task of secretary took up a lot of my time after work on the farm. I corresponded with over a dozen clubs, and over the years visited them all. Any correspondence was by hand, with a carbon backing to record a copy.

It was a unique organisation in that it was more than just social. Meetings offered a lot of variety. There were debating teams, public-speaking competitions, information nights, and presenters. There was the opportunity to do cattle and sheep judging—even at the Melbourne Show. Every club had to follow a meeting protocol and procedure that put me in good stead for the rest of my life. Socially, it was like a dream come true. There were dances, hayrides on trailers, and woolshed dances, and most important of all were the Young Farmers' Balls. They were the highlight of the year, and every club supported each other. This meant huge crowds attended. Looking back at that special era, something else now stands out. There was no alcohol. Never at a Young Farmers function did I see alcohol served or drunk. Admittedly, many were under the drinking age of 21, but it was never an issue. I find that fascinating, considering attitudes today.

Most of all, I liked the Young Farmers' dances. You could hold your partner and talk. Bands were always live, and they usually played a mixture of ballroom and a little rock-and-roll. The camaraderie between the sexes was great … we were all just good mates. Yes, relationships did develop, but often people just became mates regardless of gender. Not only did I cherish the innocence of my growing up in that era; I felt that the Young Farmers organisation was simply the icing on the cake.

However, 1964 was a year of change for me in many ways. Getting a motorbike and car licence, and going to Young Farmers events, meant I started to travel the Gippsland area, mostly attending meetings and dances. These experiences allowed me to mature, as I had a lot more responsibility in that organisation than I'd been used to.

Then, without trying, or carrying on like a film star or a charmer—or a complete dork—I met a nice young woman at a dance. After three months, we started going steady. She lived near Bairnsdale. Between courting and Young Farmers, I now had a hectic social life. I kept all my other commitments around Ensay and, somehow, fitted in the busy schedule offered by Young Farmers. Some nights, I would knock off work, get picked up, drive to somewhere like Leongatha, go to their ball, turn around and drive back to Ensay, get dropped off, get changed, and go and milk the cow—oh, the benefit of youth.

Usually, when we left to come home after Young Farmers' functions, there'd be a long drive ahead of us. I'd have a nap for an hour or so, but once we reached the road from Bairnsdale to Ensay I'd wake up. With my eyes shut, the constant twisting and turning around endless bends made me feel ill. Being awake during that last part of the journey was a bonus—it meant I could keep an eye on the driver. There were the odd occasions when I had seen them doze off. There was one time, though, when I let the side down, as it were.

We'd been to a ball in South Gippsland, and had left to come home about 2.00 a.m. We were looking at a four-hour trip; but, as usual, as we headed up into the mountains via the Omeo Highway, I was wide awake. It was always a slow trip. There could be fog, many of the bends in the road were very tight, and both people in the front would be on a hyper-alert lookout for wildlife—particularly wombats. If you ran into them, it felt like you'd hit a brick wall. Just before you reached Ensay, the road would open out, farms would replace the bush, and the bends would almost disappear. From that point on, it was only a 20-minute drive to where I worked. On this occasion, I must have dozed off the moment the road straightened slightly. Next thing, there was a screech of tyres, a crunch of metal, and a loud, jarring, scraping sound. I woke to see us rushing side-on up a high bank, and the car tearing along vertically for some 20 yards until it dropped down onto the road. Finally, it bounced this way and that, and landed on all fours, still facing in the right direction. Phew. A brief check revealed that nobody was hurt … and then we burst into raucous laughter. The four of us were covered in jelly, cream, sponge cake, and trifle.

You see, when you attended a Young Farmers' Ball it was obligatory to bring a plate for supper. We'd all obeyed the rule, but had forgotten to take the plates in when we'd arrived. So we were bringing them home again, having placed them carefully up behind the rear seat. By coincidence, my parent's car was the first on the scene. Their concern lasted all of two minutes before peals of laughter split the air. I was late for work that day.

BY 1964, my parents owned a farm at Tongio and two bush blocks, both located on Sheepstation Creek. If I wasn't tied up with Young Farmers, I still worked on all these properties most weekends and enjoyed it. However, the year 1964 started badly for me.

Bob and I were up at the Tongio farm. I was on holidays, and we were putting up a new fence. The day before, I'd used our dozer to push in a new dirt road that led up to a paddock we called the cultivation. This particular day, we'd finished putting in all the posts, and I was trimming off loose timbers before we drilled them by hand and threaded through new wires. I was using my good axe when it slipped, hit my boot, and severed the laces. It didn't hurt, so I pushed on. Admittedly, I was disappointed about the boot. They were my new Commandos—two weeks wages' worth, and waterproof as well.

I finished trimming that post and went to move on, when … *squelch, slosh.* I looked down, and realised there was blood oozing out every time I took a step. I still felt no pain, but the blood started to flow quite freely. Hell, I thought, *I'd better have a look.* Hell again—the axe had gone through the boot and my foot, and had almost come out the other side; it was a very deep cut. I hopped quickly into the Land Rover, and then an hour later I was on a bench in the Omeo hospital watching a doctor sew up the inside, then the outer layer, of the wide gap in my foot. It took ages to heal properly. The rest of my holidays were spent in a chair at Doctors Flat.

One good thing happened while I was chair-bound: Mum taught me how to knit. It was three weeks before I was walking again.

THE BUSH BLOCK, the one we called the top block, was a much better property than the one below it, called Dorrington's. It was more open, and had lighter bush on it. We'd done quite a bit of work out there, including building a new road and a dam, and now Bob decided that we should build our own log cabin. By this time we'd stopped using our axes and crosscut saw. Bob had bought a new chainsaw call a BEBO, and he felled several dozen suitable trees with it. The process of locking the logs together to build the cabin was fascinating. We had a single-roomed cabin up in no time. It had one doorway, and two windows ... or holes.

We got up early one Saturday morning, and loaded up the truck with the windows and other materials we needed to finish off the log cabin. It was exciting. I'd already made plans to do some camping out, and I was glad we'd arrived early. Our first job was to put in a window: it fitted neatly into the opening and I held it in place, and then Bob started to nail the frame to the logs. But, as he hit the nail, the window slipped backwards and started to fall. He accidentally hit the pane of glass, and it snapped, the top half having dislodged. My automatic reaction was to catch the broken pane as it fell. My hand shot through where the glass had been—just like a catch in 'slips' at the cricket—and I held on tight as my arm jammed down on the bottom half of the pane that had remained in place. I pulled it back into place and tried to line it up in the frame. Then a most amazing thing happened: we both noticed a long spurt of blood. It was spraying everywhere. One of us was bleeding. A quick look showed a deep cut right across my wrist. It wasn't red blood; it was a rich, purple colour. Quickly, we wrapped it in handkerchiefs, but the blood soaked straight through in minutes.

There was no question that the cut needed medical attention, but first we had to stop the bleeding. I took off my shirt and we wrapped it very tightly—no good. I was starting to feel faint. We knew that medical help was at least three to four hours away; but, thanks to my Boy Scouts training, I undid my boot, took out the lace, and made a tourniquet on my arm, just below the shoulder. I tightened the bootlace with a stick, and the bleeding stopped. Feeling very groggy, I hopped in the Land Rover, and Bob headed us down the steep bush track to Dorrington's block. We stopped briefly; I had a drink of water from Sheepstation Creek, and then it was a good half-hour until we reached the Omeo Highway.

My hand started to fizz and ache badly, so I released the lace ... just a fraction. Blood went everywhere, but I got the feeling back into my hand. Again, I tightened the tourniquet, and we headed off. I continued this process until we reached the Omeo hospital—release the tourniquet, get the feeling back, tighten the lace. But there was no one at the hospital ... the doctor was out, and had taken the nurse with him. We hopped back in and drove to Swifts Creek, which we'd just driven through 40 minutes before. Dot Carroll, the bush nurse, was expecting us. She sewed up the wrist. I don't know exactly what I cut in there when I severed the wrist, but I've never had much strength in it to this day. Fortunately, it healed, and I was only off work for two weeks.

AS I MENTIONED ABOVE, like all bush kids, I got my driver's licence when I turned eighteen. The test wasn't too difficult; the local policeman simply said, 'Sign here.' He was aware that many young people on farms were not only capable of driving a car, but a truck, a bulldozer, and other farm machinery as well.

For my eighteenth birthday, my parents presented me with their car keys. To be honest, at the age of eighteen, the only problem in my life was sleep: it interfered with my working and social life. The nights when I had no sleep were becoming more common. At times, this would catch up with me. Fortunately, many of the big nights out were Friday or Saturday. This was good; I could grab Mum's car, go out, come home at an ungodly hour, and then be yelled out of bed on Saturday or Sunday morning. Yes, I was still working on my parent's farm.

However, one morning after a very late night out, Dad found me asleep in a most unusual place—the lucerne-paddock gate. My arms were over the pipe on top, and my head was resting on them. I was sound asleep. I vaguely recall a Young Farmers' do I'd been to, and that I'd driven a long way home. It was very late, I hadn't wanted to disturb the animals or the household by driving in, so I'd turned off the ignition key, gone to open the front gate, opened it … and, I guess, rested for just a fraction of a moment, and …

I KEEP REFERRING to 1964. Let me just say that it was a very different year for me. I had a hectic social year, a girlfriend, a cut foot, and then a severed wrist. Yet I was fully fit and ready to play in the lightning premiership that started the new footy season mid-year.

The lightning premiership was a series of short games in which all teams competed. Held at Omeo Oval, one of the four teams would be the premier by the end of the day. I'd started to fill out a little and was looking forward to my year with the Ensie team. We were playing Omeo in the second game.

About five minutes into the game, Bertie Sam grabbed the ball and I dived at him to lay a tackle. I fell forward awkwardly and skidded along the hard ground. His boot jammed my left knee into the turf, and the stops on the sole of his footy boot sank into the top of my kneecap. It really hurt. I lay on the ground holding my knee. Gingerly, I lifted my hand a bit. Something felt funny and … Jesus … my kneecap was fully exposed. The coach, Jim, ran past me and said, 'Come on,

Baz, it was just a tap … Jesus!' He stopped, stared at this huge piece of white bone the size of a tennis ball and said, 'Shit, mate, I think you've broken ya leg. Isn't that ya leg bone or something?'

The game stopped. I wasn't going to move anything … it looked very serious. The runner, who had as much first-aid knowledge as Rover, reckoned I definitely had a broken leg, and that the funny, white protruding lump was part of the bone sticking out — very astute of him.

Mum and quite a few others came onto the ground. After a lot of staring, I was carried off. Someone's ute took me to the Omeo hospital. There, a nurse had a brief look and, after a few probes, announced that the skin over my kneecap had been prised off. She added that I was fortunate. It was a neat wound, like a knife cut. It was a large tear, and the skin had folded down below my knee — like opening a handbag, was the way she explained it to Mum. It looked a lot worse than it really was; in fact, I was in little pain … for the moment. The biggest problem was that the dirt had gotten into, around, and below the kneecap. There was also grass protruding from the layers of folded skin below my knee. The wound was about three inches across. The nurse assured everyone I was going to be okay, and left. The large contingent from the footy returned to the ground … football was serious stuff, after all. I was on my own; in fact, when the nurse left, she also didn't return for a long time.

An hour later, I was in a lot of pain. Fortunately, there was little bleeding, just a lot of pain, then more waiting … and more pain. Finally, a bloke I knew quite well walked in. His name was Reggie Tomkins. Thank God — I was busting for a pee. Reg helped me to the men's. Back in the waiting room, he asked what I was doing there and I showed him my knee. He nodded his head. He seemed oblivious to my major wound and the protruding bone. Then he told me why he was there. No, his bumping into me wasn't a social visit to check up on me. He'd come into the waiting room to lower his head and relax … for the first time in hours. His daughter, Anne, aged six, had just been in a horrific accident. It had happened on the farm. A posthole digger had entangled her, and she was badly hurt. He gave me some details.

The posthole digger is a farm implement attached to a tractor by a power take-off and three-point linkage. A large auger, it turns powerfully in a screwing motion and bores into the ground. This enables it to dig a hole roughly fifteen inches across. Reg's little daughter had been near the auger as it was grinding into the ground. She was wearing a loose cardigan, the wind was blowing, and it caught in the digger. Pulled in, the little girl became caught up, and was then screwed to the bottom of the hole. Reg became very distressed as he explained the incident. I suddenly lost interest in my knee.

When his little girl arrived at the hospital, she had a fractured skull, all the skin from the back of her head to her bottom was torn, and her condition was critical. Norma, Anne's mum, believed her little girl survived because of a miracle. By sheer chance, the Omeo doctor, John Cantwell, had had a lot of experience in West Africa, where he had seen many a fractured skull treated—and hence he'd able to perform the necessary procedure on Anne, and the little girl's condition improved immediately. Reg said it had been wonderful to hear her cry.

Now, I must admit, an accident like that put mine into some perspective, but my pain was very bad. Reg paid me a couple of visits as I sat waiting. Suddenly, he appeared briefly with a grin, and announced that he'd made a wise decision. He left and re-appeared with a small brown bottle of something.

Twenty minutes later I was smiling, talking endlessly, and insulting Reg—he was from 'above the Gap', after all … they deserve their appalling reputation. By the time the doctor got around to see me, some five hours after the accident, I was quite intoxicated. He spent ages cleaning the dirt away, put in some eleven stitches, and sent me home with strict instructions not to bend my leg. Once again, I took up Mum's knitting needles and started to knit, only this time it was more sophisticated. I learnt how to cast off, and knit both plain and pearl. I completed two scarves and a pair of bed socks.

DEAR READER, how patient you have been. I guess by now that most readers would like more detail about the term 'the Gap' that I keep using. Its use is a tradition that's been associated with the Omeo Shire for as long as I can remember. Old-timers told me it was used from the days of early settlement—and that was in the mid-1830s.

The Omeo Shire consists of high country and lower land that physically looks like a step, and to get from the lower Tambo Valley to the Omeo region requires a drive up a long, steep winding road called 'the Gap'. The Omeo area has quite severe winters; it's only an hour's drive from the snowfields of Dinner Plain and Mount Hotham. On the edge of the farming area is a large cattle station called Cobungra, which is just below the snowline.

During the summer, after the snow has thawed, good grass is available here for stock. For many years, the cattle grazed higher up in the bush on the open plains. Then, as the winter snows closed in, there would be a muster, and the cattle would return down to the station. This custom was common throughout the Omeo–Benambra area. The only cattle that grazed on the plains below the Gap were out from Ensay, up onto the plains behind the Nunyong Tablelands.

Initially, early settlement was all based on grazing land. Then gold became a major factor in the increase in population, particularly at Omeo and Cassilis, or Tongio West—both towns were very large. These new towns boasted large schools, libraries, and numerous stores and other businesses. They satisfied the human desire for knick-knacks, better living standards and, of course, the quenching of thirst.

Horse races regularly held at Omeo and other towns were well attended. From this larger population came sporting clubs, including athletics and bicycle clubs, and football and cricket clubs, just to mention a few. Along with this came rivalry—mainly between those bastards above and below the Gap. It became folklore. In the high country, as a youngster, I witnessed this in school sports and many adult games. In school sports, above-versus-below was a real conflict. To lose was to inflict shame and to cause a sense of disgrace, and reprimands were expected. Put simply, a bitter rivalry separated those above and below the Gap. Over the years, I've asked many an old-timer where it came from; apart from them raising their eyebrows at my ignorance, their replies were usually along the lines of, 'They're just ignorant and stuff, you know,' or, 'They're all inbred, those Benambra buggers, you know,' or, 'Bloody alcoholics, those Omeo bludgers. Why do you think they've got so many pubs?' or, 'That cold climate up there shrinks the brain, you know.'

Obviously, I only asked people from below the Gap for their opinions ... they were of my ilk, so to speak. My guess would be that it's the same as what happens to AFL footy supporters. If you barrack for the Bombers, well, naturally—for no other reason—you loathe the Magpies, or vice-versa.

The whole scenario reminds me of the Irish. I remember someone explaining the reason for all those years of violence in that country: *they do not know what they want, but they will fight for it anyhow.*

Yes, the term 'above' or 'below' the Gap is real, but it's based on nothing.

As mentioned, the obvious place to witness this ill feeling was sport—mainly on the footy field. My decision to play with Ensay instead of Swifts Creek was disloyal, but accepted. Had I played for Benambra ... well, I would not be writing this book.

However, there were many other subtle undertones at work, too. Rarely would you see people from below the Gap marry someone from above, or the reverse. In my own lifetime, I've witnessed controversy erupt when golf clubs pondered on amalgamation, or when the high school located at Swifts Creek served the entire shire; the rumblings can still be heard to this day, and that was four decades ago.

People from all around the Tambo Valley would drive to Swifts Creek to watch the movies on Tuesday night. No one ever drove down the Gap. There were movies at Omeo ... but I never attended them. That wasn't right. Yet it would have been quicker to drive up and down the Gap for many people.

The only places where I saw these sacred rules softened was in the pubs. Their doors were open—particularly after the footy or cricket—to anyone. This was very noticeable when it came to cricket matches. At Omeo, the ground was just across the road from the Hilltop Hotel. When one side was batting, the other players waiting to come in and bat would have more than a few beers ... usually longnecks (big bottles). If the opening batsmen were doing okay, getting a few runs, kids would go across to the pub to return with a few more bottles. It didn't matter if you were from below the Gap; the publican obliged.

DUE TO MY SELF-INFLICTED INJURIES, even apart from the ripped knee, I didn't play a lot of footy in 1964. The season was almost over by the time the large scar across my knee had healed and toughened enough for me to bend the knee fully. I played only a few games towards the end of the season, and I hung up my boots for the following year.

Then something very exciting happened. By the luck of winning a ballot or draw that involved many country footy teams, our team, the mighty blue-and-gold Ensay, would be going to the grand final in Melbourne as spectators. The grand finalists in 1964 were Melbourne and Collingwood. What a thrill. I could hardly wait.

Unlike most, I'd been to Melbourne and I'd even been to the MCG—the arena where the game would be played. Several years earlier, the RSL had sent all the Legacy boys in Victoria, including Robbie and me, to meet the English cricket team, captained by Peter May. I was still in primary school at the time. We met them in the team rooms at the MCG.

The Ensay team would be going down to Melbourne—the big smoke—in the school bus. For the tiny, isolated community of Ensay, this was a major event. Now, a bus-load of country blokes heading to Melbourne was a guarantee of certain things taking place: quite a bit of drinking, and a lot of slagging-off and camaraderie, leg-pulling, and exaggerated yarns. Furthermore, young people like me usually believed their stories. However, something unexpected happened because these blokes were generally out of their depth when it came to the city.

The bus trip to Melbourne was great. We had a team song sung to the Beatles' tune 'All My Loving', and we chanted the chorus line, 'Come on Ensay, the yellow and the blue', for most of the journey. As we approached the outskirts of the capital city, the Caulfield football oval came into view. It was beside the Caulfield Technical College, and it boasted a large pavilion or grandstand at one end. One of the blokes commented, 'There she is ... the MCG. Look at that, fellas.'

About half the bus cheered and called on the driver to stop. It was hilarious. After a lot of laughter and jibing, we continued on to Melbourne past the real MCG ... wow. This time, there was silence.

We would be staying in a hotel. That night, we gathered at a rather posh restaurant for tea. The blokes called it 'flash' and 'classy', and made comments like, 'Christ, this is 'phisticated!' and 'Hope we git a good feed.'

Then, after perusing the menu, there was serious concern expressed all round. 'No bloody mixed grill? Come on, for God's sake!' ... 'Shit, at least you'd reckon there'd be some bloody chops. And what the hell is chicken-frigging-Maryland?'

It was like my first night at the farm ... almost comical. The swearing was like morning tea in a woolshed. I noticed that most of the patrons were not very impressed.

But what really separated us Ensay blokes from the rest of the patrons was our dress. Admittedly, some of us had suits—1940s pinstripes, and the like. Others simply wore their 'good clothes'—un-ironed shirts with appalling ties, checked shirts with the top button done up, cardigans, pants with patches, dirty riding-boots ... now, I could relate to that.

Then came the highlight of the evening. One of our blokes was a bit deaf. Let's call him Chas. Being off a farm, like many, his language was colourful. That was okay; however, it was also loud. I noticed several waiters loftily tutt-tutting and consoling other patrons. We sat at a large table, and Chas, tongue-loose due to the amber fluid, was in full flight. I might add that he was still wearing his farm hat. It was a stained, sweat-brown colour, probably 20 years old. Then it happened. Possibly under instruction, or on his own initiative, a waiter approached Chas and asked to take his hat. Chas couldn't hear a word; he was stone deaf. Again the waiter inquired, and again Chas replied, 'Can't frigging hear ya, mate.'

The poor waiter raised his voice and shouted in Chas's ear. He replied, 'Oh shit, sorry, mate. You want me frigging hat, eh?' With that, Chas jumped to his feet, took off his hat—revealing a snow-white, bald head—and jammed it down on the waiter's head. The cowboy hat, being far too big, covered the waiter's ears and eyebrows. The flustered waiter turned and walked off. The entire restaurant roared with laughter.

As the evening progressed, there was a lot of mingling and frivolity. People came across and introduced themselves, bought the odd ale, and loved the country atmosphere we introduced to the restaurant. It was a memorable, fun night.

SATURDAY was the grand final. We arrived early at the MCG and had good seats near the boundary. Being an Essendon supporter, I was keen to watch the game, but had no interest in either side—Melbourne or Collingwood. Admittedly, the privilege of watching football heroes like Barassi, Dixon, Massie, and Mann, for the Demons, and Potter, Tuddenham, and Gabelich, for the Magpies, was something I was very excited about. After some early entertainment from other teams, the game started. It was everything I'd hoped for. I admired the speed of Brian Dixon, an incredible stab pass from Ron Barassi that nearly knocked Doc Roet over, and the determination of Ted Potter. The toughness of players likes Tuddenham made me wince. By the end of the first quarter, like many impartial supporters at the ground that day, I'd lost all sense of normality and had turned into a fanatical football supporter—cheering at spectacular marks, screaming at umpiring decisions, and offering endless advice to the man in white. I had turned into a frenzied, wild-eyed Demons supporter.

The game seesawed; at the last change, Collingwood led by eleven points. On reflection, the seats given to us that day were a godsend. During the last quarter, the Magpies' captain, a huge ruckman named Ray Gabelich, performed a minor sensation. Late in the quarter, with his team behind, Gabelich did a 50-yard run right in front of us, kicked a goal (finally), and put the Magpies in front. The noise—I had never heard anything like it. Gabelich played to the crowd … people cheered, bowed, and celebrated. I think most people applauded his individual effort. It was an incredible sight to watch this man fumble, stumble, hesitate, start to slow down, and finally produce that remarkable goal. It was almost in slow motion. Even the Melbourne players appeared stunned at what had just happened. The most unlikely player on the ground had not only produced a long, slow, nail-biting run as he'd tried to bounce the ball, but he'd also kicked a critical goal—the Magpies were in front by two points.

The crowd not only went bananas … in a flash, Gabelich had acquired hero status. Ned Kelly was about to be challenged as Australia's greatest. The out-of-place country hicks from Ensay went crazy. Everyone was standing up, and the Collingwood supporters were jumping up and down. The Melbourne supporters had their hands cupped around their mouths, screaming support and coaching moves that would see the Demons get home … it was the most exciting moment I'd ever experienced.

'Come on, Demons!' I was screaming insanely—no way should those bloody Magpies win.

Then, some time later, towards the end of the last quarter, the most remarkable thing I have ever witnessed in a game of football happened. I can still picture it as if it happened yesterday. A player by the name of Neil Crompton went one better than Gabelich. A Melbourne back-pocket player, he'd apparently followed his man up the ground, and ended up near the Melbourne goal. The next thing, Crompton had the ball, and he kicked a goal. Yes, the back-pocket player. The siren sounded, and Melbourne had won the premiership.

Like many, we remained at the ground for ages. It was an awesome experience. In fact, today it is recognised as one of the most memorable grand finals of all time … and I was there, in a perfect seat.

The next day, I could hardly speak. All that screaming meant I'd lost my voice. The trip back to Ensay was wonderful. Time after time, we repeated the story of the tank-like ruckman and the dashing back-pocket player.

Perhaps the other highlight was the yarn told to us by one of the young bucks in our team, who'd had a date while we'd been in Melbourne.

Now, Peter had bragged all the way down on the bus about a female called Monica. Apparently, she was a corker—yep, a stunner—and she'd invited him around to her parents' place for tea before he took her out to a dance. He'd met her at a Young Farmers' do earlier. He'd promised her that if he ever came to Melbourne, he would arrange an outing.

As you can imagine, we were excited to hear how Peter had got on. So, not long into the trip home, some blokes asked if he'd scored, whatever that meant ... perhaps the blokes thought the two of them had gone ten-pin bowling? To be honest, Pete looked different somehow. He was sort of swollen and bruised about the head. He was quiet—that wasn't like Pete. Finally, one of the blokes asked him about the lump.

Just to diverge here a little, Pete enjoyed running. On most occasions, he rarely walked from point A to B; everything was done at a jog. Any fence, gate, gutter, or steps he would leap with enthusiasm.

Now, it appears that on the evening of his inaugural date with Monica, on grand final night, he'd taken a taxi to the front of her house. Peter, who took a while to open up about this event—it took about five beers, I seem to recall—continued. 'I didn't bother with the front gate. I just gracefully leapt the front brick wall with ease. Then, at a Herb Elliot pace, I ran up the footpath, leapt the next brick wall up onto the front veranda. Bugger the steps and the side entrance; I jumped up the porch. Bam! Shit, that hurt. Next thing I know, I'm lying on the lawn, stunned, flat on my back, holding my head.'

Pete continued. 'You know, there was this bloody great pane of glass covering the veranda opening, and I hadn't seen it. I was in agony. The porch light went on, people rushed out from everywhere. Admittedly, there was a fair boom of noise as I collected that bloody window. They found me—flat on me back on the lawn, eh. I heard someone ask, "Are you okay, son?"' That would have been Monica's bloody father, I guessed. He went on.

'Then I heard a female say, "Gosh, what happened?"' Being a female voice, I supposed that must have been Monica's bloody mother. He continued.

'Then I heard someone say, "Good God, how stupid is that?"' Unfortunately, I reckoned that was Monica.

'I ignored the flaming pain and leapt to my feet,' he told us, though by now he was having to shout ... our laughter was out of control.

'But, hey, you know, once inside, even though I was feeling like shit, I put on a brave face and sat down. In no time, I was hoeing into a generous mixed grill. Bugger me, what happened then. The silly old bastard, Monica's dad, he sorta looked at me and said, "You sure you're okay, son?" I told him, sure, that I'd just tripped. Dunno why but, for some reason, I touched my forehead. Shit—there was a frigg'n great lump the size of a duck's bloody egg sticking out. Yep, just above me left flaming eye. Christ, I ask you, what's a codger supposed to bloody well do now? Anyhow, bugger it, I mumbled about suddenly feeling crook, and asked where the dunny was. Once I found a mirror, I saw that I looked like a bloody freak ... or the early stages of turning into a frigging unicorn. So I gulped down the meal and left ... on me own.'

The bus was in complete uproar. The driver had to pull over for ten minutes. The laughter continued for ages, and Pete's only response was, 'Last time you'll catch me in the big smoke.'

chapter seventeen
Endings and beginnings

MY JOB ON THE FARM AT ENSAY WAS A GOOD ONE. ALTHOUGH much of this book doesn't deal with my life on the farm, in fact, the majority of my time as a young man was spent working Monday to Friday at Kanangra. It's interesting, looking back, because when I first went there I was concerned about the myriad of skills I needed to learn. In time, however, I realised that the owners were fine people, and that they were living within a wonderful community.

Then there were bonuses. What with Swanee and then Rover, I've always felt very privileged that I spent a part of my life with talented and unique animals. When I lost Rover, I grieved as if I'd lost a close friend. No wonder older people place such a high value on their pets.

The other thing that was continually increasing while I worked was my knowledge of how to farm. By coincidence, the people who owned the farm were very progressive, and they often experimented. Few other farms in the area dared challenge the locally entrenched ways of farming.

Instead of concentrating on breeding sheep that produced

quality wool, my bosses introduced strong-woolled sheep that cut very heavy fleeces. Crossing these same sheep with a variety of rams, mainly Border Leicester, resulted in the first cross-lambs that had both meat and wool potential.

Further cross-breeding saw British breed sheep such as Romney Marsh, Southdown, and Cheviot joined to the first cross-ewes. This produced fat lambs for market after twelve to fifteen weeks, whereas most farms sold their lambs at 20 weeks or later. Further sophistication was introduced at shearing time: every fleece was weighed, and the sheep with the lighter cuts were sold off. It was the same at lambing time. Sheep that had had twins were tagged and used for the next breeding cycle. The following drop meant that our new lamb numbers were up—at a rate of approximately 120 lambs for every 100 ewes. The result of all this intensive selection and rejection of their breeding stock was a well-earned reputation for the bosses. At the annual sheep sales, their sheep were always in the top pens, and their fat lambs were highly sought-after by the top butchers.

The same applied to their cattle. Using different breeds, good-quality bulls, and good management saw the farm owners develop a similar high reputation to the one they'd gained with sheep. Today, the same farm boasts an excellent beef-cattle stud called Newcomen's Herefords.

Often, after good showers of rain, I would spend countless hours discing up paddocks, harrowing and, finally, sowing the paddocks with a variety of pasture. We tried several types of clovers, grasses, and crops like millet, rape, and oats. I realised that after several years on a farm like this I would be more than capable of running my own farm or managing a property.

Perhaps the other fortunate thing about working on the farm at Ensay was being able to work away from the farm for periods. I worked in woolsheds, carting hay, droving cattle, and at the annual sheep and cattle sales. Then there were the one-off experiences such as operating a harvester, and helping a local crop-duster pilot to locate boundaries to enable him to determine where to drop his load of superphosphate.

The owners of the farm were good people who treated me well. Sure, there's always an element of luck with employment. The job at Ensay, that wonderful community, and the era, when combined, offered me a unique experience. I never once recall feeling alone, depressed, or looking for a change in my circumstances. There were no computers, mobile phones, electronic games, takeaway foods, or television. For me, there was hard work, long hours, and a hectic social life. I'm not trying to sound honourable when I say that I believe the only thing that sometimes messed up this good life I loved was holidays. The farm at Ensay was my work, my base, and my point of contact, and my bedroom had ended up like a small office. Any permanent move away, like a holiday, required more than just packing my clothes.

Admittedly, the holidays enabled Bob and me to catch up on jobs at home and on the family farm. We often planned large projects if I had a couple of weeks off. Over the years, we fenced in many paddocks, and built roads and several dams with the 'dozer—we even completed a log cabin on the top block, as I've described. I thoroughly enjoyed the 1940's single-cylinder Flower Marshall bulldozer.

BY 1964, my parents had 500 sheep and 40 head of cattle. Our first-ever shearing took place at the neighbouring farmer's woolshed, and I recall with pride the first bales of our wool that we sent to market. As Rover and I drove the sheep back to the family farm, the blue BB (Bob and Barry) brand on the newly shorn sheeps' rumps summed up the satisfaction of years of hard work. We used the same brand on our calves. The following year, a new woolshed meant that we were ready to shear at the Tongio farm.

Come 1965, little did I realise that I was about to face major changes in my life. The first was the loss my dear, sweet friend, Rover. At the time, I was devastated. I grieved and cried in private for a long time. Not long after, I lost both my job at Ensay and the good times on the farm at home. By early 1966, I found myself conscripted into national service.

Yes, my stay at the Ensay farm ended abruptly. To be honest, it was very overwhelming and I wasn't eager to leave. With the introduction of conscription, or national service, and my marble having been drawn from the barrel, I had a duty to perform ... if I passed the medical. That's how it was in those days in the shire; it was an entrenched attitude in the Omeo area. I never experienced any dissent, objection, or ill feeling towards me for going into the army — only vague support.

My farewell at the Ensay Hall was a surprise. They were such warm and generous people, just like all the people in the high country — yes, even including those from 'above the Gap'.

No doubt, there were many changes ahead for me. Somehow, I knew that the people would never change and would always be there for me. As for my farm friends ... well, that was different. I knew I could never rekindle the special bonds I had developed with the horses and dogs. Something inside me told me that when I left I would never come back to the farm. I'd known Swanee for five years. On my last day on the farm, the dogs and horses got their pats and scratches from me. Of course, they treated it as just another day. I've always had a lot of affection for animals.

Then it was my mate's turn — Swanee, the larrikin I loved. As I said at the beginning, he was different. I walked over to him in the paddock and had a quiet chat. He stood there with his head down as I scratched behind his ears. No, he didn't try to run away, stick his rump in my face, or bite my bum.

He nudged me softly several times, rubbing his face along my ribs. Finally, I remember I turned and walked away, overcome with wonderful memories of this unique animal. Slowly, I approached the gate. I felt a push, and I fell gently against it. It was Swanee. He had walked quietly behind me. His final nudge was like a handshake from a good mate.

I left the Ensay farm for the last time one late Friday afternoon on the Bantam. When I put the stand down on my motorbike to shut the front gate and turned to snib the chain, I looked up, and there he was—Swanee, at the corner of his paddock, alongside the driveway out of the farm, his head over the fence nodding slowly up and down. I'm sure he winked at me as I left. I never saw him again.

AFTER MY DISCHARGE from the army, I returned to Ensay and the Swifts Creek area. The year was 1968. Most locals were aware that I had spent a part of my time away in Vietnam. They were hearty in their welcome. The people hadn't changed; however, I was a 'born again' in the true sense of the words. My experience away had had a profound impact on my being. Many a time in Vietnam, I would describe myself as a drunk, an old man and, finally, as almost an animal. We lived like nomads, existing in the jungle in conditions so primitive that I wonder how we coped at times. Every morning out there, my job was simple: to survive, and to help kill other human beings. My youthful innocence had been shattered; I lost that delight for life and carefree spirit I once enjoyed.

The return from life in the army to 'home' happened in less than a day, after boarding the civilian aircraft in Saigon and, much later that same day, arriving at Essendon airport.

It was too much. Too many familiar faces—Mum, Dad, and a girlfriend—were all talking in a way that was strange to me. I felt they were somehow foreign ... my own family.

Once I was back home, I almost immediately realised that the new me was a stranger in the beautiful area I loved. I couldn't deal with the virtue and naivety of the local people, when it came to war. Within days, my world shrank rapidly. Silence was my best safeguard—I decided it was best I keep my opinions and my past to myself. I smoked, swore, and drank.

Consequently, I found out what true loneliness means. For me, I believe there was little choice. How was I to answer the blank, wide-eyed looks I received when I announced I was going away again? Yes, within weeks, I turned my back on my girlfriend, my family, my friends, and my past good life. Many people were stunned when I left the district. Even more wanted an explanation. 'You must be kidding,' they said.

I wanted to hide away—to the point that, in the years that followed, I kept my recent past a secret. How does one measure the sadness that resulted after I decided to move away? Perhaps 30 years of absence might suffice.

To understand the soldier, you need to realise that he is a creature of blunt, crude training; a territorial beast intent on self-preservation at any cost. His needs are crude: to survive, and then to enjoy a brief rest swamped with food, beer, and blunt pleasure. Education, compassion, morals, wealth, and patriotism disappear ... they become irrelevant.

To understand a soldier, ask another soldier. For a sanitised version, ask our politicians; they see war and soldiers in a completely different light than do I and my mates.

AFTER THE RELEASE of my book *Well Done, Those Men*, many people wrote letters, sent me emails, or phoned me. Most appreciated the honesty, and acknowledged the difficulty I must have experienced in writing that book, which was true. Consequently, many of them had the same message: that it must have been good therapy, even healing—which was also true, but there was more to it than that.

Writing is more than my hobby; it provides me with an unseen confidant and friend. It enables me to be alone, and to ponder my life and its difficulties; then, most importantly, it gives me a sense of perspective. Now I write every day—always a diary entry, and sometimes a recollection. It might be just one sentence, but I know it will trigger a particular memory if it's needed in the future ... when I hunger for the pen or keyboard.

Since the publication of *Well Done, Those Men* I have given many talks, mainly to veterans' groups and schools. The vets' talks are great; in no time, questions and their own yarns lead off into a night of reminiscing. The school talks have also been interesting. The students have always shown respect and have asked searching questions. Their knowledge of the Vietnam era is generally meagre, and many students are amazed that this country treated Vietnam veterans so poorly upon their return from that conflict. It's not that schools won't teach that part of our history; the answer lies with the lack of suitable resources, and the decisions of curriculum branches not to promote the subject.

Sadly, the other feedback I have had from today's kids indicates that many of them have little interest in, or time for, reading or writing. Consequently, given any opportunity to do so, I encourage them to take on both of these activities.

My opinion isn't a researched or proven one. For me, it's a simple philosophy—writing allows you to explore your interior life in a way that talking to yourself or thinking doesn't. Those acts pale in comparison. To me, the written word can be re-read, altered, or mulled over like a good wine. Private thoughts, ideas, or passions can be grieved over, expressed, and vented in a way that leads to healing, wisdom, forgiveness, or compassion—capacities that we all have but, at times, struggle to find.

Reading the works of fine writers is necessary. I have found many students prefer audio books on MP3 players. That's okay. In fact, it allows the listener to close his or her eyes and enter that book entirely. As I travel only by public transport, I often listen to talking books. Recently, I've listened to *Far from the Madding Crowd*, by Thomas Hardy—what a wonderful novel. Schools should be encouraged to pursue this idea, if students don't warm to reading.

Finally, with writing, you can tell funny stories to an audience of one—yourself. Maybe you giggle at a memory. Whatever—it's you who decides whether to share the joke. On the other hand, there's the opposite: you can pour out sadness with a passion that helps dissipate the pain.

Today, writing doesn't come easily for most people. For me, the best guide is a teacher, or a good book ... looking up words that don't reveal their meaning at first glance, and then savouring a good sentence.

Consequently, I now encourage others to read and write.

As mentioned in *Well Done, Those Men*, I hesitated for ages to show anyone my original writings. After a time, a few mates read my short pieces and made grunting noises that I guessed were compliments, which led to me handing over the stack of paper that became the book. This time I got very good feedback. Still, I was reluctant to accept that it was suitable for other people to read—certainly not for publication. I had no confidence in my ability, or that it would interest other people.

To this day, I'm not sure why I wanted to show people my work. I certainly had no vision or belief that my writing would appeal to many readers. In those early writing days, I was writing prolifically. It dominated my life. I found writing a wonderful, healing activity.

I hope you find that reading it has a similar effect.

Acknowledgements

Thanks to Max Prendergast. His assistance has helped develop my writing, and his local knowledge has been of great value. To Reg and Norma Tomkins, Blake Hollands, Tom Sandy, Barry and Topsy Newcomen—like so many locals—your stories, memories, details, and encouragement have been appreciated.

Thanks also to Bill Bricknall, a fellow Vietnam veteran, who is widely read and is always supportive. And to the local writers' group—in particular, Maurs Rodwell, Cherry Stevens, Robyn Butson, and Rosemary Abbott—many thanks for your professional input and encouragement.

And to the staff at my publisher, Scribe, who have become like family, a sincere thank you.